Essential Statistics for Non-STEM Data Analysts

Get to grips with the statistics and math knowledge needed to enter the world of data science with Python

Rongpeng Li

BIRMINGHAM—MUMBAI

Essential Statistics for Non-STEM Data Analysts

Commissioning Editor: Sunith Shetty
Acquisition Editor: Devika Battike
Senior Editor: Roshan Kumar
Content Development Editor: Sean Lobo
Technical Editor: Sonam Pandey
Copy Editor: Safis Editing
Project Coordinator: Aishwarya Mohan
Proofreader: Safis Editing
Indexer: Pratik Shirodkar
Production Designer: Roshan Kawale

First published: November 2020

Production reference: 1111120

Published by Packt Publishing Ltd.
Livery Place
35 Livery Street
Birmingham
B3 2PB, UK.

ISBN 978-1-83898-484-7

www.packt.com

`Packt.com`

Subscribe to our online digital library for full access to over 7,000 books and videos, as well as industry leading tools to help you plan your personal development and advance your career. For more information, please visit our website.

Why subscribe?

- Spend less time learning and more time coding with practical eBooks and Videos from over 4,000 industry professionals

- Improve your learning with Skill Plans built especially for you

- Get a free eBook or video every month

- Fully searchable for easy access to vital information

- Copy and paste, print, and bookmark content

Did you know that Packt offers eBook versions of every book published, with PDF and ePub files available? You can upgrade to the eBook version at `packt.com` and as a print book customer, you are entitled to a discount on the eBook copy. Get in touch with us at `customercare@packtpub.com` for more details.

At `www.packt.com`, you can also read a collection of free technical articles, sign up for a range of free newsletters, and receive exclusive discounts and offers on Packt books and eBooks.

Contributors

About the author

Rongpeng Li is a data science instructor and a senior data scientist at Galvanize, Inc. He has previously been a research programmer at Information Sciences Institute, working on knowledge graphs and artificial intelligence. He has also been the host and organizer of the Data Analysis Workshop Designed for Non-STEM Busy Professionals at LA.

Michael Hansen (https://www.linkedin.com/in/michael-n-hansen/), a friend of mine, provided invaluable English language editing suggestions for this book. Michael has great attention to detail, which made him a great language reviewer. Thank you, Michael!

About the reviewers

James Mott, PhD, is a senior education consultant with extensive experience in teaching statistical analysis, modeling, data mining, and predictive analytics. He has over 30 years of experience using SPSS products in his own research, including IBM SPSS Statistics, IBM SPSS Modeler, and IBM SPSS Amos. He has also been actively teaching about these products to IBM/SPSS customers for over 30 years. In addition, he is an experienced historian with expertise in the research and teaching of 20th century United States political history and quantitative methods. His specialties are data mining, quantitative methods, statistical analysis, teaching, and consulting.

Yidan Pan obtained her PhD in system, synthetic, and physical biology from Rice University. Her research interest is profiling mutagenesis at genomic and transcriptional levels with molecular biology wet labs, bioinformatics, statistical analysis, and machine learning models. She believes that this book will give its readers a lot of practical skills for data analysis.

Packt is searching for authors like you

If you're interested in becoming an author for Packt, please visit `authors.packtpub.com` and apply today. We have worked with thousands of developers and tech professionals, just like you, to help them share their insight with the global tech community. You can make a general application, apply for a specific hot topic that we are recruiting an author for, or submit your own idea.

Table of Contents

3
Visualization with Statistical Graphs

Section 2: Essentials of Statistical Analysis

4
Sampling and Inferential Statistics

5
Common Probability Distributions

6
Parametric Estimation

7

Statistical Hypothesis Testing

Section 3: Statistics for Machine Learning

8

Statistics for Regression

5
Common Probability Distributions

6
Parametric Estimation

7
Statistical Hypothesis Testing

Section 3: Statistics for Machine Learning

8
Statistics for Regression

9
Statistics for Classification

10
Statistics for Tree-Based Methods

11
Statistics for Ensemble Methods

Section 4: Appendix

12
A Collection of Best Practices

13
Exercises and Projects

Preface

Data science has been trending for several years, and demand in the market is now really on the increase as companies, governments, and non-profit organizations have shifted toward a data-driven approach.

Many new graduates, as well as people who have been working for years, are now trying to add data science as a new skill to their resumes. One significant barrier for stepping into the realm of data science is statistics, especially for people who do not have a **science, technology, engineering, and mathematics (STEM)** background or left the classroom years ago. This book is designed to fill the gap for those people. While writing this book, I tried to explore the scattered concepts in a dot-connecting fashion such that readers feel that new concepts and techniques are *needed* rather than simply being created from thin air.

By the end of this book, you will be able to comfortably deal with common statistical concepts and computation in data science, from fundamental descriptive statistics and inferential statistics to advanced topics, such as statistics using tree-based methods and ensemble methods. This book is also particularly handy if you are preparing for a data scientist or data analyst job interview. The nice interleaving of conceptual contents and code examples will prepare you well.

Who this book is for

This book is for people who are looking for materials to fill the gaps in their statistics knowledge. It should also serve experienced data scientists as an enjoyable read. The book assumes minimal mathematics knowledge and it may appear verbose, as it is designed so that novices can use it as a self-contained book and follow the book chapter by chapter smoothly to build a knowledge base on statistics from the ground up.

What this book covers

Chapter 1, Fundamentals of Data Collection, Cleaning, and Preprocessing, introduces basic concepts in data collection, cleaning, and simple preprocessing.

Chapter 2, Essential Statistics for Data Assessment, talks about descriptive statistics, which are handy for the assessment of data quality and **exploratory data analysis** (**EDA**).

Chapter 3, Visualization with Statistical Graphs, introduces common graphs that suit different visualization scenarios.

Chapter 4, Sampling and Inferential Statistics, introduces the fundamental concepts and methodologies in sampling and the inference techniques associated with it.

Chapter 5, Common Probability Distributions, goes through the most common discrete and continuous distributions, which are the building blocks for more sophisticated real-life empirical distributions.

Chapter 6, Parametric Estimation, covers a classic and rich topic that solidifies your knowledge of statistics and probability by having you estimate parameters from accessible datasets.

Chapter 7, Statistical Hypothesis Testing, looks at a must-have skill for any data scientist or data analyst. We will cover the full life cycle of hypothesis testing, from assumptions to interpretation.

Chapter 8, Statistics for Regression, discusses statistics for regression problems, starting with simple linear regression.

Chapter 9, Statistics for Classification, explores statistics for classification problems, starting with logistic regression.

Chapter 10, Statistics for Tree-Based Methods, delves into statistics for tree-based methods, with a detailed walk through of building a decision tree from first principles.

Chapter 11, Statistics for Ensemble Methods, moves on to ensemble methods, which are meta-algorithms built on top of basic machine learning or statistical algorithms. This chapter is dedicated to methods such as bagging and boosting.

Chapter 12, Best Practice Collection, introduces several important practice tips based on the author's data science mentoring and practicing experience.

Chapter 13, Exercises and Projects, includes exercises and project suggestions grouped by chapter.

To get the most out of this book

As Jupyter notebooks can run on Google Colab, a computer connected to the internet and a Google account should be sufficient.

Software/hardware covered in the book	OS requirements
Google colab or Jupyter Notebook	Windows, macOS X, and Linux (Any)

If you are using the digital version of this book, we advise you to type the code yourself or access the code via the GitHub repository (link available in the next section). Doing so will help you avoid any potential errors related to the copying and pasting of code.

Download the example code files

You can download the example code files for this book from GitHub at `https://github.com/PacktPublishing/Essential-Statistics-for-Non-STEM-Data-Analysts`. In case there's an update to the code, it will be updated on the existing GitHub repository.

We also have other code bundles from our rich catalog of books and videos available at `https://github.com/PacktPublishing/`. Check them out!

Download the color images

We also provide a PDF file that has color images of the screenshots/diagrams used in this book. You can download it here: `https://static.packt-cdn.com/downloads/9781838984847_ColorImages.pdf`.

Conventions used

There are a number of text conventions used throughout this book.

`Code in text`: Indicates code words in text, database table names, folder names, filenames, file extensions, pathnames, dummy URLs, user input, and Twitter handles.

Here is an example: "`You can use plt.rc('ytick', labelsize='x-medium').`"

A block of code is set as follows:

```
import pandas as pd

df = pd.read_excel("PopulationEstimates.xls",skiprows=2)

df.head(8)  margin: 0;
```

Any command-line input or output is written as follows:

```
$ pip install pandas
```

Bold: Indicates a new term, an important word, or words that you see onscreen. For

example, words in menus or dialog boxes appear in the text like this. Here is an example: "
seaborn is another popular Python visualization library. With it, you can write less code to
obtain more professional-looking plots."

> **Tips or important notes**
> R is another famous programming language for data science and statistical
> analysis. There are also successful R packages. The counterpart of Matplotlib is
> the R ggplot2 package I mentioned above.

Get in touch

Feedback from our readers is always welcome.

General feedback: If you have questions about any aspect of this book, mention the book
title in the subject of your message and email us at customercare@packtpub.com.

Errata: Although we have taken every care to ensure the accuracy of our content, mistakes
do happen. If you have found a mistake in this book, we would be grateful if you would
report this to us. Please visit www.packtpub.com/support/errata, selecting your
book, clicking on the Errata Submission Form link, and entering the details.

Piracy: If you come across any illegal copies of our works in any form on the Internet,
we would be grateful if you would provide us with the location address or website name.
Please contact us at copyright@packt.com with a link to the material.

If you are interested in becoming an author: If there is a topic that you have expertise in
and you are interested in either writing or contributing to a book, please visit authors.
packtpub.com.

Reviews

Please leave a review. Once you have read and used this book, why not leave a review on the site that you purchased it from? Potential readers can then see and use your unbiased opinion to make purchase decisions, we at Packt can understand what you think about our products, and our authors can see your feedback on their book. Thank you!

For more information about Packt, please visit `packt.com`.

Section 1:
Getting Started
with Statistics for
Data Science

In this section, you will learn how to preprocess data and inspect distributions and correlations from a statistical perspective.

This section consists of the following chapters:

- *Chapter 1, Fundamentals of Data Collection, Cleaning, and Preprocessing*
- *Chapter 2, Essential Statistics for Data Assessment*
- *Chapter 3, Visualization with Statistical Graphs*

1
Fundamentals of Data Collection, Cleaning, and Preprocessing

Thank you for purchasing this book and welcome to a journal of exploration and excitement! Whether you are already a data scientist, preparing for an interview, or just starting learning, this book will serve you well as a companion. You may already be familiar with common Python toolkits and have followed trending tutorials online. However, there is a lack of a systematic approach to the statistical side of data science. This book is designed and written to close this gap for you.

As the first chapter in the book, we start with the very first step of a data science project: collecting, cleaning data, and performing some initial preprocessing. It is like preparing fish for cooking. You get the fish from the water or from the fish market, examine it, and process it a little bit before bringing it to the chef.

You are going to learn five key topics in this chapter. They are correlated with other topics, such as visualization and basic statistics concepts. For example, outlier removal will be very hard to conduct without a scatter plot. Data standardization clearly requires an understanding of statistics such as standard deviation. We prepared a GitHub repository that contains ready-to-run codes from this chapter as well as the rest.

Here are the topics that will be covered in this chapter:

- Collecting data from various data sources with a focus on data quality

- Data imputation with an assessment of downstream task requirements

- Outlier removal

- Data standardization – when and how

- Examples involving the scikit-learn preprocessing module

The role of this chapter is as a primer. It is not possible to cover the topics in an entirely sequential fashion. For example, to remove outliers, necessary techniques such as statistical plotting, specifically a box plot and scatter plot, will be used. We will come back to those techniques in detail in future chapters of course, but you must bear with it now. Sometimes, in order to learn new topics, bootstrapping may be one of a few ways to break the shell. You will enjoy it because the more topics you learn along the way, the higher your confidence will be.

Technical requirements

The best environment for running the Python code in the book is on Google Colaboratory (`https://colab.research.google.com`). Google Colaboratory is a product that runs Jupyter Notebook in the cloud. It has common Python packages that are pre-installed and runs in a browser. It can also communicate with a disk so that you can upload local files to Google Drive. The recommended browsers are the latest versions of Chrome and Firefox.

For more information about Colaboratory, check out their official notebooks: `https://colab.research.google.com`.

You can find the code for this chapter in the following GitHub repository: `https://github.com/PacktPublishing/Essential-Statistics-for-Non-STEM-Data-Analysts`

Collecting data from various data sources

There are three major ways to collect and gather data. It is crucial to keep in mind that data doesn't have to be well-formatted tables:

- **Obtaining structured tabulated data directly**: For example, the Federal Reserve (`https://www.federalreserve.gov/data.htm`) releases well-structured and well-documented data in various formats, including CSV, so that pandas can read the file into a DataFrame format.

- **Requesting data from an API**: For example, the Google Map API (`https://developers.google.com/maps/documentation`) allows developers to request data from the Google API at a capped rate depending on the pricing plan. The returned format is usually JSON or XML.

- **Building a dataset from scratch**: For example, social scientists often perform surveys and collect participants' answers to build proprietary data.

Let's look at some examples involving these three approaches. You will use the UCI machine learning repository, the Google Map API and USC President's Office websites as data sources, respectively.

Reading data directly from files

Reading data from local files or remote files through a URL usually requires a good source of publicly accessible data archives. For example, the University of California, Irvine maintains a data repository for machine learning. We will be reading the air quality dataset with `pandas`. The latest URL will be updated in the book's official GitHub repository in case the following code fails. You may obtain the file from `https://archive.ics.uci.edu/ml/machine-learning-databases/heart-disease/`. From the datasets, we are using the `processed.hungarian.data` file. You need to upload the file to the same folder where the notebook resides.

The following code snippet reads the data and displays the first several rows of the datasets:

```
import pandas as pd
df = pd.read_csv("processed.hungarian.data",
                 sep=",",
                 names = ["age","sex","cp","trestbps",
                          "chol","fbs","restecg","thalach",
                          "exang","oldpeak","slope","ca",
                          "thal","num"])
df.head()
```

This produces the following output:

	age	sex	cp	trestbps	chol	fbs	restecg	thalach	exang	oldpeak	slope	ca	thal	num
0	28	1	2	130	132	0	2	185	0	0.0	?	?	?	0
1	29	1	2	120	243	0	0	160	0	0.0	?	?	?	0
2	29	1	2	140	?	0	0	170	0	0.0	?	?	?	0
3	30	0	1	170	237	0	1	170	0	0.0	?	?	6	0
4	31	0	2	100	219	0	1	150	0	0.0	?	?	?	0

Figure 1.1 – Head of the Hungarian heart disease dataset

In the following section, you will learn how to obtain data from an API.

Obtaining data from an API

In plain English, an **Application Programming Interface** (**API**) defines protocols, agreements, or treaties between applications or parts of applications. You need to pass requests to an API and obtain returned data in JSON or other formats specified in the API documentation. Then you can extract the data you want.

> **Note**
>
> When working with an API, you need to follow the guidelines and restrictions regarding API usage. Improper usage of an API will result in the suspension of an account or even legal issues.

Let's take the Google Map Place API as an example. The Place API (`https://developers.google.com/places/web-service/intro`) is one of many Google Map APIs that Google offers. Developers can use HTTP requests to obtain information about certain geographic locations, the opening hours of establishments, and the types of establishment, such as schools, government offices, and police stations.

> **In terms of using external APIs**
>
> Like many APIs, the Google Map Place API requires you to create an account on its platform – the Google Cloud Platform. It is free, but still requires a credit card account for some services it provides. Please pay attention so that you won't be mistakenly charged.

After obtaining and activating the API credentials, the developer can build standard HTTP requests to query the endpoints. For example, the `textsearch` endpoint is used to query places based on text. Here, you will use the API to query information about libraries in Culver City, Los Angeles:

1. First, let's import the necessary libraries:

   ```
   import requests
   import json
   ```

2. Initialize the API key and endpoints. We need to replace `API_KEY` with a real API key to make the code work:

   ```
   API_KEY = Your API key goes here
   TEXT_SEARCH_URL = https://maps.googleapis.com/maps/api/
   place/textsearch/json?
   query = "Culver City Library"
   ```

3. Obtain the response returned and parse the returned data into JSON format. Let's examine it:

   ```
   response = requests.get(TEXT_SEARCH_
   URL+'query='+query+'&key='+API_KEY)
   json_object = response.json()
   print(json_object)
   ```

This is a one-result response. Otherwise, the `results` fields will have multiple entries. You can index the multi-entry `results` fields as a normal Python list object:

```
{'html_attributions': [],
 'results': [{'formatted_address': '4975 Overland Ave, Culver
City, CA 90230, United States',
    'geometry': {'location': {'lat': 34.0075635, 'lng':
-118.3969651},
     'viewport': {'northeast': {'lat': 34.00909257989272,
       'lng': -118.3955611701073},
      'southwest': {'lat': 34.00639292010727, 'lng':
-118.3982608298927}}},
    'icon': 'https://maps.gstatic.com/mapfiles/place_api/
icons/civic_building-71.png',
    'id': 'ccdd10b4f04fb117909897264c78ace0fa45c771',
    'name': 'Culver City Julian Dixon Library',
    'opening_hours': {'open_now': True},
    'photos': [{'height': 3024,
      'html_attributions': ['<a href="https://maps.google.com/
maps/contrib/102344423129359752463">Khaled Alabed</a>'],
      'photo_reference': 'CmRaAAAANT4Td01h1tkI7dTn35vAkZhx_-
mg3PjgKvjHiyh80M5UlI3wVw1cer4vkOksYR68NM9aw33ZPYGQzzXTE
8bkOwQYuSChXAWlJUtz8atPhmRht4hP4dwFgqfbJULmG5f1EhAfW1F_
cpLz76sD_81fns1OGhT4KU-zWTbuNY54_4_XozE02pLNWw',
      'width': 4032}],
    'place_id': 'ChIJrUqREx-6woARFrQdyscOZ-8',
    'plus_code': {'compound_code': '2J53+26 Culver City,
California',
     'global_code': '85632J53+26'},
    'rating': 4.2,
    'reference': 'ChIJrUqREx-6woARFrQdyscOZ-8',
    'types': ['library', 'point_of_interest', 'establishment'],
    'user_ratings_total': 49}],
 'status': 'OK'}
```

The address and name of the library can be obtained as follows:

```
print(json_object["results"][0]["formatted_address"])
print(json_object["results"][0]["name"])
```

The result reads as follows:

```
4975 Overland Ave, Culver City, CA 90230, United States
Culver City Julian Dixon Library
```

Information

An API can be especially helpful for data augmentation. For example, if you have a list of addresses that are corrupted or mislabeled, using the Google Map API may help you correct wrong data.

Obtaining data from scratch

There are instances where you would need to build your own dataset from scratch.

One way of building data is to crawl and parse the internet. On the internet, a lot of public resources are open to the public and free to use. Google's spiders crawl the internet relentlessly 24/7 to keep its search results up to date. You can write your own code to gather information online instead of opening a web browser to do it manually.

Doing a survey and obtaining feedback, whether explicitly or implicitly, is another way to obtain private data. Companies such as Google and Amazon gather tons of data from user profiling. Such data builds the core of their dominating power in ads and e-commerce. We won't be covering this method, however.

Legal issue of crawling

Notice that in some cases, web crawling is highly controversial. Before crawling a website, do check their user agreement. Some websites explicitly forbid web crawling. Even if a website is open to web crawling, intensive requests may dramatically slow down the website, disabling its normal functionality to serve other users. It is a courtesy not only to respect their policy, but also the law.

Here is a simple example that uses *regular expression* to obtain all the phone numbers from the web page of the president's office, University of Southern California: `http://departmentsdirectory.usc.edu/pres_off.html`:

1. First, let's import the necessary libraries. `re` is the Python built-in regular expression library. `requests` is an HTTP client that enables communication with the internet through the `http` protocol:

```
import re
import requests
```

2. If you look at the web page, you will notice that there is a pattern within the phone numbers. All the phone numbers start with three digits, followed by a hyphen and then four digits. Our objective now is to compile such a pattern:

```
pattern = re.compile("\d{3}-\d{4}")
```

3. The next step is to create an `http` client and obtain the response from the GET call:

```
response = requests.get("http://departmentsdirectory.usc.
edu/pres_off.html")
```

4. The `data` attribute of `response` can be converted into a long string and fed to the `findall` method:

```
pattern.findall(str(response.data))
```

The results contain all the phone numbers on the web page:

```
['740-2111',
 '821-1342',
 '740-2111',
 '740-2111',
 '740-2111',
 '740-2111',
 '740-2111',
 '740-2111',
 '740-9749',
 '740-2505',
 '740-6942',
 '821-1340',
 '821-6292']
```

In this section, we introduced three different ways of collecting data: reading tabulated data from data files provided by others, obtaining data from APIs, and building data from scratch. In the rest of the book, we will focus on the first option and mainly use collected data from the UCI Machine Learning Repository. In most cases, API data and scraped data will be integrated into tabulated datasets for production usage.

Data imputation

Missing data is ubiquitous and data imputation techniques will help us to alleviate its influence.

In this section, we are going to use the heart disease data to examine the pros and cons of basic data imputation. I recommend you read the dataset description beforehand to understand the meaning of each column.

Preparing the dataset for imputation

The heart disease dataset is the same one we used earlier in the *Collecting data from various data sources* section. It should give you a real red flag that you shouldn't take data integrity for granted. The following screenshot shows missing data denoted by question marks:

```
28,1,2,130,132,0,2,185,0,0,?,?,?,0
29,1,2,120,243,0,0,160,0,0,?,?,?,0
29,1,2,140,?,0,0,170,0,0,?,?,?,0
30,0,1,170,237,0,1,170,0,0,?,?,6,0
31,0,2,100,219,0,1,150,0,0,?,?,?,0
32,0,2,105,198,0,0,165,0,0,?,?,?,0
32,1,2,110,225,0,0,184,0,0,?,?,?,0
32,1,2,125,254,0,0,155,0,0,?,?,?,0
33,1,3,120,298,0,0,185,0,0,?,?,?,0
34,0,2,130,161,0,0,190,0,0,?,?,?,0
34,1,2,150,214,0,1,168,0,0,?,?,?,0
```

Figure 1.2 – The head of Hungarian heart disease data in VS Code (CSV rainbow extension enabled)

First, let's do an `info()` call that lists column data type information:

```
df.info()
```

> **Note**
>
> `df.info()` is a very helpful function that provides you with pointers for your next move. It should be the first function call when given an unknown dataset.

The following screenshot shows the output obtained from the preceding function:

```
<class 'pandas.core.frame.DataFrame'>
RangeIndex: 294 entries, 0 to 293
Data columns (total 14 columns):
age         294 non-null int64
sex         294 non-null int64
cp          294 non-null int64
trestbps    294 non-null object
chol        294 non-null object
fbs         294 non-null object
restecg     294 non-null object
thalach     294 non-null object
exang       294 non-null object
oldpeak     294 non-null float64
slope       294 non-null object
ca          294 non-null object
thal        294 non-null object
num         294 non-null int64
dtypes: float64(1), int64(4), object(9)
memory usage: 32.3+ KB
```

Figure 1.3 – Output of the info() function call

If pandas can't infer the data type of a column, it will interpret it as objects. For example, the **chol** (cholesterol) column contains missing data. The missing data is a question mark treated as a string, but the remainder of the data is of the **float** type. The records are collectively called objects.

Python's type tolerance

As Python is pretty error-tolerant, it is a good practice to introduce a necessary type check. For example, if a column mixes the numerical values, instead of using numerical values to check truth, explicitly check its type and write two branches. Also, it is advised to avoid type conversion on columns with data type objects. Remember to make your code completely deterministic and future-proof.

Now, let's replace the question mark with the NaN values. The following code snippet declares a function that can handle three different cases and treat them appropriately. The three cases are listed here:

- The record value is "?".

- The record value is of the integer type. This is treated independently because columns such as num should be binary. Floating numbers will lose the essence of using 0-1 encoding.

- The rest includes valid strings that can be converted to float numbers and original float numbers.

The code snippet will be as follows:

```
import numpy as np
def replace_question_mark(val):
    if val == "?":
        return np.NaN
    elif type(val)==int:
        return val
    else:
        return float(val)
df2 = df.copy()
for (columnName, _) in df2.iteritems():
    df2[columnName] = df2[columnName].apply(replace-question_
mark)
```

Now we call the info() function and the head() function, as shown here:

```
df2.info()
```

You should expect that all fields are now either floats or integers, as shown in the following output:

```
<class 'pandas.core.frame.DataFrame'>
RangeIndex: 294 entries, 0 to 293
Data columns (total 14 columns):
age         294 non-null int64
sex         294 non-null int64
cp          294 non-null int64
trestbps    293 non-null float64
chol        271 non-null float64
fbs         286 non-null float64
restecg     293 non-null float64
thalach     293 non-null float64
exang       293 non-null float64
oldpeak     294 non-null float64
slope       104 non-null float64
ca          3 non-null float64
thal        28 non-null float64
num         294 non-null int64
dtypes: float64(10), int64(4)
memory usage: 32.3 KB
```

Figure 1.4 – Output of info() after data type conversion

Now you can check the number of non-null entries for each column, and different columns have different levels of completeness. age and sex don't contain missing values, but ca contains almost no valid data. This should guide you on your choices of data imputation. For example, strictly dropping all the missing values, which is also considered a way of data imputation, will almost remove the complete dataset. Let's check the shape of the DataFrame after the default missing value drops. You see that there is only one row left. We don't want it:

```
df2.dropna().shape
```

A screenshot of the output is as follows:

```
1 df2.dropna().shape
```

(1, 14)

Figure 1.5 – Removing records containing NaN values leaves only one entry

Before moving on to other more mainstream imputation methods, we would love to perform a quick review of our processed DataFrame.

Check the head of the new DataFrame. You should see that all question marks are replaced by NaN values. NaN values are treated as legitimate numerical values, so native NumPy functions can be used on them:

```
df2.head()
```

The output should look as follows:

	age	sex	cp	trestbps	chol	fbs	restecg	thalach	exang	oldpeak	slope	ca	thal	num
0	28	1	2	130.0	132.0	0.0	2.0	185.0	0.0	0.0	NaN	NaN	NaN	0
1	29	1	2	120.0	243.0	0.0	0.0	160.0	0.0	0.0	NaN	NaN	NaN	0
2	29	1	2	140.0	NaN	0.0	0.0	170.0	0.0	0.0	NaN	NaN	NaN	0
3	30	0	1	170.0	237.0	0.0	1.0	170.0	0.0	0.0	NaN	NaN	6.0	0
4	31	0	2	100.0	219.0	0.0	1.0	150.0	0.0	0.0	NaN	NaN	NaN	0

Figure 1.6 – The head of the updated DataFrame

Now, let's call the describe() function, which generates a table of statistics. It is a very helpful and handy function for a quick peak at common statistics in our dataset:

```
df2.describe()
```

Here is a screenshot of the output:

	age	sex	cp	trestbps	chol	fbs	restecg	thalach	exang	oldpeak	slope	ca	thal	num
count	294.000000	294.000000	294.000000	293.000000	271.000000	286.000000	293.000000	293.000000	293.000000	294.000000	104.000000	3.0	28.000000	294.000000
mean	47.826531	0.724490	2.982993	132.583618	250.848708	0.069930	0.218430	139.129693	0.303754	0.586054	1.894231	0.0	5.642857	0.360544
std	7.811812	0.447533	0.965117	17.626568	67.657711	0.255476	0.460868	23.589749	0.460665	0.908648	0.338995	0.0	1.615074	0.480977
min	28.000000	0.000000	1.000000	92.000000	85.000000	0.000000	0.000000	82.000000	0.000000	0.000000	1.000000	0.0	3.000000	0.000000
25%	42.000000	0.000000	2.000000	120.000000	209.000000	0.000000	0.000000	122.000000	0.000000	0.000000	2.000000	0.0	5.250000	0.000000
50%	49.000000	1.000000	3.000000	130.000000	243.000000	0.000000	0.000000	140.000000	0.000000	0.000000	2.000000	0.0	6.000000	0.000000
75%	54.000000	1.000000	4.000000	140.000000	282.500000	0.000000	0.000000	155.000000	1.000000	1.000000	2.000000	0.0	7.000000	1.000000
max	66.000000	1.000000	4.000000	200.000000	603.000000	1.000000	2.000000	190.000000	1.000000	5.000000	3.000000	0.0	7.000000	1.000000

Figure 1.7 – Output from the describe() call

> **Understanding the describe() limitation**
>
> Note that the describe() function only considers valid values. In this sample, the average age value is more trustworthy than the average thal value. Do also pay attention to the metadata. A numerical value doesn't necessarily have a numerical meaning. For example, a thal value is encoded to integers with given meanings.

Now, let's examine the two most common ways of imputation.

Imputation with mean or median values

Imputation with mean or median values only works on numerical datasets. Categorical variables don't contain structures, such as one label being larger than another. Therefore, the concepts of mean and median won't apply.

There are several advantages associated with mean/median imputation:

- It is easy to implement.

- Mean/median imputation doesn't introduce extreme values.

- It does not have any time limit.

However, there are some statistical consequences of mean/median imputation. The statistics of the dataset will change. For example, the histogram for cholesterol prior to imputation is provided here:

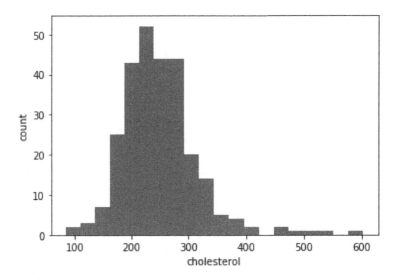

Figure 1.8 – Cholesterol concentration distribution

The following code snippet does the imputation with the mean. Following imputation the with mean, the histogram shifts to the right a little bit:

```
chol = df2["chol"]
plt.hist(chol.apply(lambda x: np.mean(chol) if np.isnan(x) else
x), bins=range(0,630,30))
plt.xlabel("cholesterol imputation")
plt.ylabel("count")
```

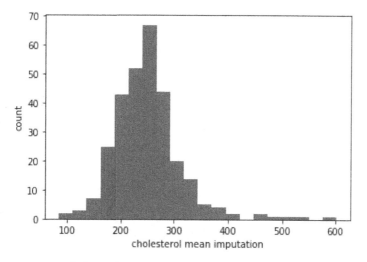

Figure 1.9 – Cholesterol concentration distribution with mean imputation

Imputation with the median will shift the peak to the left because the median is smaller than the mean. However, it won't be obvious if you enlarge the bin size. Median and mean values will likely fall into the same bin in this eventuality:

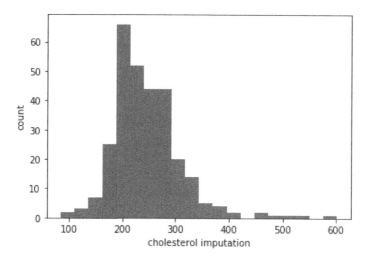

Figure 1.10 – Cholesterol imputation with median imputation

The good news is that the shape of the distribution looks rather similar. The bad news is that we probably increased the level of concentration a little bit. We will cover such statistics in *Chapter 3, Visualization with Statistical Graphs*.

> **Note**
>
> In other cases where the distribution is not centered or contains a substantial ratio of missing data, such imputation can be disastrous. For example, if the waiting time in a restaurant follows an exponential distribution, imputation with mean values will probably break the characteristics of the distribution.

Imputation with the mode/most frequent value

The advantage of using the most frequent value is that it works well with categorical features and, without a doubt, it will introduce bias as well. The slope field is categorical in nature, although it looks numerical. It represents three statuses of a slope value as positive, flat, or negative.

The following code snippet will reveal our observation:

```
plt.hist(df2["slope"],bins = 5)
plt.xlabel("slope")
plt.ylabel("count");
```

Here is the output:

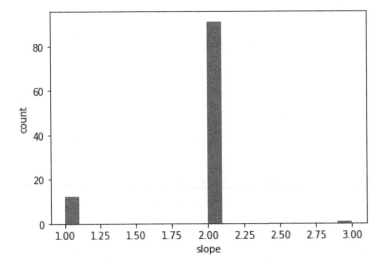

Figure 1.11 – Counting of the slope variable

Without a doubt, the mode is 2. Following imputation with the mode, we obtain the following new distribution:

```
plt.hist(df2["slope"].apply(lambda x: 2 if np.isnan(x) else
x),bins=5)
plt.xlabel("slope mode imputation")
plt.ylabel("count");
```

In the following graph, pay attention to the scale on *y*:

```
1 chol = df2["slope"]
2 plt.hist(chol.apply(lambda x: 2 if np.isnan(x) else x),bins=20)
3 plt.xlabel("slope mode imputation")
4 _ = plt.ylabel("count")
```

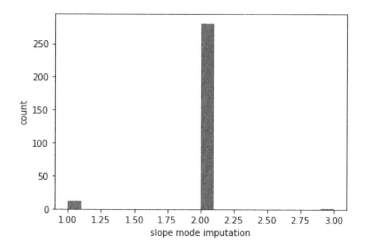

Figure 1.12 – Counting of the slope variable after mode imputation

Replacing missing values with the mode in this case is disastrous. If positive and negative values of slope have medical consequences, performing prediction tasks on the preprocessed dataset will depress their weights and significance.

Different imputation methods have their own pros and cons. The prerequisite is to fully understand your business goals and downstream tasks. If key statistics are important, you should try to avoid distorting them. Also, do remember that collecting more data is always an option.

Outlier removal

Outliers can stem from two possibilities. They either come from mistakes or they have a story behind them. In principle, outliers should be very rare, otherwise the experiment/survey for generating the dataset is intrinsically flawed.

The definition of an **outlier** is tricky. Outliers can be legitimate because they fall into the long tail end of the population. For example, a team working on financial crisis prediction establishes that a financial crisis occurs in one out of 1,000 simulations. Of course, the result is not an outlier that should be discarded.

It is often good to keep original *mysterious* outliers from the raw data if possible. In other words, the reason to remove outliers should only come from outside the dataset – only when you already know the originals. For example, if the heart rate data is strangely fast and you know there is something wrong with the medical equipment, then you can remove the bad data. The fact that you know the sensor/equipment is wrong can't be deduced from the dataset itself.

Perhaps the best example for including outliers in data is the discovery of Neptune. In 1821, Alexis Bouvard discovered substantial deviations in Uranus' orbit based on observations. This led him to hypothesize that another planet may be affecting Uranus' orbit, which was found to be Neptune.

Otherwise, discarding mysterious outliers is risky for downstream tasks. For example, some regression tasks are sensitive to extreme values. It takes further experiments to decide whether the outliers exist for a reason. In such cases, don't remove or correct outliers in the data preprocessing steps.

The following graph generates a scatter plot for the **trestbps** and **chol** fields. The highlighted data points are possible outliers, but I probably will keep them for now:

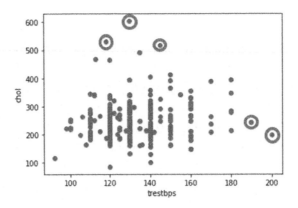

Figure 1.13 – A scatter plot of two fields in heart disease dataset

Like missing data imputation, outlier removal is tricky and depends on the quality of data and your understanding of the data.

It is hard to discuss systemized outlier removal without talking about concepts such as quartiles and box plots. In this section, we looked at the background information pertaining to outlier removal. We will talk about the implementation based on statistical criteria in the corresponding sections in *Chapter 2*, *Essential Statistics for Data Assessment*, and *Chapter 3*, *Visualization with Statistical Graphs*.

Data standardization – when and how

Data standardization is a common preprocessing step. I use the terms standardization and normalization interchangeably. You may also encounter the concept of rescaling in literature or blogs.

Standardization often means shifting the data to be zero-centered with a standard deviation of 1. The goal is to bring variables with different units/ranges down to the same range. Many machine learning tasks are sensitive to data magnitudes. Standardization is supposed to remove such factors.

Rescaling doesn't necessarily bring the variables to a common range. This is done by means of customized mapping, usually linear, to scale original data to a different range. However, the common approach of *min-max* scaling does transform different variables into a common range [0, 1].

People may argue about the difference between standardization and normalization. When comparing their differences, normalization will refer to normalizing different variables to the same range [0, 1], and min-max scaling is considered a normalization algorithm. However, there are other normalization algorithms as well. Standardization cares more about the mean and standard deviation.

Standardization also transforms the original distribution closer to a Gaussian distribution. In the event that the original distribution is indeed Gaussian, standardization outputs a standard Gaussian distribution.

> **When to perform standardization**
>
> Perform standardization when your downstream tasks require it. For example, the *k-nearest neighbors* method is sensitive to variable magnitudes, so you should standardize the data. On the other hand, *tree-based* methods are not sensitive to different ranges of variables, so standardization is not required.

There are mature libraries to perform standardization. We first calculate the standard deviation and mean of the data, subtract the mean from every entry, and then divide by the standard deviation. Standard deviation describes the level of variety in data that will be discussed more in *Chapter 2, Essential Statistics for Data Assessment.*

Here is an example involving vanilla Python:

```
stdChol = np.std(chol)
meanChol = np.mean(chol)
chol2 = chol.apply(lambda x: (x-meanChol)/stdChol)
plt.hist(chol2,bins=range(int(min(chol2)), int(max(chol2))+1,
1));
```

The output is as follows:

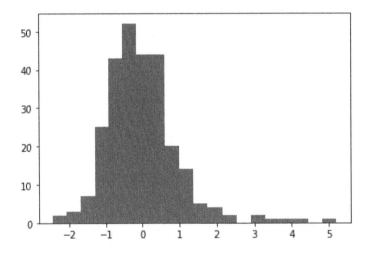

Figure 1.14 – Standardized cholesterol data

Note that the standardized distribution looks more like a Gaussian distribution now.

Data standardization is irreversible. Information will be lost in standardization. It is only recommended to do so when no original information, such as magnitudes or original standard deviation, will be required later. In most cases, standardization is a safe choice for most downstream data science tasks.

In the next section, we will use the scikit-learn preprocessing module to demonstrate tasks involving standardization.

Examples involving the scikit-learn preprocessing module

For both imputation and standardization, scikit-learn offers similar APIs:

1. First, *fit* the data to learn the imputer or standardizer.

2. Then, use the fitted object to *transform* new data.

In this section, I will demonstrate two examples, one for imputation and another for standardization.

> **Note**
>
> Scikit-learn uses the same syntax of *fit* and *predict* for predictive models. This is a very good practice for keeping the interface consistent. We will cover the machine learning methods in later chapters.

Imputation

First, create an imputer from the `SimpleImputer` class. The initialization of the instance allows you to choose missing value forms. It is handy as we can feed our original data into it by treating the question mark as a missing value:

```python
from sklearn.impute import SimpleImputer
imputer = SimpleImputer(missing_values=np.nan, strategy="mean")
```

Note that `fit` and `transform` can accept the same input:

```python
imputer.fit(df2)
df3 = pd.DataFrame(imputer.transform(df2))
```

Now, check the number of missing values – the result should be 0:

```python
np.sum(np.sum(np.isnan(df3)))
```

Standardization

Standardization can be implemented in a similar fashion:

```python
from sklearn import preprocessing
```

The scale function provides the default zero-mean, one-standard deviation transformation:

```
df4 = pd.DataFrame(preprocessing.scale(df2))
```

> **Note**
>
> In this example, categorical variables represented by integers are also zero-mean, which should be avoided in production.

Let's check the standard deviation and mean. The following line outputs infinitesimal values:

```
df4.mean(axis=0)
```

The following line outputs values close to 1:

```
df4.std(axis=0)
```

Let's look at an example of `MinMaxScaler`, which transforms every variable into the range [0, 1]. The following code fits and transforms the heart disease dataset in one step. It is left to you to examine its validity:

```
minMaxScaler = preprocessing.MinMaxScaler()
df5 = pd.DataFrame(minMaxScaler.fit_transform(df2))
```

Let's now summarize what we have learned in this chapter.

Summary

In this chapter, we covered several important topics that usually emerge at the earliest stage of a data science project. We examined their applicable scenarios and conservatively checked some consequences, either numerically or visually. Many arguments made here will be more prominent when we cover other more sophisticated topics later.

In the next chapter, we will review probabilities and statistical concepts, including the mean, the median, quartiles, standard deviation, and skewness. I am sure you will then have a deeper understanding of concepts such as outliers.

2
Essential Statistics for Data Assessment

In *Chapter 1, Fundamentals of Data Collection, Cleaning, and Preprocessing*, we learned about data collection, basic data imputation, outlier removal, and standardization. Hence, this will provide you with a good foundation to understand this chapter.

In this chapter, you are going to learn how to examine the **essential statistics** for data assessment. Essential statistics are also often referred to as **descriptive statistics**. Descriptive statistics provide simple, quantitative summaries of datasets, usually combined with descriptive graphics. For example, descriptive statistics can demonstrate the tendency of centralization or measures of the variability of features, and so on.

Descriptive statistics are important. Correctly represented descriptive statistics give you a precise summary of the datasets at your disposal. In this chapter, we will learn to extract information and make quantitative judgements from descriptive statistics. Just a heads-up at this point. Besides descriptive statistics, another kind of statistics is known as **inferential statistics**, which tries to learn information from the distribution of the population that the dataset was generated or sampled from. In this chapter, we assume the data covers a whole population rather than a subset sampled from a distribution. We will see the differences between the two statistics in later chapters as well. For now, don't worry.

The following topics will be covered in this chapter:

- Classifying numerical and categorical variables
- Understanding mean, median, and mode
- Learning about variance, standard deviation, percentiles, and skewness
- Knowing how to handle categorical variables and mixed data types
- Using bivariate and multivariate descriptive statistics

Classifying numerical and categorical variables

Descriptive statistics are all about **variables**. You must know what you are describing to define corresponding descriptive statistics.

A variable is also referred to as a **feature** or **attribute** in other literature. They all mean the same thing: a single column in a tabulated dataset.

In this section, you will examine the two most important variable types, **numerical** and **categorical**, and learn to distinguish between them. Categorical variables are *discrete* and usually represent a classification property of entry. Numerical variables are *continuous* and descriptive quantitatively. Descriptive statistics that can be applied to one kind of variable may not be applied to another one, hence distinguishing between them precedes analytics.

Distinguishing between numerical and categorical variables

In order to understand the differences between the two types of variables with the help of an example, I will be using the population estimates dataset released by the United States Department of Agriculture by way of a demonstration. It contains the estimated population data at county level for the United States from 2010 to 2018. You can obtain the data from the official website, https://www.ers.usda.gov/data-products/county-level-data-sets/download-data/, or the book's GitHub repository.

The following code snippet loads the data and examines the first several rows:

```
import pandas as pd
df = pd.read_excel("PopulationEstimates.xls",skiprows=2)
df.head(8)
```

The output is a table with more than 140 columns. Here are two screenshots showing the beginning and trailing columns:

	FIPS	State	Area_Name	Rural-urban_Continuum Code_2003	Rural-urban_Continuum Code_2013	Urban_Influence_Code_2003	Urb
0	0	US	United States	NaN	NaN	NaN	
1	1000	AL	Alabama	NaN	NaN	NaN	
2	1001	AL	Autauga County	2.0	2.0	2.0	
3	1003	AL	Baldwin County	4.0	3.0	5.0	
4	1005	AL	Barbour County	6.0	6.0	6.0	
5	1007	AL	Bibb County	1.0	1.0	1.0	
6	1009	AL	Blount County	1.0	1.0	1.0	
7	1011	AL	Bullock County	6.0	6.0	6.0	

8 rows × 149 columns

Figure 2.1 – First 6 columns of the dfad() output

In the preceding dataset, there is a variable called *Rural-urban_Continuum Code_2013*. It takes the value of integers. This leads to pandas autointerpreting this variable; pandas auto-interprets it as numerical. Instead, however, the variable is actually categorical.

Should you always trust libraries?

Don't always trust what functions from Python libraries give you. They may be wrong, and the developer, which is you, has to make the final decision.

After some research, we found the variable description on this page: https://www.ers.usda.gov/data-products/rural-urban-continuum-codes/. According to the code standard published in 2013, the *Rural-urban_Continuum Code_2013* variable indicates how urbanized an area is.

The meaning of *Rural-urban_Continuum Code_2013* is shown in *Figure 2.2*.

Metropolitan Counties*

Code	Description
1	Counties in metro areas of 1 million population or more
2	Counties in metro areas of 250,000 to 1 million population
3	Counties in metro areas of fewer than 250,000 population

Nonmetropolitan Counties

4	Urban population of 20,000 or more, adjacent to a metro area
5	Urban population of 20,000 or more, not adjacent to a metro area
6	Urban population of 2,500 to 19,999, adjacent to a metro area
7	Urban population of 2,500 to 19,999, not adjacent to a metro area
8	Completely rural or less than 2,500 urban population, adjacent to a metro area
9	Completely rural or less than 2,500 urban population, not adjacent to a metro area

Figure 2.2 – Interpretation of Rural-urban_Continuum Code_2013

> **Note**
>
> Pandas makes intelligent auto-interpretations of variable types, but oftentimes
> it is wrong. It is up to the data scientist to investigate the exact meaning of the
> variable type and then change it.

Many datasets use integers to represent categorical variables. Treating them as numerical
values may result in serious consequences in terms of downstream tasks such as machine
learning, mainly because artificial *distances* between numerical values will be introduced.

On the other hand, numerical variables often have a *direct* quantitative meaning. For
example, R_NET_MIG_2013 means the rate of net immigration in 2013 for a specific
area. A histogram plot of this numerical variable gives a more descriptive summary of
immigration trends in the States, but it makes little sense plotting the code beyond simple
counting.

Let's check the net immigration rate for the year 2013 with the following code snippet:

```
plt.figure(figsize=(8,6))
plt.rcParams.update({'font.size': 22})
plt.hist(df["R_NET_MIG_2013"],bins=np.linspace(np.nanmin(df["R_
NET_MIG_2013"]),np.nanmax(df["R_NET_MIG_2013"]),num=100))
plt.title("Rate of Net Immigration Distribution for All
Records, 2013");
```

The result appears as follows.

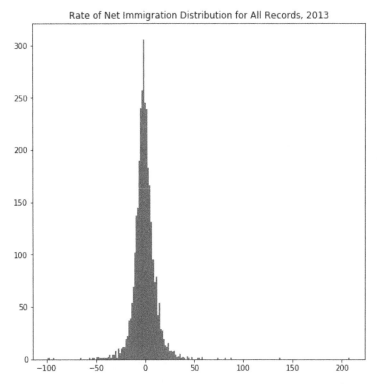

Figure 2.3 – Distribution of the immigration rate for all records in datasets

Here are the observations drawn from *Figure 2.3*:

- In either categorical or numerical variables, structures can be introduced to construct special cases. A typical example is *date* or *time*. Depending on the scenarios, date and time can be treated as categorical variables as well as numerical variables with a semi-continuous structure.

- It is common to convert numerical variables to categorical variables on the basis of a number of rules. The rural-urban code is a typical example. Such a conversion is easy for conveying a first impression.

Now that we have learned how to distinguish between numerical and categorical variables, let's move on to understanding a few essential concepts of statistics, namely, mean, median, and mode.

Understanding mean, median, and mode

Mean, median, and mode describe the central tendency in some way. Mean and median are only applicable to numerical variables whereas mode is applicable to both categorical and numerical variables. In this section, we will be focusing on mean, median, and mode for numerical variables as their numerical interactions usually convey interesting observations.

Mean

Mean, or arithmetical mean, measures the *weighted center* of a variable. Let's use n to denote the total number of entries and i as the index. The mean $\bar{x}$ reads as follows:

$$\bar{x} = \frac{\sum x_i}{n}$$

Mean is influenced by the value of every entry in the population.

Let me give an example. In the following code, I will generate 1,000 random numbers from 0 to 1 uniformly, plot them, and calculate their mean:

```
import random
random.seed(2019)
plt.figure(figsize=(8,6))
rvs = [random.random() for _ in range(1000)]
plt.hist(rvs, bins=50)
plt.title("Histogram of Uniformly Distributed RV");
```

The resulting histogram plot appears as follows:

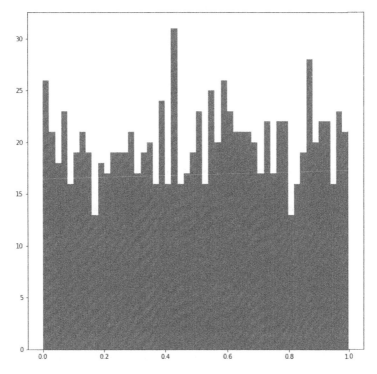

Figure 2.4 – Histogram distribution of uniformly distributed variables between 0 and 1

The mean is around `0.505477`, pretty close to what we surmised.

Median

Median measures the *unweighted center* of a variable. If there is an odd number of entries, the median takes the value of the central one. If there is an even number of entries, the median takes the value of the mean of the central two entries. Median may not be influenced by every entry's value. On account of this property, median is more *robust* or *representative* than the mean value. I will use the same set of entries as in previous sections as an example.

The following code calculates the median:

```
np.median(rvs)
```

The result is 0.5136755026003803. Now, I will be changing one entry to 1,000, which is 1,000 times larger than the maximal possible value in the dataset and repeat the calculation:

```
rvs[-1]=1000
print(np.mean(rvs))
print(np.median(rvs))
```

The results are 1.5054701085937803 and 0.5150437661964872. The mean increased by roughly 1, but the median is robust.

The relationship between mean and median is usually interesting and worth investigating. Usually, the combination of a larger median and smaller mean indicates that there are more points on the bigger value side, but that an extremely small value also exists. The reverse is true when the median is smaller than the mean. We will demonstrate this with some examples later.

Mode

The mode of a set of values is the most frequent element in a set. It is evident in a histogram plot such that it represents the peak(s). If the distribution has only one mode, we call it unimodal. Distributions with two peaks that don't have to have equal heights are referred to as bimodal.

> **Bimodals and bimodal distribution**
>
> Sometimes, the definition of bimodal is corrupted. The property of being **bimodal** usually refers to the property of having two modes, which, according to the definition of mode, requires the same height of peaks. However, the term **bimodal distribution** often refers to a distribution with two local maxima. Double-check your distribution and state the modes clearly.

The following code snippet demonstrates two distributions with unimodal and bimodal shapes, respectively:

```
r1 = [random.normalvariate(0.5,0.2) for _ in range(10000)]
r2 = [random.normalvariate(0.2,0.1) for _ in range(5000)]
r3 = [random.normalvariate(0.8,0.2) for _ in range(5000)]

fig, axes = plt.subplots(1,2,figsize=(12,5))
axes[0].hist(r1,bins=100)
axes[0].set_title("Unimodal")
```

```
axes[1].hist(r2+r3,bins=100)
axes[1].set_title("Bimodal");
```

The resulting two subplots appear as follows:

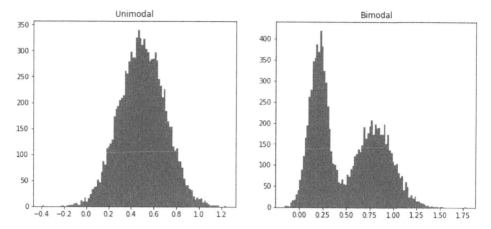

Figure 2.5 – Histogram of unimodal and bimodal datasets with one mode and two modes

So far, we have talked about mean, median and mode, mean, median and mode, which are the first three statistics of a dataset. They are the start of almost all exploratory data analysis.

Learning about variance, standard deviation, quartiles, percentiles, and skewness

In the previous section, we studied the mean, median, and mode. They all describe, to a certain degree, the properties of the central part of the dataset. In this section, we will learn how to describe the *spreading* behavior of data.

Variance

With the same notation, variance for the population is defined as follows:

$$\sigma^2 = \frac{\sum(x_i - \bar{x})^2}{n}$$

Intuitively, the further away the elements are from the mean, the larger the variance. Here, I plotted the histogram of two datasets with different variances. The one on the left subplot has a variance of 0.09 and the one on the right subplot has a variance of 0.009, 10 times smaller.

The following code snippet generates samples from the two distributions and plots them:

```
r1 = [random.normalvariate(0.5,0.3) for _ in range(10000)]
r2 = [random.normalvariate(0.5,0.1) for _ in range(10000)]

fig, axes = plt.subplots(1,2,figsize=(12,5))
axes[0].hist(r1,bins=100)
axes[0].set_xlim([-1,2])
axes[0].set_title("Big Variance")
axes[1].hist(r2,bins=100)
axes[1].set_title("Small Variance")
axes[1].set_xlim([-1,2]);
```

The results appear as follows:

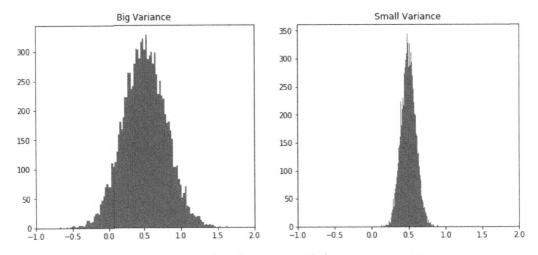

Figure 2.6 – Big and small variances with the same mean at 0.5

The following code snippet generates a scatter plot that will demonstrate the difference more clearly. The variable on the *x* axis spreads more widely:

```
plt.figure(figsize=(8,8))
plt.scatter(r1,r2,alpha=0.2)
plt.xlim(-1,2)
plt.ylim(-1,2)
plt.xlabel("Big Variance Variable")
```

```
plt.ylabel("Small Variance Variable")
plt.title("Variables With Different Variances");
```

The result looks as follows:

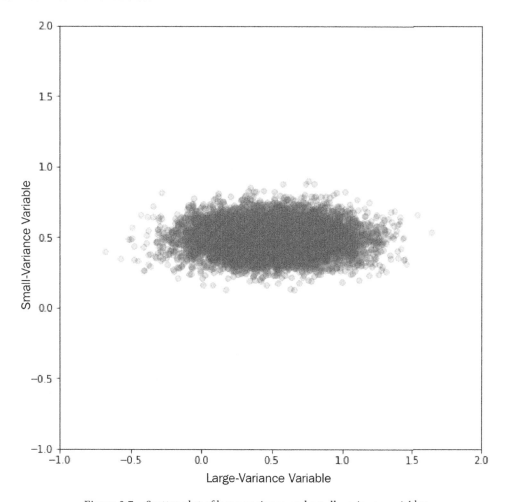

Figure 2.7 – Scatter plot of large-variance and small-variance variables

The spread in the *x* axis is significantly larger than the spread in the *y* axis, which indicates the differences in variance magnitude. A common mistake is not getting the range correct. Matplotlib will, by default, try to determine the ranges. You need to use a code such as `plt.xlim()` to force it, otherwise the result is misleading.

Standard deviation

Standard deviation is the square root of the variance. It is used more commonly to measure the level of dispersion since it has the same unit as the original data. The formula for the standard deviation of a population reads as follows:

$$\sigma = \sqrt{\frac{\sum(x_i - \bar{x})^2}{n}}$$

Standard deviation is extremely important in scientific graphing. A standard deviation is often plotted together with the data and represents an estimate of variability.

For this chapter, I will be using the net immigration rate for Texas from 2011 to 2018 as an example. In the following code snippet, I will first extract the county-level data, append the means and standard deviations to a list, and then plot them at the end. The standard deviation is obtained using `numpy.std()` and the error bar is plotted using `matplotlib.pyplot.errorbar()`:

```
dfTX = df[df["State"]=="TX"].tail(-1)


YEARS = [year for year in range(2011,2019)]
MEANS = []
STDS = []
for i in range(2011,2019):
    year = "R_NET_MIG_"+str(i)
    MEANS.append(np.mean(dfTX[year]))
    STDS.append(np.std(dfTX[year]))


plt.figure(figsize=(10,8))
plt.errorbar(YEARS,MEANS,yerr=STDS)
plt.xlabel("Year")
plt.ylabel("Net Immigration Rate");
```

The output appears as shown in the following figure:

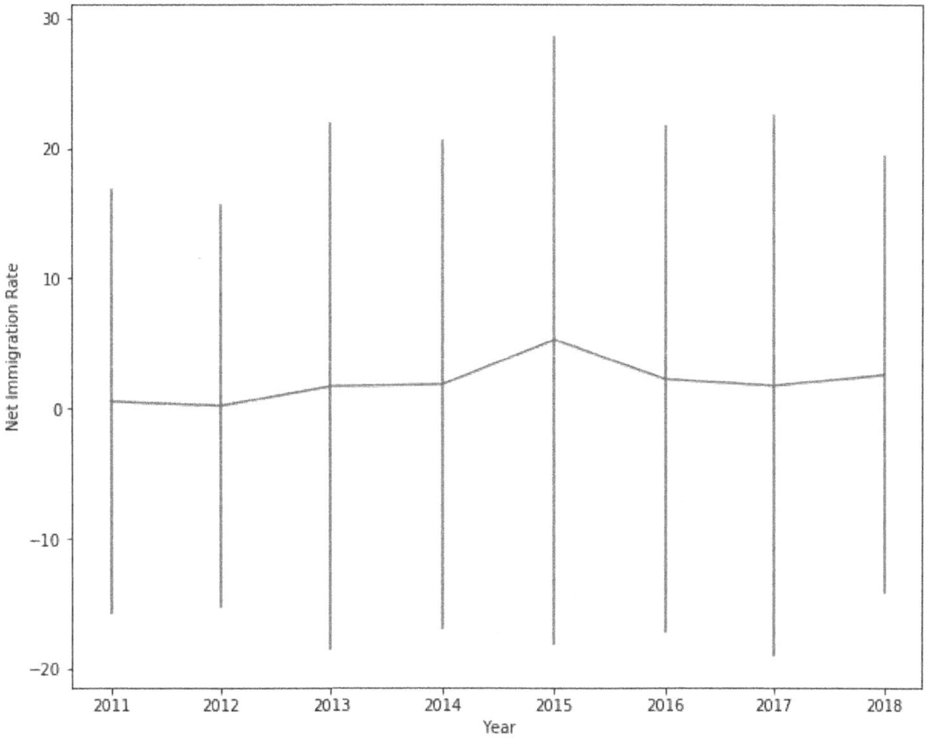

Figure 2.8 – Net immigration rate across counties in Texas from 2011 to 2018

We can see in *Figure 2.8* that although the net immigration in Texas is only slightly positive, the standard deviation is huge. Some counties may have a big positive net rate, while others may potentially suffer from the loss of human resources.

Quartiles

Quartiles are a special kind of quantile that divide data into a number of equal portions. For example, quartiles divide data into four equal parts with the ½ quartile as the median. Deciles and percentiles divide data into 10 and 100 equal parts, respectively.

The first quartile, also known as the lower quartile Q_1 takes the value such that 25% of all the data lies below it. The second quartile is the median. The third quartile, Q_3, is also known as the upper quartile and 25% of all values lie above it.

Quartiles are probably the most commonly used **quantiles** because they are associated with a statistical graph called a **boxplot**. Let's use the same set of Texas net immigration data to study it.

The function in NumPy is `quantile()` and we specify a list of quantiles as an argument for the quantiles we want to calculate, as in the following single-line code snippet:

```
np.quantile(dfTX["R_NET_MIG_2013"],[0.25,0.5,0.75])
```

The output reads as follows:

```
array([-7.83469971,  0.87919226,  8.84040759])
```

The following code snippet visualizes the quartiles:

```
plt.figure(figsize=(12,5))
plt.hist(dfTX["R_NET_MIG_2013"],bins=50,alpha=0.6)
for quartile in np.quantile(dfTX["R_NET_
MIG_2013"],[0.25,0.5,0.75]):
plt.axvline(quartile,linestyle=':',linewidth=4)
```

As you can see from the following output, the vertical dotted lines indicate the three quartiles:

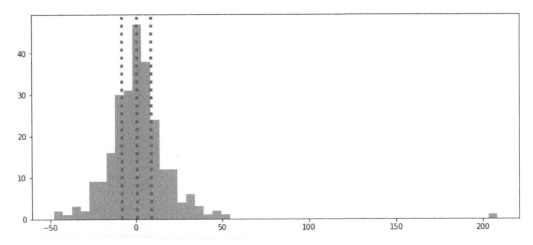

Figure 2.9 – Quartiles of the net immigration data in 2013

The lower and upper quartiles keep exactly 50% of the data values in between. $Q_3 - Q_1$ is referred to as the interquartile range called **Interquartile Range (IQR)** and it plays an important role in outlier detection. We will see more about this soon.

Skewness

Skewness differs from the three measures of variability we discussed in the previous subsections. It measures the direction the data takes and the extent to which the data distribution tilts. Skewness is given as shown in the following equation:

$$Sk = \frac{\bar{x} - mode}{\sigma}$$

Various definitions of skewness

The skewness we defined earlier is precisely referred to as Pearson's first skewness coefficient. It is defined through the mode, but there are other definitions of skewness. For example, skewness can be defined through the median.

Skewness is unitless. If the mean is larger than the mode, skewness is positive, and we say the data is skewed to the right. Otherwise, the data is skewed to the left.

Here is the code snippet that generates two sets of skewed data and plots them:

```
r1 = [random.normalvariate(0.5,0.4) for _ in range(10000)]
r2 = [random.normalvariate(0.1,0.2) for _ in range(10000)]
r3 = [random.normalvariate(1.1,0.2) for _ in range(10000)]


fig, axes = plt.subplots(1,2,figsize=(12,5))
axes[0].hist(r1+r2,bins=100,alpha=0.5)
axes[0].axvline(np.mean(r1+r2), linestyle=':',linewidth=4)
axes[0].set_title("Skewed To Right")
axes[1].hist(r1+r3,bins=100,alpha=0.5)
axes[1].axvline(np.mean(r1+r3),linestyle=':',linewidth=4)
axes[1].set_title("Skewed to Left");
```

The vertical dotted line indicates the position of the mean as follows:

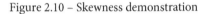

Figure 2.10 – Skewness demonstration

Think about the problem of income inequality. Let's say you have a plot of the histogram of the population with different amounts of wealth. A larger value just like where the x axis value indicates the amount of wealth and the y axis value indicates the portion of the population that falls into a certain wealth amount range. A larger x value means more wealth. A larger y value means a greater percentage of the population falls into that range of wealth possession. Positive skewness (the left subplot in *Figure 2.10*) means that even though the average income looks good, this may be driven up by a very small number of super rich individuals when the majority of people earn a relatively small income. Negative skewness (the right subplot in *Figure 2.10*) indicates that the majority may have an income above the mean value, so there might be some very poor people who may need help.

A revisit of outlier detection

Now, let's use what we have learned to revisit the outlier detection problem.

The **z-score**, also known as the **standard score**, is a good criterion for detecting outliers. It measures the distance between an entry and the population mean, taking the population variance into consideration:

$$z = \frac{x - \bar{x}}{\sigma}$$

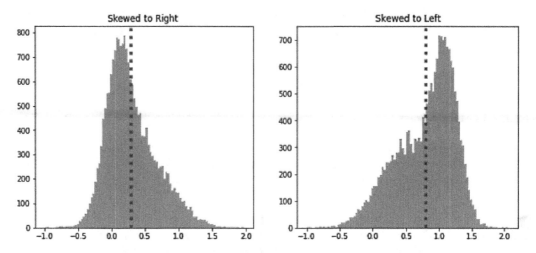

If the underlying distribution is normal, a situation where a z-score is greater than 3 or less than 0 only has a probability of roughly 0.27%. Even if the underlying distribution is not normal, Chebyshev's theorem guarantees a strong claim such that at most $1\backslash k\char`^2$, where k is an integer, of the total population can fall outside k standard deviations.

As an example, the following code snippet generates 10,000 data points that follow a normal distribution:

```
random.seed(2020)
x = [random.normalvariate(1, 0.5) for _ in range(10000)]
plt.figure(figsize=(10,8))
plt.hist(x,bins=100,alpha=0.5);
styles = [":","--","-."]
for i in range(3):
    plt.axvline(np.mean(x) + (i+1)*np.std(x),
                linestyle=styles[i],
                linewidth=4)
    plt.axvline(np.mean(x) - (i+1)*np.std(x),
                linestyle=styles[i],
                linewidth=4)
plt.title("Integer Z values for symmetric distributions");
```

In the generated histogram plot, the dotted line indicates the location where $z = \pm 1$. The dashed line indicates the location of $z = \pm 2$. The dashed dotted line indicates the location of $z = \pm 3$:

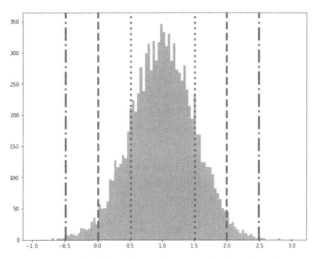

Figure 2.11 – Integer z value boundaries for normally distributed symmetric data

If we change the data points, the distribution will change, but the z-score criteria will remain valid. As you can see in the following code snippet, an asymmetric distribution is generated rather than a normal distribution:

```
x = [random.normalvariate(1, 0.5) + random.expovariate(2) for _
in range(10000)]
```

This produces the following output:

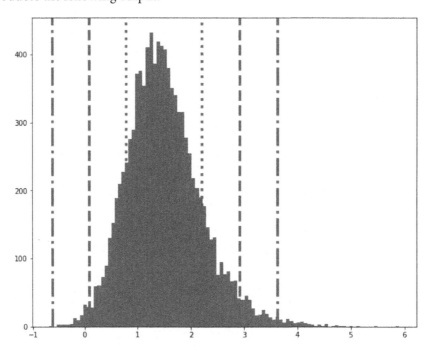

Figure 2.12 – Integer z value boundaries for asymmetric data

Note on the influence of extreme outliers

A drawback of the z-score is that the mean itself is also influenced by extreme outliers. The median can replace a mean to remove this effect. It is flexible to set different criteria in different production cases.

We have covered several of the most important statistics to model variances in a dataset. In the next section, let's work on the data types of features.

Knowing how to handle categorical variables and mixed data types

Categorical variables usually have simpler structures or descriptive statistics than continuous variables. Here, we introduce the two main descriptive statistics and talk about some interesting cases when converting continuous variables to categorical ones.

Frequencies and proportions

When we discussed the mode for categorical variables, we introduced `Counter`, which outputs a dictionary structure whose key-value pair is the element-counting pair. The following is an example of a counter:

```
Counter({2.0: 394, 3.0: 369, 6.0: 597, 1.0: 472, 9.0: 425, 7.0:
434, 8.0: 220, 4.0: 217, 5.0: 92})
```

The following code snippet illustrates frequency as a bar plot where the absolute values of counting become intuitive:

```
counter = Counter(df["Rural-urban_Continuum Code_2013"].
dropna())
labels = []
x = []
for key, val in counter.items():
    labels.append(str(key))
    x.append(val)
plt.figure(figsize=(10,8))
plt.bar(labels,x)
plt.title("Bar plot of frequency");
```

What you will get is the bar plot that follows:

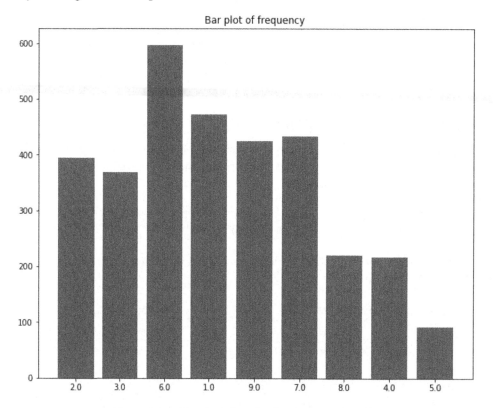

Figure 2.13 – Bar plot of rural-urban continuum code

For proportionality, simply divide each count by the summation of counting, as shown in the following code snippet:

```
x = np.array(x)/sum(x)
```

The shape of the bar plot remains the same, but the *y* axis ticks change. To better check the relative size of components, I have plotted a pie plot with the help of the following code snippet:

```
plt.figure(figsize=(10,10))
plt.pie(x=x,labels=labels,)
plt.title("Pie plot for rural-urban continuum code");
```

What you get is a nice pie chart as follows:

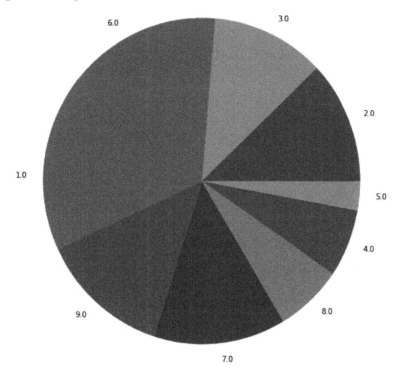

Figure 2.14 – Pie plot of rural-urban continuum code

It becomes evident that code 2.0 contains about twice as many samples as code 8.0 does.

Unlike the mean and median, categorical data does have a mode. We are going to reuse the same data:

```
Counter(df["Rural-urban_Continuum Code_2013"].dropna())
```

The output reads as follows:

```
Counter({2.0: 394, 3.0: 369, 6.0: 597, 1.0: 472, 9.0: 425, 7.0:
434, 8.0: 220, 4.0: 217, 5.0: 92})
```

The mode is 6.0.

> **Note**
>
> The mode means that the counties with urban populations of 2,500 to 19,999 adjacent to a metro area are most prevalent in the United States, and not the number 6.0.

Transforming a continuous variable to a categorical one

Occasionally, we may need to convert a continuous variable to a categorical one. Let's take lifespan as an example. The 80+ age group is supposed to be very small. Each of them will represent a negligible data point in classification tasks. If they can be grouped together, the noise introduced by the sparsity of this age group's individual points will be reduced.

A common way to perform categorization is to use quantiles. For example, quartiles will divide the datasets into four parts with an equal number of entries. This avoids issues such as data imbalance.

For example, the following code indicates the cut-offs for the categorization of the continuous variable net immigration rate:

```
series = df["R_NET_MIG_2013"].dropna()
quantiles = np.quantile(series,[0.2*i for i in range(1,5)])
plt.figure(figsize=(10,8))
plt.hist(series,bins=100,alpha=0.5)
plt.xlim(-50,50)
for i in range(len(quantiles)):
    plt.axvline(quantiles[i],linestyle=":",
                linewidth=4)
plt.title("Quantiles for net immigration data");
```

As you can see in the following output, the dotted vertical lines split the data into 5 equal sets, which are hard to spot with the naked eye. I truncated the x axis to select the part between -50 and 50. The result looks as follows:

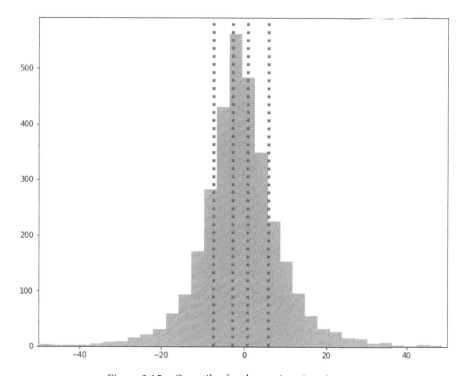

Figure 2.15 – Quantiles for the net immigration rate

Note on the loss of information

Categorization destroys the rich structure in continuous variables. Only use it when you absolutely need to.

Using bivariate and multivariate descriptive statistics

In this section, we briefly talk about bivariate descriptive statistics. Bivariate descriptive statistics apply two variables rather than one. We are going to focus on correlation for continuous variables and cross-tabulation for categorical variables.

Covariance

The word *covariance* is often incorrectly used as *correlation*. However, there are a number of fundamental differences. Covariance usually measures the joint variability of two variables, while correlation focuses more on the strength of variability. Correlation coefficients have several definitions in different use cases. The most common descriptive statistic is the Pearson correlation coefficient. We will also be using it to describe the covariance of two variables. The correlation coefficient for variables x and y from a population is defined as follows:

$$\rho(x, y) = \frac{\frac{1}{n}\sum_{i=1}^{n}(x_i - \bar{x})(y_i - \bar{x})}{\sigma_x \sigma_y}$$

Let's first examine the expression's sign. The coefficient becomes positive when x is greater than its mean and y is also greater than its own mean.

Another case is when x and y are both smaller than their means, respectively. The products sum together and then get *normalized* by the standard deviation of each variable. So, a positive coefficient indicates that x and y vary jointly in the same direction. You can make a similar argument about negative coefficients.

In the following code snippet, we select the net immigration rates for counties in Texas as our datasets and use the `corr()` function to inspect the correlation coefficient across years:

```
corrs = dfTX[['R_NET_MIG_2011','R_NET_MIG_2012', 'R_NET_
MIG_2013', 'R_NET_MIG_2014', 'R_NET_MIG_2015','R_NET_MIG_2016',
'R_NET_MIG_2017', 'R_NET_MIG_2018']].corr()
```

The output is a so-called *correlation matrix* whose diagonal elements are the self-correlation coefficients, which are just 1:

	R_NET_MIG_2011	R_NET_MIG_2012	R_NET_MIG_2013	R_NET_MIG_2014	R_NET_MIG_2015	R_NET_MIG_201
R_NET_MIG_2011	1.000000	-0.025355	0.476505	-0.021194	0.407675	0.03031
R_NET_MIG_2012	-0.025355	1.000000	0.028037	0.555593	-0.027442	0.04825
R_NET_MIG_2013	0.476505	0.028037	1.000000	-0.007720	0.713877	0.02416
R_NET_MIG_2014	-0.021194	0.555593	-0.007720	1.000000	-0.226211	0.17700
R_NET_MIG_2015	0.407675	-0.027442	0.713877	-0.226211	1.000000	0.22386
R_NET_MIG_2016	0.030318	0.048258	0.024169	0.177007	0.223869	1.00000
R_NET_MIG_2017	0.344111	-0.187224	0.310188	-0.148383	0.568450	0.59568
R_NET_MIG_2018	0.492326	0.049451	0.376498	0.185914	0.476637	0.44369

Figure 2.16 – Correlation matrix for the net immigration rate

A good way to visualize this matrix is to use the `heatmap()` function from the Seaborn library. The following code snippet generates a nice heatmap:

```
import seaborn as sns
plt.figure(figsize=(10,8))
plt.rcParams.update({'font.size': 12})
sns.heatmap(corrs,cmap="YlGnBu");
```

The result looks as follows:

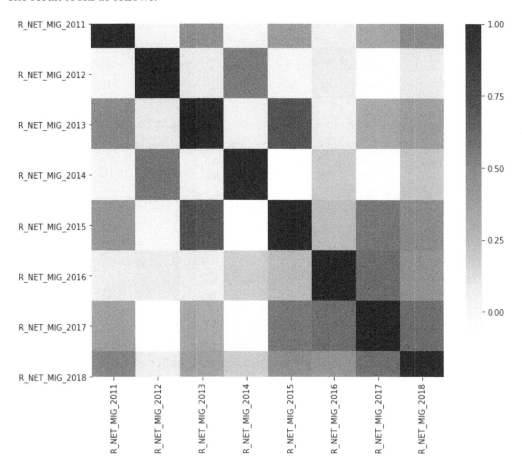

Figure 2.17 – Heatmap of a correlation matrix for net immigration rates in Texas

We do see an interesting pattern that odd years correlate with one another more strongly, and even years correlate with each other more strongly, too. However, that is not the case between even - and odd - numbered years. Perhaps there is a 2-year cyclic pattern and the heatmap of the correlation matrix just helped us discover it.

Cross-tabulation

Cross-tabulation can be treated as a discrete version of correlation detection for categorical variables. It helps derive innumerable insights and sheds light on downstream task designs.

Here is an example. I am creating a list of weather information and another list of a golfer's decisions on whether to go golfing. The `crosstab()` function generates the following table:

```
weather = ["rainy","sunny","rainy","windy","windy",
           "sunny","rainy","windy","sunny","rainy",
           "sunny","windy","windy"]
golfing = ["Yes","Yes","No","No","Yes","Yes","No","No",
           "Yes","No","Yes","No","No"]


dfGolf = pd.DataFrame({"weather":weather,"golfing":golfing})
pd.crosstab(dfGolf.weather, dfGolf.golfing, margins=True)
```

golfing	No	Yes	All
weather			
rainy	3	1	4
sunny	0	4	4
windy	4	1	5
All	7	6	13

Figure 2.18 – Cross-tabulation for golfing decisions

As you can see, the columns and rows give the exact counts, which are identified by the column name and row name. For a dataset with a limited number of features, this is a handy way to inspect imbalance or bias.

We can tell that the golfer goes golfing if the weather is sunny, and that they seldom go golfing on rainy or windy days.

With that, we have come to the end of the chapter!

Summary

Statistics or tools to assess datasets were introduced and demonstrated in this chapter. You should be able to identify different kinds of variables, compute corresponding statistics, and detect outliers. We do see graphing as an essential part of descriptive statistics.

In the next chapter, we will cover the basics of Python plotting, the advanced customization of aesthetics, and professional plotting techniques.

3
Visualization with Statistical Graphs

A picture is worth a thousand words. Humans rely on visual input for more than 90% of all information obtained. A statistical graph can demonstrate trends, explain reasons, or predict futures much better than words if done right.

Python data ecosystems come with a lot of great tools for visualization. The three most important ones are Matplotlib, seaborn, and plotly. The first two are mainly for static plotting, while plotly is capable of interactive plotting and is gaining in popularity gradually.

In this chapter, you will focus on static plotting, which is the backbone of data visualization. We have already extensively used some plots in previous chapters to illustrate concepts.

In this chapter, we will approach them in a systematic way. The topics that will be covered in this chapter are as follows:

- Picking the right plotting types for different tasks
- Improving and customizing visualization with advanced aesthetic customization
- Performing statistical plotting tailored for business queries
- Building stylish and professional plots for presentations or reports

Let's start with the basic Matplotlib library.

Basic examples with the Python Matplotlib package

In this chapter, we will start with the most basic functionalities of the Matplotlib package. Let's first understand the elements to make a perfect statistical graph.

Elements of a statistical graph

Before we dive into Python code, I will give you an overview of how to decompose the components of a statistical graph. I personally think the philosophy that embeds the R ggplot2 package is very concise and clear.

> **Note**
>
> R is another famous programming language for data science and statistical analysis. There are also successful R packages. The counterpart of Matplotlib is the R ggplot2 package mentioned previously.

ggplot2 is a very successful visualization tool developed by Hadley Wickman. It decomposes a statistical plot into the following three components:

- **Data**: The data must have the information to display; otherwise, the plotting becomes totally misleading. The data can be transformed, such as with categorization, before being visualized.

- **Geometries**: Geometry here means the types of plotting. For example, bar plot, pie plot, boxplot, and scatter plot are all different types of plotting. Different geometries are suitable for different visualization purposes.

- **Aesthetics**: The size, shape, color, and positioning of visual elements, such as the title, ticks, and legends, all belong to aesthetics. A coherent collection of aesthetic elements can be bundled together as a theme. For example, Facebook and The Economist have very distinguishable graphical themes.

Let's use the birth rate and death rate data for Texas counties grouped by urbanization level as an example. Before that, let's relate this data with the three components mentioned previously:

- The data is the *birth rate and death rate data*, which determines the location of the scattered points.

- The geometry is a *scatter plot*. If you use a line plot, you are using the wrong type of plot because there isn't a natural ordering structure in the dataset.

- There are many aesthetic elements, but the most important ones are the *size* and the *color* of the spots. How they are determined will be detailed when we reach the second section of this chapter.

Incorporating this data into a graph gives a result that would look something like this:

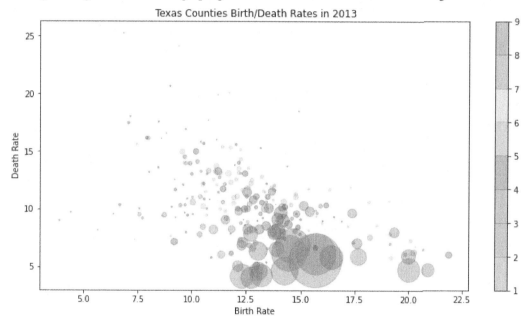

Figure 3.1 – Example for elements of statistical graphing

Geometry is built upon data, and the aesthetics will only make sense if you have the right data and geometry. In this chapter, you can assume we already have the right data. If you have the wrong data, you will end up with graphs that make no sense and are oftentimes misleading.

In this section, let's focus mainly on geometry. In the following sections, I will talk about how to transform data and customize aesthetics.

Exploring important types of plotting in Matplotlib

Let's first explore the most important plotting types one by one.

Simple line plots

A simple line plot is the easiest type of plotting. It represents only a binary mapping relationship between two ordered sets. Stock price versus date is an example; temperature versus time is another.

The following code snippet generates a list of evenly spaced numbers and their sine and plots them. Please note that the libraries only need to be imported once:

```
import numpy as np
import matplotlib.pyplot as plt
%matplotlib inline
fig = plt.figure()
x = np.linspace(0, 10, 1000)
plt.plot(x, np.sin(x));
```

This generates the following output:

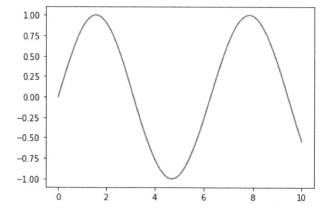

Figure 3.2 – A simple line plot of the sine function

You can add one or two more simple line plots; Matplotlib will decide the default color of the lines for you. The following snippet will add two more trigonometric functions:

```
fig = plt.figure(figsize=(10,8))
x = np.linspace(0, 10, 100)
plt.plot(x, np.sin(x),linestyle=":",linewidth=4)
plt.plot(x,np.cos(x),linestyle="--",linewidth=4)
plt.plot(x,np.cos(2*x),linestyle="-.",linewidth=4);
```

Different sets of data are plotted with dashed lines, dotted lines, and dashed-dotted lines, as shown in the following figure:

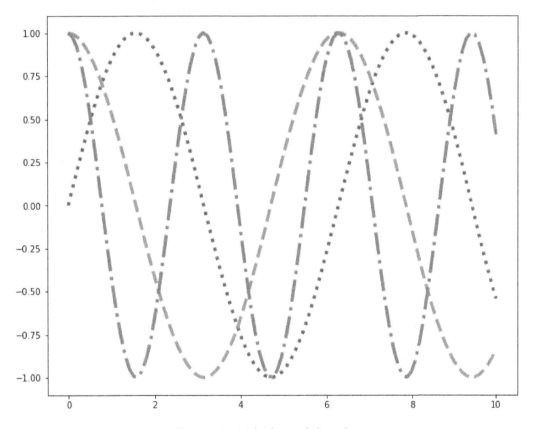

Figure 3.3 – Multiple simple line plots

Now that we have understood a simple line plot, let's move on to the next type of plotting – a histogram plot.

Histogram plots

We used a histogram plot extensively in the previous chapter. This type of plot groups data into bins and shows the counts of data points in each bin with neighboring bars.

The following code snippet demonstrates a traditional one-dimensional histogram plot:

```
x1 = np.random.laplace(0, 0.8, 500)
x2 = np.random.normal(3, 2, 500)
plt.hist(x1, alpha=0.5, density=True, bins=20)
plt.hist(x2, alpha=0.5, density=True, bins=20);
```

The following output shows the histogram plots overlapping each other:

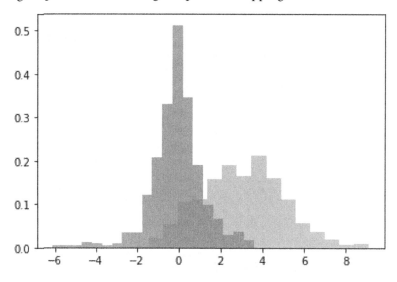

Figure 3.4 – A one-dimensional histogram

Here, density is normalized, so the histogram is no longer a frequency count but a probability count. The transparency level, the alpha value, is set to 0.5, so the histogram underline is displayed properly.

Boxplot and outlier detection

A two-dimensional histogram plot is especially helpful for visualizing correlations between two quantities. We will be using the immigration data we used in the *Classifying numerical and categorical variables* section in *Chapter 2, Essential Statistics for Data Assessment*, as an example.

The good thing about a boxplot is that it gives us a very good estimation of the existence of outliers. The following code snippet plots the Texas counties' net immigration rate of 2017 in a boxplot:

```
import pandas as pd
df = pd.read_excel("PopulationEstimates.xls",skiprows=2)
dfTX = df[df["State"]=="TX"].tail(-1)
plt.boxplot(dfTX['R_NET_MIG_2017']);
```

The plot looks as in the following figure:

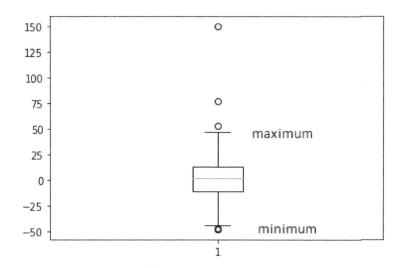

Figure 3.5 – A boxplot of the 2017 net immigration rate of Texas counties

What we generated is a simple boxplot. It has a box with a horizontal line in between. There are **minimum** and **maximum** data points, which are represented as short horizontal lines. However, there are also data points above the maximum and below the minimum. You may also wonder what they are since there are already maximum and minimum data points. We will solve these issues one by one.

Let's understand the box first. The top and bottom of the box are the ¾ quartile and the ¼ quartile, respectively. This means exactly *50%* of the data is in the box. The distance between the ¼ quartile and the ¾ quartile is called the **Interquartile Range (IQR)**. Clearly, the shorter the box is, the more centralized the data points are. The orange line in the middle represents the **median**.

The position of the maximum is worked out as the sum of the ¾ quartile and 1.5 times the IQR. The minimum is worked out as the difference between the ¼ quartile and 1.5 times the IQR. What still lies outside of the range are considered **outliers**. In the preceding boxplot, there are four outliers. For example, if the distribution is normal, a data point being an outlier has a probability of roughly 0.7%, which is small.

> **Note**
>
> A boxplot offers you a visual approach to detect outliers. In the preceding example, 1.5 times the IQR is not a fixed rule, and you can choose a cut-off for specific tasks.

Scatter plots

A scatter plot is very useful for visually inspecting correlations between variables. It is especially helpful to display data at a different time or date from different locations in the same graph. Readers usually find it difficult to tell minute distribution differences from numerical values, but a scatter plot makes them easy to spot.

For example, let's plot the birth rate and death rate for all the Texas counties in 2013 and 2017. It becomes somewhat clear that from 2013 to 2017, some data points with the highest death rate disappear, while the birth rates remain unchanged. The following code snippet does the job:

```
plt.figure(figsize=(8,6))
plt.scatter(dfTX.R_birth_2013,dfTX.R_
death_2013,alpha="0.5",label="2013")
plt.scatter(dfTX.R_birth_2017,dfTX.R_
death_2017,alpha="0.5",label="2017")
plt.legend()
plt.xlabel("Birth Rate")
plt.ylabel("Death Rate")
plt.title("Texas Counties Birth/Death Rates");
```

The output looks as in the following figure:

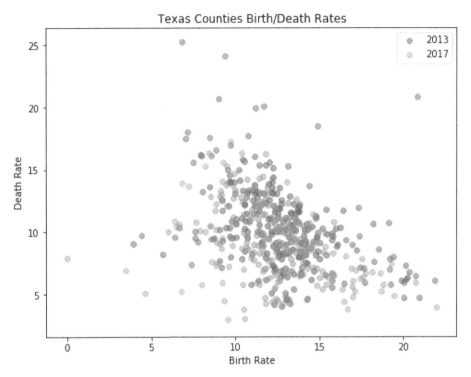

Figure 3.6 – A scatter plot of the birth rate and death rate in Texas counties

Note

The scatter plot shown in *Figure 3.6* doesn't reveal one-to-one dynamics. For example, we don't know the change in the birth rate or death rate of a specific county, and it is possible, though unlikely, that county *A* and county *B* exchanged their positions in the scatter plot. Therefore, a basic scatter plot only gives us distribution-wise information, but no more than that.

Bar plots

A bar plot is another common plot to demonstrate trends and compare several quantities side by side. It is better than a simple line chart because sometimes line charts can be misleading without careful interpretation.

For example, say I want to see the birth rate and death rate data for Anderson County in Texas from 2011 to 2018. The following short code snippet would prepare the column masks to select features and examine the first row of the DataFrame, which is the data for Anderson County:

```
birthRates = list(filter(lambda x: x.startswith("R_
birth"),dfTX.columns))
```
```
deathRates = list(filter(lambda x: x.startswith("R_
death"),dfTX.columns))
```
```
years = np.array(list(map(lambda x: int(x[-4:]), birthRates)))
```

The Anderson County information can be obtained by using the `iloc` method, as shown in the following snippet:

```
dfTX.iloc[0]
```

Figure 3.7 shows the first several columns and the last several ones of the Anderson County data:

```
FIPS                                      48001
State                                        TX
Area_Name                       Anderson County
Rural-urban_Continuum Code_2003               5
Rural-urban_Continuum Code_2013               7
                                  ...
R_NET_MIG_2014                        -0.0518018
R_NET_MIG_2015                          -2.83995
R_NET_MIG_2016                         -0.729192
R_NET_MIG_2017                           12.2665
R_NET_MIG_2018                         -0.80847
Name: 2568, Length: 149, dtype: object
```

Figure 3.7 – Anderson County data

> **Note**
>
> `DataFrame.iloc[]` in `pandas` allows you to slice a DataFrame by the index field.

The following code snippet generates a simple line plot:

```
plt.figure(figsize=(10,6))
width=0.4
plt.plot(years-width/2, dfTX.iloc[0][birthRates], label= "birth
rate")
plt.plot(years+width/2, dfTX.iloc[0][deathRates],label="death
rate")
plt.xlabel("years")
plt.ylabel("rate")
plt.legend()
plt.title("Anderson County birth rate and death rate");
```

The following figure shows the output, which is a simple line plot with the dotted line being the birth rate and the dashed line being the death rate, by default:

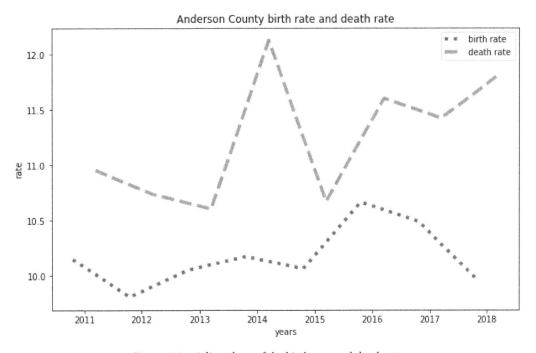

Figure 3.8 – A line chart of the birth rate and death rate

Without carefully reading it, you can derive two pieces of information from the plot:

- The death rates change dramatically across the years.
- The death rates are much higher than the birth rates.

Even though the *y* - axis tick doesn't support the two claims presented, admit it, this is the first impression we get without careful observation.

However, with a bar plot, this illusion can be eliminated early. The following code snippet will help in generating a bar plot:

```
plt.figure(figsize=(10,6))
width=0.4
plt.bar(years-width/2, dfTX.iloc[0][birthRates],
        width=width, label= «birth rate», alpha = 1)
plt.bar(years+width/2, dfTX.iloc[0][deathRates],
        width=width, label="death rate", alpha = 1)
plt.xlabel("years")
plt.ylabel("rate")
plt.legend()
plt.title("Anderson County birth rate and death rate");
```

I slightly shifted `year` to be the *X* value and selected `birthRates` and `deathRates` with the `iloc[]` method we introduced earlier. The result will look as shown in *Figure 3.9*:

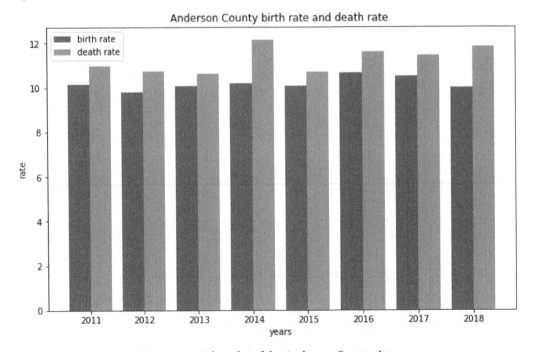

Figure 3.9 – A bar plot of the Anderson County data

The following is now much clearer:

- The death rate is higher than the birth rate but not as dramatically as the line plot suggests.

- The rates do not change dramatically across the years, except in 2014.

The bar plot will, by default, show the whole scale of the data, therefore eliminating the earlier illusion.

Note how I used the `width` parameter to shift the two sets of bars so that they can be properly positioned.

Advanced visualization customization

In this section, you are going to learn how to customize the plots from two perspectives, the *geometry* and the *aesthetics*. You will see examples and understand how the customization works.

Customizing the geometry

There isn't enough time nor space to cover every detail of geometry customization. Let's learn by understanding and following examples instead.

Example 1 – axis-sharing and subplots

Continuing from the previous example, let's say you want the birth rate and the population change to be plotted on the same graph. However, the numerical values of the two quantities are drastically different, making the birth rate basically indistinguishable. There are two ways to solve this issue. Let's look at each of the ways individually.

Axis-sharing

We can make use of both the left-hand y axis and the right-hand Y axis to represent different scales. The following code snippet copies the axes with the `twinx()` function, which is the key of the whole code block:

```
figure, ax1 = plt.subplots(figsize=(10,6))
ax1.plot(years, dfTX.iloc[0][birthRates], label= "birth
rate",c="red")
ax2 = ax1.twinx()
ax2.plot(years, dfTX.iloc[0][popChanges][1:], label="population
change")
```

```
ax1.set_xlabel("years")
ax1.set_ylabel("birth rate")
ax2.set_ylabel("population change")
ax1.legend()
ax2.legend()
plt.title("Anderson County birth rate and population change");
```

As you can see, the preceding code snippet does three things, in order:

1. Creates a figure instance and an axis instance, `ax1`

2. Creates a twin of `ax1` and plots the two sets of data on two different axes

3. Creates labels for two different axes, shows the legend, sets the title, and so on

The following is the output:

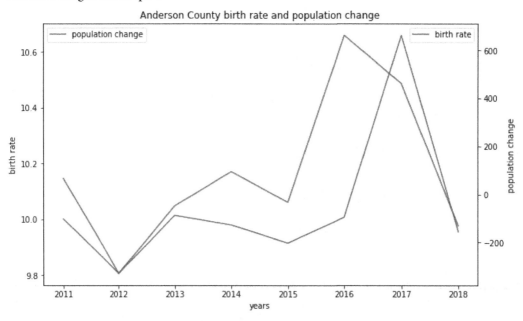

Figure 3.10 – Double Y axes example

The output looks nice, and both trends are clearly visible.

Subplots

With subplots, we can also split the two graphs into two subplots. The following code snippet creates two stacked subplots and plots the dataset on them separately:

```
figure, axes = plt.subplots(2,1,figsize=(10,6))
axes[0].plot(years, dfTX.iloc[0][birthRates], label= "birth
rate",c="red")
axes[1].plot(years, dfTX.iloc[0][popChanges][1:],
label="population change")
axes[1].set_xlabel("years")
axes[0].set_ylabel("birth rate")
axes[1].set_ylabel("population change")
axes[0].legend()
axes[1].legend()
axes[0].set_title("Anderson County birth rate and population
change");
```

> **Note**
>
> The subplots function takes 2 and 1 as two arguments. This means the layout will have 2 rows but 1 column. So, the *axes* will be a two-element list.

The output of the previous code will look as follows:

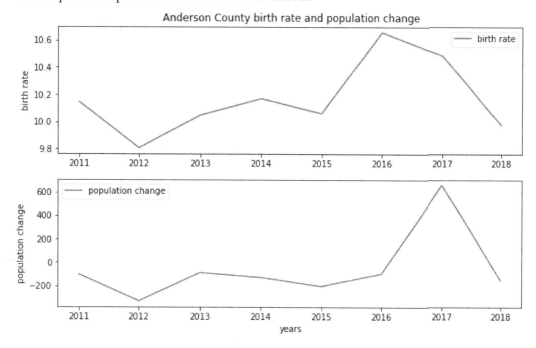

Figure 3.11 – Birth rate and population subplots example

The two plots will adjust the scale of the *Y* axis automatically. The advantage of using subplots over a shared axis is that subplots can support the addition of more complicated markups, while a shared axis is already crowded.

Example 2 – scale change

In this second example, we will be using the dataset for the total number of coronavirus cases in the world published by WHO. At the time of writing this book, the latest data I could obtain was from March 15, 2020. You can also obtain the data from the official repository of this book.

The following code snippet loads the data and formats the date column into a date data type:

```python
coronaCases = pd.read_csv("total_cases_03_15_2020.csv")
from datetime import datetime
coronaCases["date"] = coronaCases["date"].apply(lambda x:
datetime.strptime(x, "%Y-%m-%d"))
```

Then, we plot the data for the world and the US. The output of the previous code snippet will look like this:

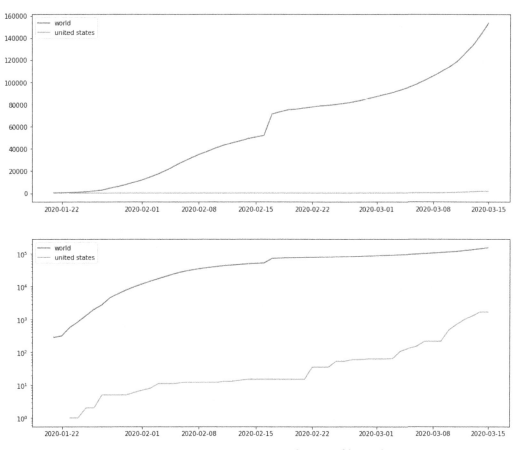

Figure 3.12 – Coronavirus cases in linear and log scales

Note how I changed the second subplot from a linear scale to a log scale. Can you work out the advantage of doing so?

On a linear scale, because the cases in the world are much larger than the cases in the US, the representation of cases in the US is basically a horizontal line, and the details in the total case curve at the early stage are not clear. In the log-scale plot, the Y axis changes to a logarithm scale, so exponential growth becomes a somewhat linear line, and the numbers in the US are visible now.

Customizing the aesthetics

Details are important, and they can guide us to focus on the right spot. Here, I use one example to show the importance of aesthetics, specifically the markers. A good choice of markers can help readers notice the most important information you want to convey.

Example – markers

Suppose you want to visualize the birth rate and death rate for counties in Texas but also want to inspect the rates against the total population and `rural_urban_continuum_code` for a specific year.

In short, you have *four* quantities to inspect, so which geometry will you choose and how will you represent the quantities?

> **Note**
>
> The continuum code is a discrete variable, but the other three are continuous variables. To represent a discrete variable that doesn't have numerical relationships between categories, you should choose colors or markers over others, which may suggest numerical differences.

A naïve choice is a scatter plot, as we did earlier. This is shown in the following code snippet:

```python
plt.figure(figsize=(12,6))
plt.scatter(dfTX.R_birth_2013,
            dfTX.R_death_2013,
            alpha=0.4,
            s = dfTX.POP_ESTIMATE_2013/1000,
            )
plt.xlabel("Birth Rate")
plt.ylabel("Death Rate")
plt.title("Texas Counties Birth/Death Rates in 2013");
```

Note that I set the s parameter, the size of the default marker, to be 1 unit for every 1,000 of the population.

The output already looks very informative:

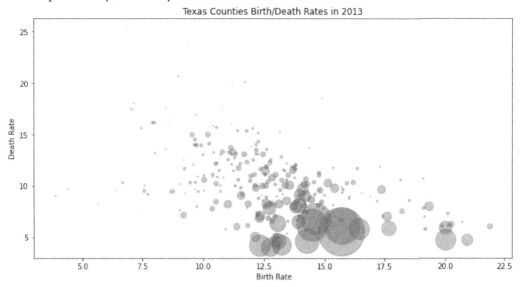

Figure 3.13 – The birth rate and death rate in Texas

However, this is probably not enough because we can't tell whether the region is a rural area or an urban area. To do this, we need to introduce a color map.

> **Note**
>
> A color map maps a feature to a set of colors. In Matplotlib, there are many different color maps. For a complete list of maps, check the official document at `https://matplotlib.org/3.2.0/tutorials/colors/colormaps.html`.

The following code snippet maps `rural_urban_continuum_code` to colors and plots the color bar. Although the code itself is numerical, the color bar ticks contain no numerical meaning:

```
plt.figure(figsize=(12,6))
plt.scatter(dfTX.R_birth_2013,
            dfTX.R_death_2013,
            alpha=0.4,
            s = dfTX.POP_ESTIMATE_2013/1000,
            c= dfTX["Rural-urban_Continuum Code_2003»],
            cmap =  'Dark2',
            )
```

```
plt.colorbar()
plt.xlabel("Birth Rate")
plt.ylabel("Death Rate")
plt.title("Texas Counties Birth/Death Rates in 2013");
```

The output looks much easier to interpret:

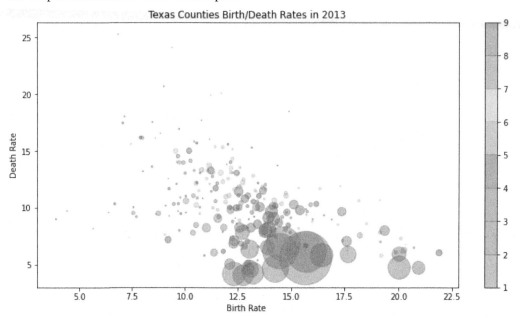

Figure 3.14 – The birth rate and death rate in Texas (revised)

From this plotting, counties with smaller code numbers have a bigger population, a relatively moderate birth rate, but a lower death rate. This is possibly due to the age structure because cities are more likely to attract younger people. This information can't be revealed without adjusting the aesthetics of the graph.

Query-oriented statistical plotting

The visualization should always be guided by business queries. In the previous section, we saw the relationship between birth and death rates, population, and code, and with that, we designed how the graph should look.

In this section, we will see two more examples. The first example is about preprocessing data to meet the requirement of the plotting API in the `seaborn` library. In the second example, we will integrate simple statistical analysis into plotting, which will also serve as a teaser for our next chapter.

Example 1 – preparing data to fit the plotting function API

`seaborn` is another popular Python visualization library. With it, you can write less code to obtain more professional-looking plots. Some APIs are different, though.

Let's plot a boxplot. You can check the official documentation at `https://seaborn.pydata.org/generated/seaborn.boxplot.html`. Let's try to use it to plot the birth rates from different years for Texas counties.

However, if you look at the DataFrame that the `seaborn` library imported, it looks different from what we used earlier:

```
import seaborn as sns
tips = sns.load_dataset("tips")
tips.head()
```

The output looks as follows:

	total_bill	tip	sex	smoker	day	time	size
0	16.99	1.01	Female	No	Sun	Dinner	2
1	10.34	1.66	Male	No	Sun	Dinner	3
2	21.01	3.50	Male	No	Sun	Dinner	3
3	23.68	3.31	Male	No	Sun	Dinner	2
4	24.59	3.61	Female	No	Sun	Dinner	4

Figure 3.15 – Head of tips, a seaborn built-in dataset

The syntax of plotting a boxplot is shown in the following snippet:

```
ax = sns.boxplot(x="day", y="total_bill", data=tips)
```

The output is as follows:

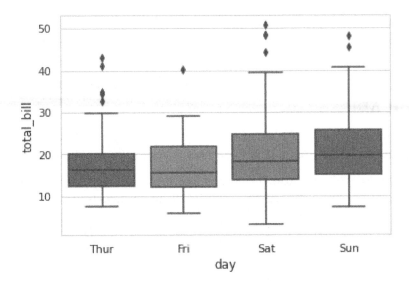

Figure 3.16 – The seaborn tips boxplot

> **Note**
>
> It is hard to generate such a beautiful boxplot with one-line code using the Matplotlib library. There is always a trade-off between control and easiness. In my opinion, seaborn is a good choice if you have limited time for your tasks.

Notice that the x parameter, day, is a column name in the tips DataFrame, and it can take several values: Thur, Fri, Sat, and Sun. However, in the Texas county data, records for each year are separated as different columns, which is much *wider* than the tidy tips DataFrame.

To convert a wide table into a long table, we need the pandas melt function: https://pandas.pydata.org/pandas-docs/stable/reference/api/pandas.melt.html.

The following code snippet selects the birth rate-related columns and transforms the table into a longer, thinner format:

```
birthRatesDF = dfTX[birthRates]
birthRatesDF["index"] = birthRatesDF.index;
birthRatesDFLong = pd.melt(birthRatesDF,id_
vars=["index"],value_vars = birthRatesDF.columns[:-1])
birthRatesDFLong["variable"] = birthRatesDFLong["variable"].
apply(lambda x: int(x[-4:]))
```

The long-format table now looks as in the following figure:

	index	variable	value
0	2568	2011	10.146205
1	2569	2011	17.197473
2	2570	2011	14.259472
3	2571	2011	10.043969
4	2572	2011	7.243954
...	...	...	...
2027	2817	2018	9.170208
2028	2818	2018	17.489652
2029	2819	2018	11.936818
2030	2820	2018	17.068802
2031	2821	2018	13.779856

2032 rows × 3 columns

Figure 3.17 – Long format of the birth rates data

Now, the seaborn API can be used directly, as follows:

```
plt.figure(figsize=(10,8))
sns.boxplot(x="variable", y="value", data=birthRatesDFLong)
plt.xlabel("Year")
plt.ylabel("Birth Rates");
```

The following will be the output:

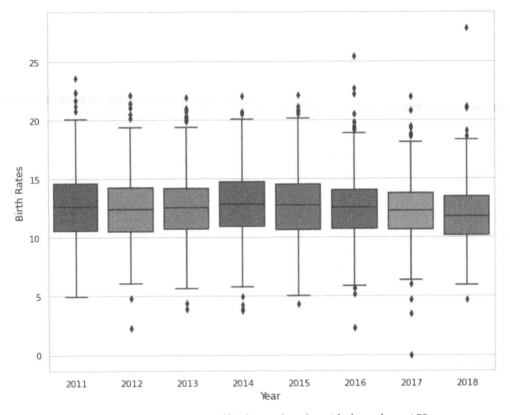

Figure 3.18 – Texas counties' birth rates boxplot with the seaborn API

Nice, isn't it? You've learned how to properly transform the data into the formats that the library APIs accept. Good job!

Example 2 – combining analysis with plain plotting

In the second example, you will see how one-line code can add inference flavor to your plots. Suppose you want to examine the birth rate and the natural population increase rate in the year 2017 *individually*, but you also want to check whether there is some correlation between the two.

To summarize, we need to do the following:

1. Examine the individual distributions of each quantity.
2. Examine the correlation between these two quantities.
3. Obtain a mathematical visual representation of the two quantities.

seaborn offers the `jointplot` function, which you can make use of. It enables you to combine univariate plots and bivariate plots. It also allows you to add annotations with statistical implications.

The following code snippet shows the univariate distribution, bivariate scatter plot, an estimate of univariate density, and bivariate linear regression information in one command:

```
g = sns.jointplot("R_NATURAL_INC_2017", "R_birth_2017",
data=dfTX, kind="reg",height=10)
```

The following graph shows the output:

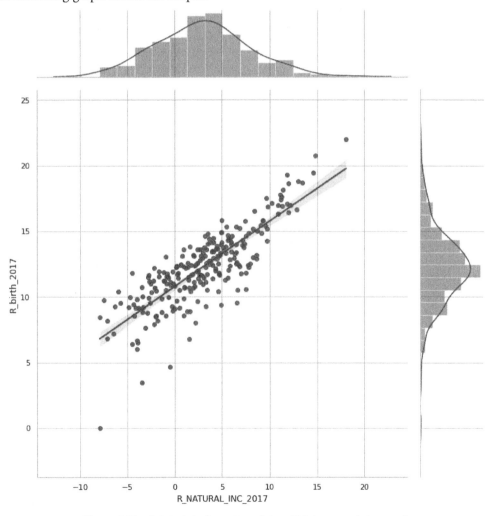

Figure 3.19 – Joint plot of a scatter plot and histogram plot example

> **Tip**
> By adding inference information, density estimation, and the linear regression part to an exploratory graph, we can make the visualization very professional.

Presentation-ready plotting tips

Here are some tips if you plan to use plots in your professional work.

Use styling

Consider using the following tips to style plots:

- You should consider using a style that accommodates your PowerPoint or slides. For example, if your presentation contains a lot of grayscale elements, you shouldn't use colorful plots.

- You should keep styling consistent across the presentation or report.

- You should avoid using markups that are too fancy.

- Be aware of the fact that sometimes people only have grayscale printing, so red and green may be indistinguishable. Use different markers and textures in this case.

For example, the following code replots the joint plot in grayscale style:

```
with plt.style.context('grayscale'):
    plt.figure(figsize=(12,6))
    g = sns.jointplot("R_NATURAL_INC_2017", "R_birth_2017",
data=dfTX, kind="reg",height=10)
```

The result is as follows:

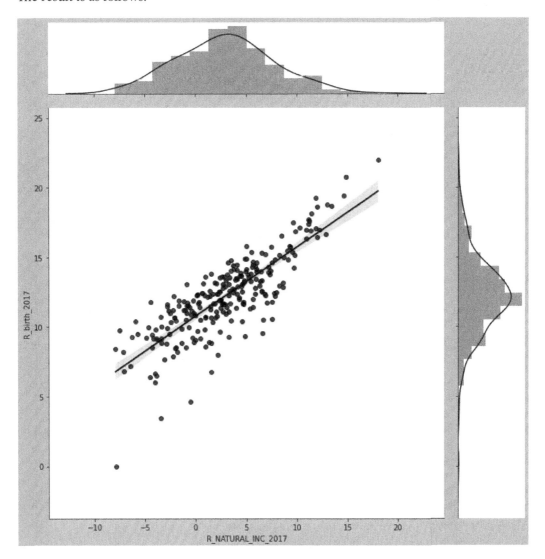

Figure 3.20 – Replot with grayscale style

Font matters a lot

Before the end of this chapter, I would like to share my tips for font choice aesthetics:

- Font size is very important. It makes a huge difference. What you see on a screen can be very different from what you see on paper or on a projector screen. For example, you can use `plt.rc('ytick', labelsize='x-medium')` to specify the `xtick` size of your graph.

- Be aware that the font size usually won't scale when the graph scales. You should test it and set it explicitly, if necessary.

- Font family is also important. The font family of graphs should match the font of the paper. Serif is the most common one. Use the following code to change the default fonts to serif: `plt.rc('font', family='serif')`.

Let's summarize what we have learned in this chapter.

Summary

In this chapter, we discussed the most important plots in Python. Different plots suit different purposes, and you should choose them accordingly. The default settings of each plot may not be perfect for your needs, so customizations are necessary. You also learned the importance of choosing the right geometries and aesthetics to avoid problems in your dataset, such as significant quantity imbalance or highlighting features to make an exploratory argument.

Business queries are the starting point of designing a statistical plot. We discussed the necessity of transforming data to fit a function API and choosing proper plotting functions to answer queries without hassle.

In the next chapter, let's look at some probability distributions. After all, both the histogram plot and the density estimation plot in a joint plot try to uncover the probability distributions behind the dataset.

Section 2:
Essentials of
Statistical Analysis

Section 2 covers the most fundamental and classical contents of statistical analysis at the undergraduate level. However, the statistical analysis we'll get into is applied to messy real-word datasets. This section will give you a taste of statistical analysis as well as sharpening your math skills for further chapters.

This section consists of the following chapters:

- *Chapter 4, Sampling and Inferential Statistics*
- *Chapter 5, Common Probability Distributions*
- *Chapter 6, Parametric Estimation*
- *Chapter 7, Statistical Hypothesis Testing*

4
Sampling and Inferential Statistics

In this chapter, we focus on several difficult sampling techniques and basic inferential statistics associated with each of them. This chapter is crucial because in real life, the data we have is, most likely, only a small portion of a whole set. Sometimes, we also need to perform sampling on a given large dataset. Common reasons for sampling are listed as follows:

- The analysis can run quicker when the dataset is small.
- Your model doesn't benefit much from having gazillions of pieces of data.

Sometimes, you also don't want sampling. For example, sampling a small dataset with sub-categories may be detrimental. Understanding how sampling works will help you to avoid various kinds of pitfalls.

The following topics will be covered in this chapter:

- Understanding fundamental concepts in sampling techniques
- Performing proper sampling under different scenarios
- Understanding statistics associated with sampling

We begin by clarifying the concepts.

Understanding fundamental concepts in sampling techniques

In *Chapter 2*, *Essential Statistics for Data Assessment*, I emphasized that statistics such as mean and variance were used to describe the population. The intent is to help you distinguish between the population and samples. With a population at hand, the information is complete, which means all statistics you calculated will be authentic since you have everything. With a sample, the information you have only relates to a small portion, or a subset of the population.

What exactly is a population?

A population is the *whole* set of entities under *study*. If you want to study the average monthly income of all American women, then the population includes every woman in the United States. Population will change if the study or the question changes. If the study is about finding the average monthly income of all Los Angeles women, then a subset of the population for the previous study becomes the whole population of the current study.

Certain populations are accessible for a study. For example, it probably only takes 1 hour to measure kids' weights in a single kindergarten. However, it is both economically and temporally impractical to obtain income information for American women or even Los Angeles women. In order to get a good estimate of such an answer, sampling is required.

A **sample** is a subset of the population under study. The process of obtaining a sample is called **sampling**. For example, you could select 1,000 Los Angeles women and make this your sample. By collecting their income information, you can infer the average income of all Los Angeles women.

As you may imagine, selecting 1,000 people will likely give us a more confident estimation of the statistics. The sampling size matters because more entries will increase the likelihood of representing more characteristics of the original population.

What is more important is the way how sampling is done. if you randomly select people walking on the street in Hollywood, you probably will significantly overestimate the true average income. If you go to a college campus to interview students, you will likely find an underestimated statistic because students won't have a high income in general.

Another related concept is the accessible population. The whole population under study is also referred to as the target population, which is supposed to be the set to study. However, sometimes only part of it is accessible. The key characteristic is that the sampling process is restricted by accessibility. As regards a study of the income of all Los Angeles women, an accessible population may be very small. Even for a small accessible population, researchers or survey conductors can only sample a small portion of it. This makes the sampling process crucially important.

Failed sampling

Failed sampling can lead to disastrous decision making. For example, in earlier times when phones were not very accessible to every family, if political polling was conducted based on phone directories, the result could be wildly inaccurate. The fact of having a phone indicated a higher household income, and their political choices may not reveal the characteristics of the whole community or region. In the 1936 Presidential election between Roosevelt and Landon, such a mistake resulted in an infamous false Republican victory prediction by *Literary Digest*.

In the next section, you will learn some of the most important sampling methods. We will still be using the Texas population data. For your reference, the following code snippet reads the dataset and creates the dfTX DataFrame:

```
import pandas as pd
df = pd.read_excel("PopulationEstimates.xls",skiprows=2)
dfTX = df[df["State"]=="TX"].tail(-1)
```

The first several columns of the dfTX DataFrame appear as follows:

	FIPS	State	Area_Name	Rural-urban_Continuum Code_2003	Rural-urban_Continuum Code_2013	Urban_Influence_Code_2003	Urban_Influence_Code_2013
2568	48001	TX	Anderson County	5.0	7.0	8.0	8.0
2569	48003	TX	Andrews County	6.0	6.0	5.0	5.0
2570	48005	TX	Angelina County	5.0	5.0	8.0	8.0
2571	48007	TX	Aransas County	2.0	2.0	2.0	2.0
2572	48009	TX	Archer County	3.0	3.0	2.0	2.0

Figure 4.1 – First several columns of the dfTX DataFrame

Next, let's see how different samplings are done.

Performing proper sampling under different scenarios

The previous section introduced an example of misleading sampling in political polling. The correctness of a sampling approach will change depending on its content. When telephones were not accessible, polling by phone was a bad practice. However, now everyone has a phone number associated with them and, in general, the phone number is largely random. If a polling agency generates a random phone number and makes calls, the bias is likely to be small. You should keep in mind that the standard of judging a sampling method as right or wrong should always depend on the scenario.

There are two major ways of sampling: probability sampling and non-probability sampling. Refer to the following details:

- **Probability sampling**, as the name suggests, involves random selection. In probability sampling, each member has an equal and known chance of being selected. This theoretically guarantees that the results obtained will *ultimately* reveal the behavior of the population.

- **Non-probability sampling**, where subjective sampling decisions are made by the researchers. The sampling process is usually more convenient though.

The dangers associated with non-probability sampling

Yes. Here I do indeed refer to non-probability sampling as being dangerous, and I am not wrong. Here I list the common ways of performing non-probability sampling and we will discuss each in detail:

- Convenience sampling

- Volunteer sampling

- Purposive sampling

There are two practical reasons why people turn to non-probability sampling. Non-probability sampling is *convenient*. It usually costs much less to obtain an initial exploratory result with non-probability sampling than probability sampling. For example, you can distribute shopping surveys in a supermarket parking lot to get a sense of people's shopping habits on a Saturday evening. But your results will likely change if you do it on a Monday morning. For example, people might tend to buy more alcohol at the weekend. Such sampling is called **convenience sampling**.

Convenience sampling is widely used in a pilot experiment/study. It can avoid wasting study resources on improper directions or find hidden issues at the early stages of study. It is considered unsuitable for a major study.

Two other common non-probability sampling methods are **volunteer sampling** and **purposive sampling**. Volunteer sampling relies on the participants' own self-selection to join the sampling. A purposive selection is highly judgmental and subjective such that researchers will manually choose participants as part of the sample.

A typical example of volunteer sampling is a survey conducted by a political figure with strong left- or right-wing tendencies. Usually, only their supporters will volunteer to spend time taking the survey and the results will be highly biased, tending to support this person's political ideas.

An exaggerated or even hilarious example of purposive sampling is asking people whether they successfully booked a plane ticket on the plane. The result is obvious because it is done on the plane.

You may notice that such sampling techniques are widely and deliberately used in everyday life, such as in commercials or political campaigns, in an extremely disrespectful way. Many surveys conclude the results before they were performed.

Be careful with non-probability sampling

Non-probability sampling is not wrong. It is widely used. For inexperienced researchers or data scientists who are not familiar with the domain knowledge, it is very easy to make mistakes with non-probability sampling. The non-probability sampling method should be justified carefully to avoid mistakes such as ignoring the fact that people who own a car or a telephone in 1936 were likely Republican.

In the next section, you are going to learn how to perform sampling safely. Also, since probability sampling doesn't involve much subjective judgement, you are going to see some working code again.

Probability sampling – the safer approach

I refer to probability sampling as a safer sampling approach because it avoids serious distribution distortion due to human intervention in most cases. Here I introduce three ways of probability sampling. They are systematic and objective, and are therefore more likely to lead to unbiased results. We will spend more time on them. As before, I will list them first:

- Simple random sampling
- Stratified random sampling
- Systematic random sampling

Let's start with simple random sampling.

Simple random sampling

The first probability sampling is **Simple Random Sampling (SRS)**.

Let's say we have a study that aims to find the mean and standard deviation of the counties' populations in Texas. If it is not possible to perform this in all counties in Texas, simple random sampling can be done to select a certain percentage of counties in Texas.

The following code shows the total number of counties and plots their population distributions.

The following code selects 10%, which is 25 counties, of all of all the counties' populations in 2018. First, let's take a look at our whole dataset's distribution:

```
plt.figure(figsize=(10,6))
plt.rcParams.update({'font.size': 22})
plt.hist(dfTX["POP_ESTIMATE_2018"],bins=100)
plt.title("Total number of counties: {}".format(len(dfTX["POP_
ESTIMATE_2018"])))
plt.axvline(np.mean(dfTX["POP_
ESTIMATE_2018"]),c="r",linestyle="--")
plt.xlabel("Population")
plt.ylabel("Count");
```

The result is a highly skewed distribution with few very large population outliers. The dashed line indicates the position of the mean:

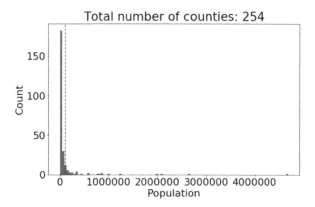

Figure 4.2 – Population histogram plotting of all 254 Texas counties

Most counties have populations of below half a million and fewer than 5 counties have population in excess of 2 million.

The population mean is 112,999, according to the following one-line code:

```
np.mean(dfTX["POP_ESTIMATE_2018"])
```

Now, let's use the `random.sample()` function from the `random` module to select 25 non-repetitive samples and plot the distribution. To make the result reproducible, I set the random seed to be 2020.

> **Note on reproducibility**
>
> To make your analysis such that it involves reproducible randomness, set a random seed so that *randomness* becomes deterministic.

The following code snippet selects 25 counties' data and calculates the mean population figure:

```
random.seed(2020)
plt.figure(figsize=(10,6))
sample = random.sample(dfTX["POP_ESTIMATE_2018"].to_list(),25)
plt.hist(sample,bins=100)
plt.axvline(np.mean(sample),c="r")
plt.title("Mean of sample population: {}".format(np.mean(sample)))
```

```
plt.xlabel("Population")
plt.ylabel("Count");
```

The result appears as follows. Notice that the sample's mean is about 50% smaller than the population's mean:

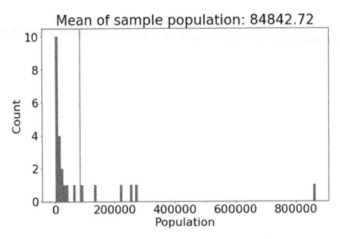

Figure 4.3 – Simple random sample results

We can do this several more times to check the results since the sampling will be different each time. The following code snippet calculates the mean of the sample 100 times and visualizes the distribution of the sampled mean. I initialize the random seed so that it becomes reproducible.

The following code snippet repeats the SRS process 100 times and calculates the mean for each repetition. Then, plot the histogram of the means. I call the number of occasions (100) `trials`, and the size of each sample (25) `numSample`:

```
numSample = 25
trials = 100
random.seed(2020)
sampleMeans = []
for i in range(trials):
    sample = random.sample(dfTX["POP_ESTIMATE_2018"].to_
list(),numSample)
    sampleMeans.append(np.mean(sample))
plt.figure(figsize=(10,8))
plt.hist(sampleMeans,bins=25)
plt.title("Distribution of the {} sample means for sample size
```

```
of {}".format(trials, numSample))
plt.gca().xaxis.set_tick_params(rotation=45)
plt.xlabel("Sample Mean")
plt.ylabel("Count");
```

The result looks somewhat like the original distribution of the population:

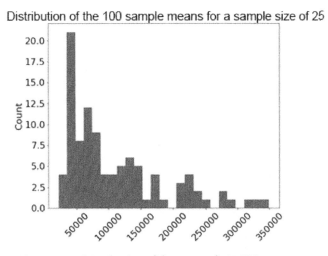

Figure 4.4 – Distribution of the mean of 100 SRS processes

However, the distribution shape will change drastically if you modify the sample size or number of trials. Let me first demonstrate the change in sample size. In the following code snippet, the number of samples takes values of 25 and 100 and the number of trials is 1000. Note that the distribution is normed, so the scale becomes comparable:

```
numSamples = [25,100]
colors = ["r","b"]
trials = 1000
random.seed(2020)
plt.figure(figsize=(10,8))
sampleMeans = []
for j in range(len(numSamples)):
    for i in range(trials):
        sample = random.sample(dfTX["POP_ESTIMATE_2018"].to_
list(),numSamples[j])
        sampleMeans.append(np.mean(sample))
    plt.hist(sampleMeans,color=colors[j],
alpha=0.5,bins=25,label="sample size: {}".
```

```
format(numSamples[j]),density=True)
```
```
plt.legend()
```
```
plt.title("Distribution density of means of 1000 SRS, \nwith
respect to sample sizes")
```
```
plt.xlabel("Sample Mean")
```
```
plt.ylabel("Density");
```

You can clearly see the influence of sample size on the result in the following graph:

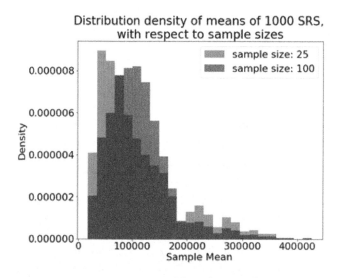

Figure 4.5 – Demonstration of the influence of sample size

In short, if you choose a bigger sample size, it is more likely that you will obtain a larger estimation of the mean of the population data. It is not counter-intuitive because the mean is very susceptible to extreme values. With a larger sample size, the extreme values, those > 1 million, are more likely to be selected and therefore increase the chance that the sample mean is large.

I will leave it to you to examine the influence of the number of trials. You can run the following code snippet to find out. The number of trials should only influence accuracy:

```
numSample = 100
colors = ["r","b"]
trials = [1000,5000]
random.seed(2020)
plt.figure(figsize=(10,8))
sampleMeans = []
for j in range(len(trials)):
    for i in range(trials[j]):
        sample = random.sample(dfTX["POP_ESTIMATE_2018"].to_
list(),numSample)
        sampleMeans.append(np.mean(sample))
    plt.hist(sampleMeans,color=colors[j],
alpha=0.5,bins=25,label="trials: {}".
format(trials[j]),density=True)
plt.legend();
plt.title("Distribution density of means of 1000 SRS and 5000
SRS")
plt.xlabel("Sample Mean")
plt.ylabel("Density");
```

Most of the code is the same as the previous one, except the number of trials now takes another value, that is, 5000 in line 3.

Stratified random sampling

Another common method of probability sampling is stratified random sampling. **Stratifying** is a process of aligning or arranging something into categories or groups. In stratified random sampling, you should first classify or group the population into categories and then select elements from each group randomly.

The advantage of stratified random sampling is that every group is guaranteed to be represented in the final sample. Sometimes this is important. For example, if you want to sample the income of American women without SRS, it is likely that most samples will fall into high-population states such as California and Texas. Information about small states will be *completely* lost. Sometimes you want to sacrifice the absolute equal chance to include the representativeness.

For the Texas county population data, we want to include all counties from different urbanization levels. The following code snippet examines the urbanization code level distribution:

```
from collections import Counter
Counter(dfTX["Rural-urban_Continuum Code_2013"])
```

The result shows *some* imbalance:

```
Counter({7.0: 39,
         6.0: 65,
         5.0: 6,
         2.0: 25,
         3.0: 22,
         1.0: 35,
         8.0: 20,
         9.0: 29,
         4.0: 13})
```

If we want equal representativeness from each urbanization group, such as two elements from each group, stratified random sampling is likely the only way to do it. In SRS, the level 5 data will have a very low chance of being sampled.

Think about the choice between sampling equal numbers of entries in each level/strata or a proportional number of entries as a choice between selecting senators and House representatives.

Note

In the United States, each state has two senators, regardless of the population and state size. The number of representatives in the House reflects how large the state's population is. The larger the population, the more representatives the state has in the House.

The following code snippet samples four representatives from each urbanization level and prints out the mean. Note that the code is not optimized for performance but for readability:

```
random.seed(2020)
samples = []
for level in sorted(np.unique(dfTX["Rural-urban_Continuum
Code_2013"])):
```

```
    samples += random.sample(dfTX[dfTX["Rural-urban_Continuum
Code_2013"]==level]["POP_ESTIMATE_2018"].to_list(),4)
print(np.mean(samples))
```

The result is about `144010`, so not bad.

Let's do this four more times and check the distribution of the sample mean. The following code snippet performs stratified random sampling 1,000 times and plots the distribution of means:

```
plt.figure(figsize=(10,8))
plt.hist(sampleMeans,bins=25);
plt.title("Sample mean distribution, with stratified random
sampling ")
plt.gca().xaxis.set_tick_params(rotation=45)
plt.xlabel("Sample Mean")
plt.ylabel("Count");
```

The following results convey some important information. As you can tell, the sampled means are pretty much centered around the true mean of the population:

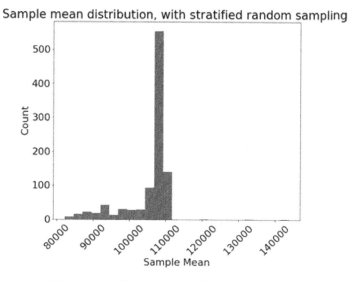

Figure 4.6 – Distribution of sample means from stratified random sampling

To clarify the origin of this odd shape, you need to check the mean of each group. The following code snippet does the job:

```
plt.figure(figsize=(10,8))
levels = []
codeMeans = []
for level in sorted(np.unique(dfTX["Rural-urban_Continuum
Code_2013"])):
    codeMean = np.mean(dfTX[dfTX["Rural-urban_Continuum
Code_2013"]==level]["POP_ESTIMATE_2018"])
    levels.append(level)
    codeMeans.append(codeMean)
plt.plot(levels,codeMeans,marker=10,markersize=20)
plt.title("Urbanization level code versus mean population")
plt.xlabel("Urbanization level code (2013)")
plt.ylabel("Population mean");
```

The result looks like the following:

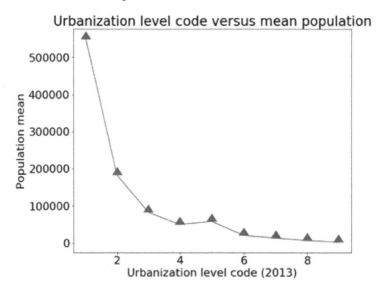

Figure 4.7 – Urbanization level code versus the mean population

Note that the larger the urbanization level code, the smaller the mean population. Stratified random sampling takes samples from each group, so an improved performance is not surprising.

Recall that the urbanization level is a categorical variable, as we introduced it in *Chapter 2, Essential Statistics for Data Assessment*. The previous graph is for visualization purposes only. It doesn't tell us information such as that the urbanization difference between levels 3 and 2 is the same as the difference between levels 5 and 6.

Also notice that it is important to choose a correct stratifying criterion. For example, classifying counties into different levels based on the first letter in a county name doesn't make sense here.

Systematic random sampling

The last probability sampling method is likely the easiest one. If the population has an order structure, you can first select one at random, and then select every *n*-th member after it. For example, you can sample the students by ID on campus or select households by address number.

The following code snippet takes every tenth of the Texas dataset and calculates the mean:

```
random.seed(2020)
idx = random.randint(0,10)
populations = dfTX["POP_ESTIMATE_2018"].to_list()
samples = []
samples.append(populations[idx])
while idx + 10 < len(populations):
    idx += 10
    samples.append(populations[idx])
print(np.mean(samples))
```

The result is 158799, so not bad.

Systematic random sampling is easy to implement and understand. It naturally avoids potential clustering in the data. However, it assumes a natural randomness in the dataset such that manipulation of the data may cause false results. Also, you have to know the size of the population beforehand in order to determine a sampling interval.

We have covered three ways of probability sampling. Combining previous non-probability sampling techniques, you have six methods at your disposal. Each of the sampling techniques has its own pros and cons. Choose wisely in different cases. In the next section, we will study some statistics associated with sampling techniques that will help us make such decisions.

Understanding statistics associated with sampling

In the previous section, you saw something like a histogram plot of the samples' means. We used the histogram to show the *quality* of the sampled mean. If the distribution of the mean is centered around the true mean, I claim it has a better quality. In this section, we will go deeper into it.

Instead of using Texas population data, I will be using artificial uniform distributions as examples. It should be easier for you to grasp the quantitative intuition if the distribution underlining the population is clear.

Sampling distribution of the sample mean

You have seen the distribution of the sampled mean in the previous section. There are some questions remaining. For example, what is the systematic relationship between the sample size and the sample mean? What is the relationship between the number of times of sampling and the sample mean's distribution?

Assume we have a population that can only take values from integers 1 to 10 with equal probability. The population is very large, so we can sample as many as we want. Let me perform an experiment by setting the sample size to 4 and then calculate the sample mean. Let's do the sampling 100 times and check the distribution of the sample mean. We did similar computational experiments for the Texas population data, but here you can obtain the theoretical mean and standard deviation of the uniform distribution beforehand.

The theoretical mean and standard deviation of the distribution can be calculated in one line:

```
print(np.mean([i for i in range(1,11)]))
print(np.sqrt(np.mean([(i-5.5)**2 for i in range(1,11)])))
```

The mean is 5.5 and the standard deviation is about 2.87.

The following code snippet performs the computational experiment and plots the distribution of the sample mean:

```
trials = 100
sampleSize = 4
random.seed(2020)
sampleMeans = []
candidates = [i for i in range(1,11)]
```

```
plt.rcParams.update({'font.size': 18})
for i in range(trials):
    sampleMean = np.mean([random.choice(candidates) for _ in
range(sampleSize)])
    sampleMeans.append(sampleMean)
plt.figure(figsize=(10,6))
plt.hist(sampleMeans, bins=25);
plt.axvline(5.5,c="r", linestyle="--")
plt.title("Sample mean distribution, trial: {}, sample size:
{}".format(trials, sampleSize))
plt.xlabel("Sample mean")
plt.ylabel("Count");
```

I used the dashed vertical line to highlight the location of the true population mean. The visualization can be seen here:

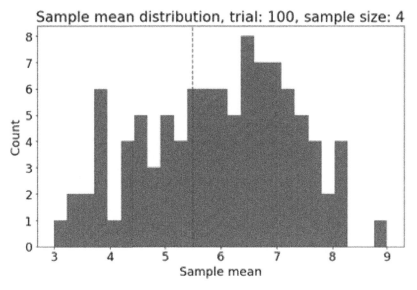

Figure 4.8 – Sample mean distribution for 100 trials with a sample size of 4

Let's also take a note of the sample means' standard deviation:

```
np.mean(sampleMeans)
```

The result is 5.9575.

Now, let's repeat the process by increasing the number of trials to 4, 16, 64, and 100, keeping sampleSize = 4 unchanged. I am going to use a subplot to do this.

The follow code snippet first declares a function that returns the sample means as a list:

```
def obtainSampleMeans(trials = 100, sampleSize = 4):
    sampleMeans = []
    candidates = [i for i in range(1,11)]
    for i in range(trials):
        sampleMean = np.mean([random.choice(candidates) for _
in range(sampleSize)])
        sampleMeans.append(sampleMean)
    return sampleMeans
```

The following code snippet makes use of the function we declared and plots the result of the experiments:

```
random.seed(2020)
figure, axes = plt.subplots(4,1,figsize=(8,16))
figure.tight_layout()
times = [4,16,64,100]
for i in range(len(times)):
    sampleMeans = obtainSampleMeans(100*times[i],4)
    axes[i].hist(sampleMeans,bins=40,density= True);
    axes[i].axvline(5.5,c="r")
    axes[i].set_title("Sample mean distribution, trial: {},
sample size: {}".format(100*times[i], 4));
print("mean: {}, std: {}".format(np.mean(sampleMeans),np.
std(sampleMeans)))
```

You may observe an interesting trend where the distributions assume an increasingly smooth shape. Note that the skipping is due to the fact that the possible sample values are all integers:

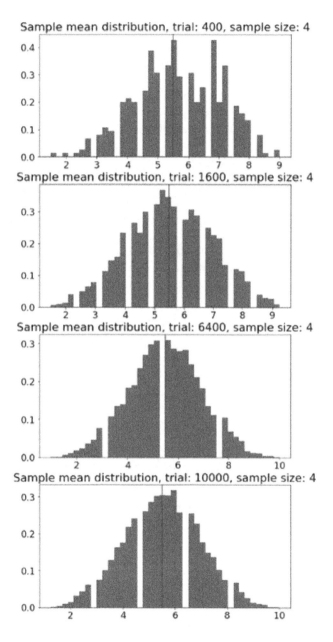

Figure 4.9 – Sample mean distribution with 400, 1,600, 6,400, and 10,000 trials

There are two discoveries here:

- As the number of trials increases, the sample means' distribution becomes smoother and bell-shaped.

- When the number of trials reaches a certain level, the standard deviation doesn't seem to change.

To verify the second claim, you need to compute the standard deviation of the sample means. I will leave this to you. The result is listed here. As regards the four different numbers of trials, the standard deviations are all around 1.44. Here is the output of the code snippet showing no significant decrease in standard deviation:

```
trials: 400, mean: 5.64, std: 1.4078218992472025
trials: 1600, mean: 5.53390625, std: 1.4563112832464553
trials: 6400, mean: 5.4877734375, std: 1.4309896472527093
trials: 10000, mean: 5.51135, std: 1.4457899838842432
```

Next, let's study the influence of the number of trials. The following code snippet does the trick. In order to obtain more data points for future analysis, I am going to skip some plotting results, but you can always check the official notebook of the book for yourself. I am going to stick to `trials = 6400` for this experiment:

```
random.seed(2020)
sizes = [2**k for k in range(1,9)]
figure, axes = plt.subplots(8,1,figsize=(8,4*8))
figure.tight_layout()
for i in range(len(sizes)):
    sampleMeans = obtainSampleMeans(6400,sizes[i])
    axes[i].hist(sampleMeans,bins=np.linspace(np.
min(sampleMeans),np.max(sampleMeans),40),density= True);
    axes[i].axvline(5.5,c="r", linestyle="--")
    axes[i].set_title("Sample mean distribution, trial: {},
sample size: {}".format(6400, sizes[i]));
    axes[i].set_xlim(0,10)
print("mean: {}, std: {}".format(np.mean(sampleMeans),np.
std(sampleMeans)))
```

Let's check the `sampleSize = 16` result:

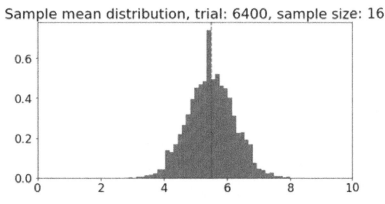

Figure 4.10 – Sample mean distribution; sample size = 16

If the sample size increases eightfold, you obtain the following:

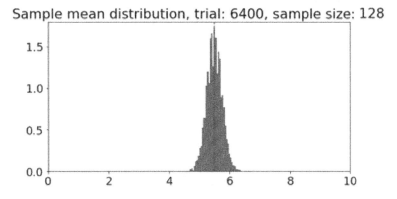

Figure 4.11 – Sample mean distribution; sample size = 128

We do see that the standard error of the sample mean shrinks when the sample size increases. The estimates of the population mean are more precise, hence a tighter and tighter histogram. We will study this topic more quantitatively in the next subsection.

Standard error of the sample mean

The sample mean's standard error decreases when the sample size increases. We will do some visualization to find out the exact relationship. The standard error is the standard deviation of a statistic of a sampling distribution. Here, the statistic is the mean.

> **The thought experiment tip**
>
> A useful technique for checking a monotonic relationship is to perform a thought experiment. Imagine the sample size is 1, then, when the number of trials increases to infinity, basically we will be calculating the statistics of the population itself. On the other hand, if the sample size increases to a very large number, then every sample mean will be very close to the true population mean, which leads to small variance.

Here, I plotted the relationship between the size of the sample and the standard deviation of the sample mean. The following code snippet does the job:

```
random.seed(2020)
sizes = [2**k for k in range(1,9)]
ses = []
figure, axes = plt.subplots(8,1,figsize=(8,4*8))
for i in range(len(sizes)):
    sampleMeans = obtainSampleMeans(6400,sizes[i])
ses.append(np.std(sampleMeans))
```

Due to space limitations, here we only show two of the eight sub-figures:

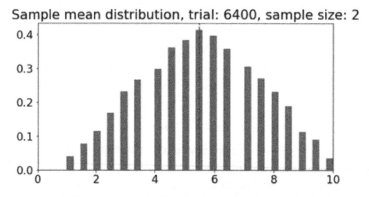

Figure 4.12 – Sample mean distribution when the sample size is 2

With a larger sample size, we have the following diagram:

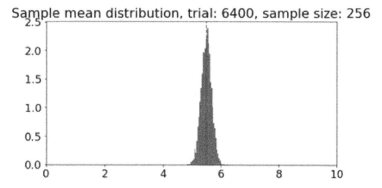

Figure 4.13 – Sample mean distribution when the sample size is 256

Then we plot the relationship in a simple line chart:

```
plt.figure(figsize=(8,6))
plt.plot(sizes,ses)
plt.title("Standard Error of Sample Mean Versus Sample Size")
plt.xlabel("Sample Size")
plt.ylabel("Standard Error of Sample Mean");
```

What you get is a following curve:

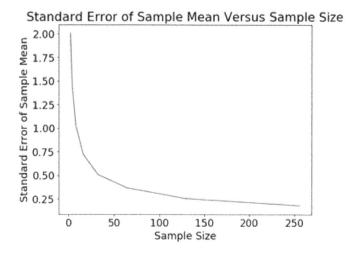

Figure 4.14 – The sample mean standard error decreases with the sample size

Now, let's perform a transformation of the standard error so the relationship becomes clear:

```
plt.figure(figsize=(8,6))
plt.plot(sizes,[1/ele**2 for ele in ses])
plt.title("Inverse of the Square of Standard Error \nversus
Sample Size")
plt.xlabel("Sample Size")
plt.ylabel("Transformed Standard Error of Sample Mean");
```

The output becomes a straight linear line:

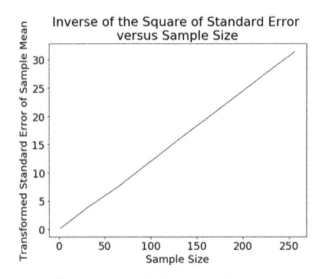

Figure 4.15 – Standard error transformation

There is a linear relationship between the sample size and the inverse of the square of the standard error. Let's use n to denote the sample size:

$$\sigma_n \propto \frac{1}{\sqrt{n}}$$

Now, recall that if the sample size is 1, we are basically calculating the population itself. Therefore, the relationship is exactly the following:

$$\sigma_n = \frac{\sigma}{\sqrt{n}}$$

This equation is useful for estimating the true population standard deviation.

> **Note on replacement**
>
> I used the `random.choice()` function for `sampleSize` times in this example. This suggests that I am sampling from an infinitely large population, or sampling with replacements. However, in the first section, when sampling Texas population data, I used the `random.sample(sampleSize)` function to sample a finite dataset without replacements.

The analysis of the sample mean will still apply, but the standard error's coefficient will be different. You will pick up a finite population correction factor that is related to the population size. We won't go deeper into this topic due to content limitation.

The central limit theorem

One last topic to discuss in this chapter is probably one of the most important theorems in statistics. You may notice that the shape of the sample mean distribution tends to a bell-shaped distribution, indeed, a normal distribution. This is due to one of the most famous and important theorems in statistics – the **Central Limit Theorem** (**CLT**).

The CLT states that, given a sufficiently large sample size, the sampling distribution of the mean for a variable will approximate a normal distribution regardless of that variable's distribution in the population.

Recall that the example distribution I used is the simplest discrete uniform distribution. You can already see that the sample mean follows the bell-shaped distribution, which is equivalent to checking the sample sum. The CLT is very strong. Normal distribution is the most important distribution among many others, as we will cover in the next chapter. Mathematicians developed a lot of theories and tools relating to normal distribution. The CLT enables us to apply those tools to other distributions as well.

Proving the CLT is beyond the scope of this introductory book. However, you are encouraged to perform the following thought experiment and do a computational experiment to verify it.

You toss an unfair coin that favors heads, and record the heads as 1 and tails as 0. A set of tossings contains n tossings. If n equals 1, you can do m sets of tossing and count the sum of each set's results. What you can get is m binary numbers, either 0 or 1, with 1 more likely than 0.

If $n = 10$, the sum of a set can now take values from 0 to 10 and will likely have an average greater than 5 because the coin is unfair. However, now you have a *spread* of the possible outcomes, no longer binary. As n increases, the sum of the tossing set keeps increasing, but it will likely increase at a more *stable* rate, probably around 0.7?

Casually speaking, the sum *hides* the intrinsic structure of the original distribution. To verify this amazing phenomenon, perform some computational experiments. The code snippets in this chapter provides useful skeletons.

Summary

In this chapter, you learned important but often undervalued concepts such as population, samples, and sampling methods. You learned the right ways to perform sampling as well as the pitfalls of dangerous sampling methods. We also made use of several important distributions in this chapter.

In the next chapter, you are going to systematically learn some common important distributions. With these background concepts solidified, we can then move on to inferential statistics with confidence.

5
Common Probability Distributions

In the previous chapter, we discussed the concepts of population and sampling. In most cases, it is not likely that you will find a dataset that perfectly obeys a well-defined distribution. However, common probability distributions are the backbone of data science and serve as the first approximation of real-world distributions.

The following topics will be covered in this chapter:

- Understanding important concepts in probability
- Understanding common discrete probability distributions
- Understanding common continuous probability distributions
- Learning about joint and conditional distribution
- Understanding the power law and black swan

Recall the famous saying, *there is nothing more practical than good theory*. The theory of probability is beyond greatness. Let's get started!

Understanding important concepts in probability

First of all, we need to clarify some fundamental concepts in probability theory.

Events and sample space

The easiest and most intuitive way to understand probability is probably through the idea of counting. When tossing a fair coin, the probability of getting a heads is one half. You count two possible results and associate the probability of one half with each of them. And the sum of all the associated non-overlapping events, not including having a coin standing on its edge, must be unity.

Generally, probability is associated with *events* within a sample space, S. In the coin tossing example, tossing the coin is considered a random experiment; it has two possible outcomes, and the collection of all outcomes is the sample space. The outcome of having a heads/tails is an event.

Note that an event is not necessarily single-outcome, for example, tossing a dice and defining an event as having a result larger than 4. The event contains a subset of the six-outcome sample space. If the dice is fair, it is intuitive to say that such an event having a result larger than 4 is associated with the probability $P(A) = \frac{1}{3}$.

The probability of the whole sample space is 1 and any probability lies between 0 and 1. If an event A contains no outcomes, the probability is 0.

Such intuition doesn't only apply to discrete outcomes. For continuous cases such as the arrival time of a bus between 8 A.M. and 9 A.M., you can define the sample space S as the whole-time interval from 8 A.M. to 9 A.M. An event A can be a bus arriving between 8:30 and 8:40, while another event B can be a bus arriving later than 8:50. A has a probability of $P(A) = \frac{1}{6}$ and B has a probability of $P(B) = \frac{1}{6}$ as well.

Let's use $\cup$ and $\cap$ to denote the union and intersection of two events. The following three axioms for probability calculation will hold:

- $P(A) > 0$ for any event $A \subseteq S$
- $P(S) = 1$
- If A, B are mutually exclusive, then $P(A \cup B) = P(A) + P(B)$

This leaves to you to verify that if A, B are not mutually exclusive, the following relationship holds: $P(A \cup B) = P(A) + P(B) - P(A \cap B)$

The probability mass function and the probability density function

Both the **Probability Mass Function** (**PMF**) and the **Probability Density Function** (**PDF**) we are invented to describe the *point density* of a distribution. PMF can be used to describe the probability of discrete events, whereas PDF can be used to describe continuous cases. Let's look at some examples to understand these functions better.

PMF

PMF associates each single outcome of a discrete probability with a probability. For example, the following table represents a PMF for our coin-tossing experiment:

Outcome	Probability
Head	0.5
Tail	0.5

Figure 5.1 – Probability of coin tossing outcomes

If the coin is biased toward heads, then the probability of having heads will be larger than 0.5, but the sum will remain as 1.

Let's say you toss two fair dice. What is the PMF for the sum of the outcomes? We can achieve the result by counting. The table cells contain the sum of the two outcomes:

Results	1	2	3	4	5	6
1	2	3	4	5	6	7
2	3	4	5	6	7	8
3	4	5	6	7	8	9
4	5	6	7	8	9	10
5	6	7	8	9	10	11
6	7	8	9	10	11	12

Figure 5.2 – Sum of two dice-tossing outcomes

We can then build a PMF table as shown in the following table. As you can see, the probability associated with each outcome is different. Also note that the sample space changes its definition when we change the random experiment. In these two-dice cases, the sample space S becomes *all the outcomes of the possible sums*:

Sum of outcomes	Probability
2	$\frac{1}{36}$
3	$\frac{1}{18}$
4	$\frac{1}{12}$
5	$\frac{1}{9}$
6	$\frac{5}{36}$
7	$\frac{1}{6}$
8	$\frac{5}{36}$
9	$\frac{1}{9}$
10	$\frac{1}{12}$
11	$\frac{1}{18}$
12	$\frac{1}{36}$

Figure 5.3 – Probability of the sum of dice tossing

Let's denote the one dice's outcome as A and another as B. You can verify that $P(A.B) = P(A).P(B)$. In this case, the easiest example is the case of that sum being *2* and *12*.

The following code snippet can simulate the experiment as we know that each dice generates the possible outcome equally. First, generate all the possible outcomes:

```
import random
import numpy as np
dice = [1,2,3,4,5,6]
probs = [1/6,1/6,1/6,1/6,1/6,1/6]
sums = sorted(np.unique([dice[i] + dice[j] for i in range(6)
for j in range(6)]))
```

The following code then calculates all the associated probabilities. I iterated every possible pair of outcomes and added the probability product to the corresponding result. Here, we make use of the third axiom declared earlier, and the relationship we just claimed:

```
from collections import OrderedDict
res = OrderedDict()
for s in sums:
    res[s] = 0
    for i in range(6):
        for j in range(6):
            if dice[i]+dice[j]==s:
                res[s] += probs[i]*probs[j]
```

> **Note on code performance**
> The code is not optimized for performance but for readability.

OrderedDict creates a dictionary that maintains the order of the key as the order in which the keys are created.

Let's check the results and plot them with a bar plot. Since the dictionary is ordered, it is OK to plot keys() and values() directly as x and height as per the function's API:

```
plt.figure(figsize=(8,6))
plt.rcParams.update({'font.size': 22})
plt.bar(res.keys(),res.values())
plt.title("Probabilities of Two Dice Sum")
plt.xlabel("Sum Value")
plt.ylabel("Probability");
```

Let's check out the beautiful symmetric result:

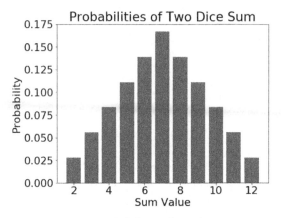

Figure 5.4 – Probabilities of two dice sums

You can check the sum of the values by using `sum(res.values())`.

PDF

PDF is the equivalent of PMF for continuous distribution. For example, a uniform distribution at interval [0,1] will have a PDF of $f_X(x) = P(x) = 1$ for any x in the range.

The requirements for a PDF to be valid are straightforward from the axioms for a valid probability. A PDF must be non-negative and integrates to 1 in the range where it takes a value.

Let's check a simple example. Suppose the PDF of the bus' arrival time looks as follows:

Figure 5.5 – PDF of the bus arrival time

You may check that the shaded region does have an area of 1. The bus has the highest probability of arriving at 8:30 and a lower probability of arriving too early or too late. This is a terrible bus service anyway.

Unlike PMF, a PDF's value can take an arbitrarily high number. The highest probability for the two-dice outcome is $\frac{1}{6}$, but the highest value on the PDF graph is 2. This is one crucial difference between PDF and PMF. A *single point* on the PDF function doesn't hold the same meaning as a value in the PMF table. Only the integrated **Area Under the Curve (AUC)** represents a meaningful probability. For example, in the previous PDF, the probability that the bus will arrive between 8:24 A.M. (*8.4* on the *x*-axis) and 8:36 A.M. (*8.6* on the x-axis) is the area of the central lightly shaded part, as shown in the following graph:

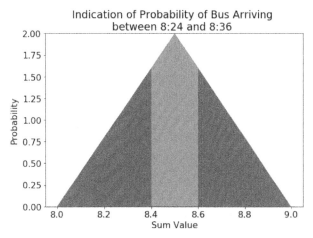

Figure 5.6 – Probability that a bus will arrive between 8:24 A.M. and 8:36 A.M.

> **Note on the difference between PMF/PDF plots and histogram plots**
>
> Don't confuse the PMF or PDF plots with the histogram plots you saw in previous chapters. A histogram shows data distribution, whereas the PMF and PDF are not backed by any data but theoretical claims. It is not possible to schedule a bus that obeys the preceding weird PDF strictly, but when we estimate the mean arrival time of the bus, the PDF can be used as a simple approachable tool.

Integrating a PDF up to a certain value x gives you the **Cumulative Distribution Function (CDF)**, which is shown as the following formula: $F_X(x) = \int_{-\infty}^{x} f_X(x)$. It takes values between 0 and 1. A CDF contains all the information a PDF contains. Sometimes it is easier to use a CDF instead of a PDF in order to solve certain problems.

Subjective probability and empirical probability

From another perspective, you can classify probabilities into two types:

- Subjective probability, or theoretical probability

- Empirical probability, or objective probability

Let's look at each of these classifications in detail.

Subjective probability stems from a theoretical argument without any observation of the data. You check the coin and think it is a fair one, and then you come up with an equal probability of heads and tails. You don't require any observations or random experiments. All you have is *a priori* knowledge.

On the other hand, empirical probability is deduced from observations or experiments. For example, you observed the performance of an NBA player and estimated his probability of 3-point success for next season. Your conclusion comes from *a posteriori* knowledge.

If theoretical probability exists, by the *law of large numbers*, given sufficient observations, the observed frequency will approximate the theoretical probability infinitely closely. For the content of this book, we won't go into details of the proof, but the intuition is clear.

In a real-world project, you may wish to build a robust model to obtain a subjective probability. Then, during the process of observing random experiment results, you adjust the probability to reflect the observed correction.

Understanding common discrete probability distributions

In this section, we will introduce you to some of the most important and common distributions. I will first demonstrate some examples and the mechanism behind them that exhibits corresponding probability. Then I will calculate the expectation and variance of the distribution, show you samples that generated from the probability, and plot its histogram plot and boxplot.

The expectation of X that follows a distribution is the *mean* value that X can take. For example, with PDF $f_X(x)$, the mean is calculated as follows:

$$E(x) = \int_{-\infty}^{\infty} f_X(x)x dx$$

The variance measures the spreading behavior of the distribution and is calculated as follows:

$$Var(x) = \int_{-\infty}^{\infty} f_X(x)\big(x - E(x)\big)^2 dx$$

μ and σ^2 are the common symbols for expectation and variance.

X is called a *random variable*. Note that it is the outcome of a random experiment. However, not all random variables represent outcomes of events. For example, you can take $Y = exp(X)$, and Y is also a random variable, but not an outcome of a random experiment. You can calculate the expectation and variance of any random variable.

We have three discrete distributions to cover. They are as follows:

- Bernoulli distribution
- Binomial distribution
- Poisson distribution

Now, let's look at these in detail one by one.

Bernoulli distribution

Bernoulli distribution is the simplest discrete distribution that originates from a Bernoulli experiment. A Bernoulli experiment resembles a general coin-tossing scenario. The name comes from Jakob I. Bernoulli, a famous mathematician in the 1600s.

A Bernoulli experiment has two outcomes, and the answer is usually binary that one outcome excludes another. For example, the following are all valid Bernoulli experiments:

- Randomly ask a person whether they are married.
- Buy a lottery ticket to win the lottery.
- Whether a person will vote for Trump in 2020.

If one event is denoted as a success with probability p, then the opposite is denoted as a failure with probability *1 - p*.

Using X to denote the outcome and x to denote the outcome's realization, where we set *x = 1* to be a success and *x = 0* to be a failure, the PMF can be concisely written as follows:

$$f_X(x) = p^x(1 - p)^{(1-x)}$$

> **Note on notations**
>
> As you may have already noticed, the uppercase letter is used to denote the outcome or event itself, whereas the lowercase letter represents a specific realization of the outcome. For example, x can represent the realization that X takes the value of *married* in one experiment. X denotes the event itself.

Given the definitions, the mean is as follows:

$$p * 1 + (1 - p) * 0 = p$$

The variance is as follows:

$$(0 - p)^2(1 - p) + (1 - p)^2 p = p(1 - p)$$

The following code performs a computational experiment with `p = 0.7` and `sample size = 1000`:

```
p = 0.7
samples = [random.random() < 0.7 for _ in range(1000)]
print(np.mean(samples),np.var(samples))
```

Since the result is straightforward, we won't get into it. You are welcome to examine it.

Binomial distribution

Binomial distribution is built upon the Bernoulli distribution. Its outcome is the sum of a collection of *independent* Bernoulli experiments.

> **Note on the concept of independency**
>
> This is the first time that we have used the word *independent* explicitly. In a two-coin experiment, it is easy to imagine the fact that tossing one coin won't influence the result of another in any way. It is enough to understand *independent* this way and we will go into its mathematical details later.

Let's say you do n Bernoulli experiments, each with a probability of success p. Then we say the outcome X follows a binomial distribution parametrized by n and p. The outcome of the experiment can take any value k as long as k is smaller than or equal to n. The PMF reads as follows:

$$f(k, n, p) = P(X = k) = \frac{n!}{k!\,(n-k)!} p^k (1 - p)^{n-k}$$

The first term represents the combination of selecting *k* successful experiments out of *n*. The second term is merely a product of independent Bernoulli distribution PMF.

The expectation/mean of the binomial distribution is *np* and the variance is *np(1 – p)*. This fact follows the results of the sums of independent random variables. The mean is the sum of means and the variance is the sum of the variance.

Let's do a simple computational example, tossing a biased coin with *P(Head) = 0.8* 100 times and plotting the distribution of the sum with 1,000 trials. The following code snippet first generates the theoretical data points:

```
X = [i for i in range(1,101)]
p = 0.8
Fx = [np.math.factorial(n)/(np.math.factorial(n-k)*np.math.
factorial(k))*p**k*(1-p)**(n-k) for k in X]
```

Then the following code snippet conducts the experiment and the plotting:

```
random.seed(2020)
n = 100
K = []
for trial in range(1000):
    k = np.sum([random.random() < p for _ in range(n)])
    K.append(k)
plt.figure(figsize=(8,6))
plt.hist(K,bins=30,density=True,label="Computational Experiment
PMF");
plt.plot(X,Fx,color="r",label="Theoretical PMF",linestyle="--")
plt.legend();
```

The result looks as follows:

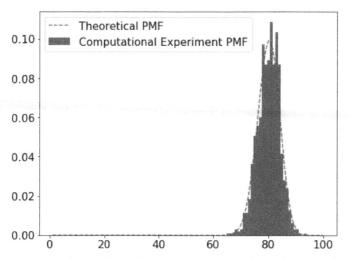

Figure 5.7 – Binomial distribution, theoretical, and simulation results

The simulated values and the theoretical values agree pretty well. Now, we'll move on to another important distribution.

Poisson distribution

The last discrete distribution we will cover is Poisson distribution. It has a PMF as shown in the following equation, where λ is a parameter:

$$P(X = k) = \frac{e^{-\lambda}\lambda^k}{k!}$$

k can take values of positive integers. This distribution looks rather odd, but it appears in nature everywhere. Poisson distribution can describe the times a random event happens during a unit of time. For example, the number of people calling 911 in the United States every minute will obey a Poisson distribution. The count of gene mutations per unit of time also follows a Poisson distribution. Let's first examine the influence of the value λ. The following code snippet plots the theoretical PMF for different values of λ:

```
lambdas = [2,4,6,16]
K = [k for k in range(30)]
plt.figure(figsize=(8,6))
for i,l in enumerate(lambdas):
    plt.plot(K, [np.exp(-l)*l**k/np.math.factorial(k) for k in
K],
            label=str(l),
```

```
              marker=i*2)
plt.legend()
plt.ylabel("Probability")
plt.xlabel("Values")
plt.title("Parameterized Poisson Distributions");
```

The result looks as follows:

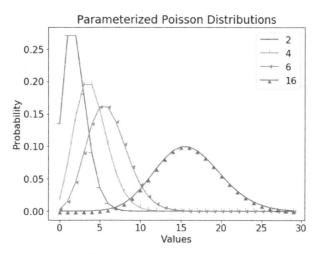

Figure 5.8 – Poisson distribution with various λ values

The trend is that the larger λ is, the larger the mean and variance will become. This observation is true. Indeed, the mean and variance of Poisson distribution are both λ.

The `numpy.random.poisson()` function can easily generate Poisson distribution samples. The computational experiment is left to you. You can try and conduct computational experiments on your own for further practice.

Understanding the common continuous probability distribution

In this section, you will see the three most important continuous distributions:

- Uniform distribution
- Exponential distribution
- Gaussian/normal distribution

Let's look at each of these in detail.

Uniform distribution

Uniform distribution is an important uniform distribution. It is useful computationally because many other distributions can be simulated with uniform distribution. In earlier code examples, I used `random.random()` in the simulation of the Bernoulli distribution, which itself generates a uniform random variable in the range *[0,1]*.

For a uniformly distributed random variable on *[0,1]*, the mean is 0.5 and the variance is $\frac{1}{12}$. This is a good number to remember for a data scientist role interview.

For a general uniform distribution, If the range is *[a,b]*, the PDF reads as $P(X = x) = \frac{1}{b-a}$ if *x* is in the range *[a,b]*. The mean and variance become $\frac{b+a}{2}$ and $\frac{(b-a)^2}{12}$, respectively. If you remember calculus, check it yourself. We will skip the computational experiments part for simplicity and move on to exponential distribution.

Exponential distribution

The exponential distribution function is another important continuous distribution function. In nature, it mostly describes the time difference between independent random distribution. For example, the time between two episodes of lightning in a thunderstorm or the time between two 911 calls. Recall that the number of 911 calls in a unit of time follows the Poisson distribution. Exponential distribution and Poisson distribution do have similarities.

The PDF for exponential distribution is also parameterized by λ. The value *x* can only take non-negative values. Its PDF observes the following form:

$$f(x, \lambda) = \lambda e^{-\lambda x}$$

Because of the monotonicity of the PDF, the maximal value always happens at *x = 0*, where *f(0,λ) = λ*. The following code snippet plots the PDF for different λ:

```python
lambdas = [0.2,0.4,0.8,1.0]
K = [0.5*k for k in range(15)]
plt.figure(figsize=(8,6))
for i,l in enumerate(lambdas):
    plt.plot(K, [np.exp(-l*k)*l for k in K],
            label=str(l),
        marker=i*2)
plt.legend()
plt.ylabel("Probability")
```

```
plt.xlabel("Values")
plt.title("Parameterized Exponential Distributions");
```

The result looks as follows:

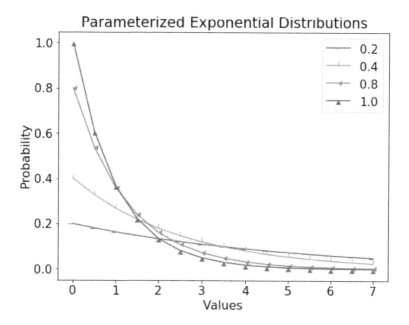

Figure 5.9 – Exponential distribution with various λ

The larger λ is, the higher the peak at 0 is, but the faster the distribution decays. A smaller λ gives a lower peak, but a *fatter tail*.

Integrating the product of x and PDF gives us the expectation and variance. First the expectation reads as follows:

$$E(x) = \int_0^\infty x\lambda e^{-\lambda x}\mathrm{d}x = \frac{1}{\lambda}$$

The variance reads as follows:

$$Var(x) = \int_0^\infty \left(x - E(x)\right)^2 \lambda e^{-\lambda x}\mathrm{d}x = \frac{1}{\lambda^2}$$

The result agrees with the graphical story. The larger λ is, the thinner the tail is, and hence the smaller the expectation is. Meanwhile, the peakier shape brings down the variance.

Next, we will investigate normal distribution.

Normal distribution

We have used the term *normal distribution* quite often in previous chapters without defining it precisely.

A one-dimensional normal distribution has a PDF as follows. μ and σ^2 are the parameters as expectation and standard deviation:

$$f(x) = \frac{1}{\sigma\sqrt{2\pi}} e^{-\frac{(x-\mu)^2}{2\sigma^2}}$$

A standard normal function has an expectation of 0 and a variance of 1. Therefore, its PDF reads as follows in a simpler form:

$$f(x) = \frac{1}{\sqrt{2\pi}} e^{-\frac{x^2}{2}}$$

> **Qualitative argument of a normal distribution PDF**
>
> The standard normal distribution PDF is an even function, so it is symmetric with a symmetric axis $x = 0$. Its PDF also monotonically decays from its peak at a faster rate than the exponential distribution PDF because it has a squared form.

Transforming the standard PDF to a general PDF, the expectation μ on the exponent shifts the position of the symmetric axis and the variance σ^2 determines how quick the decay is.

The universality of normal distribution is phenomenal. For example, the human population's height and weight roughly follow a normal distribution. The number of leaves on trees in a forest will also roughly follow a normal distribution. From the CLT, we know that the sample sum from a population of any distribution will ultimately tend to follow a normal distribution.

Take the tree leaves example, and imagine that the probability of growing a leaf follows a very sophisticated probability. The total number of leaves on a tree will, however, cloud the details of the sophistication of the probability, but gives you a normal distribution. A lot of phenomena in nature follow a similar pattern: what we observe is a collection or summation of lower-level mechanisms. This is how the CLT makes normal distribution so universal and important.

For now, let's focus on a one-dimensional one.

Let's plot several normal distribution PDFs with different expectations, [-1, 0 and 1], with the following code snippet:

```
mus = [-1,0,1]
K = [0.2*k-5 for k in range(50)]
plt.figure(figsize=(8,6))
for i,mu in enumerate(mus):
    plt.plot(K, [1/(np.sqrt(2*np.pi))*np.exp(-(k-mu)**2/2) for k in K],
             label=str(mu),
             marker=i*2)
plt.legend()
plt.ylabel("Probability")
plt.xlabel("Values")
plt.title("Parameterized Normal Distributions");
```

The result looks as follows:

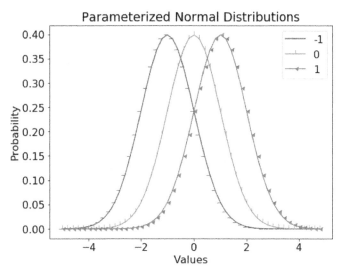

Figure 5.10 – Normal distribution with different expectations

I will leave the exercise with a different variance to you.

Normal distribution has a deep connection with various statistical tests. We will cover the details in *Chapter 7, Statistical Hypothesis Testing*.

Learning about joint and conditional distribution

We have covered basic examples from discrete probability distributions and continuous probability distributions. Note that all of them describe the distribution of a single experiment outcome. How about the probability of the simultaneous occurrence of two events/outcomes? The proper mathematical language is joint distribution.

Suppose random variables X and Y denote the height and weight of a person. The following probability records the probability that $X = x$ and $Y = y$ simultaneously, which is called a **joint distribution**. A joint distribution is usually represented as shown in the following equation:

$$P(X = x, Y = y)$$

For a population, we may have $P(X = 170cm, Y = 75kg) = 0.25$. You may ask the question: What is the probability of a person being 170 cm while weighing 75 kg? So, you see that there is a condition that we already know this person weighs 75 kg. The expression for a conditional distribution is a ratio as follows:

$$P(X = 170cm | Y = 75kg) = \frac{P(X = 170cm, Y = 75kg)}{P(Y = 75kg)}$$

The notation $P(X|Y)$ represents the *conditional distribution* of X given Y. Conditional distributions are everywhere, and people often misread them by ignoring the conditions. For example, does the following argument make sense?

> *Most people have accidents within 5 miles of their home, therefore, the further away you drive, the safer you are.*

What's wrong with this claim? It claims the probability $P(death \mid more\ than\ 5\ miles\ away)$ to be small as compared to $P(death \mid less\ than\ 5\ miles\ away)$ given the fact that $P(death \mid less\ than\ 5\ miles\ away)$ is larger than $P(death \mid more\ than\ 5\ miles\ away)$. It intentionally ignores the fact that the majority of commutes take place within short distances of the home in its phrasing of the claim. The denominator is simply too small on the right-hand side in the following equation:

$$P(death \mid more\ than\ 5\ miles\ away) = \frac{P(death, more\ than\ 5\ miles\ away)}{P(more\ than\ 5\ miles\ away)}$$

I hope you are able to spot such tricks and understand the essence of these concepts.

Independency and conditional distribution

Now, we can explore the true meaning of independency. In short, there are two equivalent ways to declare two random variables independent. $P(X = x, Y = y) = P(X = x)P(Y = y)$ for any x, y and $P(X = x | Y = y) = P(X = x)$ for any x, y. You can check that they are indeed equivalent. We see an independent relationship between X and Y implies that a conditional distribution of a random variable X over Y doesn't *really* depend on the random variable Y.

If you can decompose the PDF/PMF of a joint probability into a product of two PDFs/PMFs that one only contains one random variable and another only contains another random variable, then the two random variables are independent.

Let's look at a quick example. You toss a coin three times. X denotes the event when you see two or more heads and Y denotes the event when the sum of heads is odd. Are X and Y independent? Let's do a quick calculation to obtain the probabilities:

$$P(X = True) = \frac{1}{2}, \quad P(Y = True) = \frac{1}{2}, \quad P(X = True, Y = True) = \frac{1}{4}.$$

You can verify the remaining three cases to check that X and Y are indeed independent.

The idea of conditional distribution is key to understanding many behaviors: for example, the survival bias. For all the planes returning from the battlefield, if the commander reinforces those parts where the plane got shot, will the air force benefit from it? The answer is probably no. The commander is not looking at the whole probability, but a conditional probability distribution based on the fact the plane *did* return. To make the correct judgement, the commander should reinforce those parts where the plane was not shot. It is likely that a plane that got shot in those areas didn't make it back.

Conditional probability is also crucial to understanding the classical classification algorithm: the Bayes-based classifier. Adding an independence requirement to the features of the data, we simplify the algorithm further to the naïve Bayes classifier. We will cover these topics in *Chapter 9, Working with Statistics for Classification Tasks*.

Understanding the power law and black swan

In this last section, I want to give you a brief overview of the so-called power law and black swan events.

The ubiquitous power law

What is the power law? If you have two quantities such that one varies according to a power relationship of another, and independent of the initial sizes, then you have a power law relationship. Many distributions have a power law shape, rather than normal distributions: $P(X = x) = Cx^{-\alpha}$. The exponential distribution we saw previously is one such example.

For a real-word example, the frequency of words in most languages follows a power law. The English letter frequencies also roughly follow a power law. e appears the most often, with a frequency of 11%. The following graph taken from Wikipedia (`https://en.wikipedia.org/wiki/Letter_frequency`) shows a typical example of such a power law:

Letter ⬍	Relative frequency in the English language ▲	
z	0.077%	
q	0.095%	
x	0.150%	
j	0.153%	
v	0.978%	
k	1.292%	
b	1.492%	
p	1.929%	
y	1.994%	
g	2.015%	
c	2.202%	
f	2.228%	
m	2.406%	
w	2.560%	
u	2.758%	
l	4.025%	
d	4.253%	
h	6.094%	
s	6.327%	
n	6.749%	
o	7.507%	
i	7.546%	
r	7.587%	
a	8.497%	
t	9.356%	
e	11.162%	

Figure 5.11 – Frequency of English letters

What's amazing about a power law is not only its universality, but also its lack of well-defined mean and variance in some cases. For example, when α is larger than 2, the expectation of such a power law distribution will explode to infinity, while when α is larger than 3, the variance will also explode.

Be aware of the black swan

Simply put, a lack of well-defined variance implications is known as black swan behavior. A black swan event is a rare event that is hard to predict or compute scientifically. However, black swan events have a huge impact on history, science, or finance, and make people rationalize black swan events in hindsight.

> **Note**
> Before people found black swans in Australia, Europeans believed that all swans were white. The term *black swan* was coined to represent ideas that were considered impossible.

Here are some of the typical examples of black swan events:

- The 2020 coronavirus outbreak
- The 2008 financial crisis
- The assassination of Franz Ferdinand, which sparked World War I

People can justify those events afterward, which make black swans totally inescapable, but no one was prepared to prevent the occurrence of those black swans beforehand.

Beware of black swan events in the distribution you are working on. Remember, in the case of our Texas county population data in *Chapter 4, Sampling and Inference Statistics*, that most of the counties have small populations, but quite a few have populations that are 10 times above the average. If you have sampled your data on a fair number of occasions and didn't see these outliers, you may be inclined toward making incorrect estimations.

Summary

In this chapter, we covered the basics of common discrete and continuous probability distributions, examined their statistics, and also visualized the PDFs. We also talked about joint distribution, conditional distribution, and independency. We also briefly covered power law and black swan behavior.

Many distributions contain parameters that dictate the behavior of the probability distribution. Suppose we know a sample comes from a population that follows a certain distribution; how do you find the parameter of the distribution? This will be the topic of our next chapter: parametric estimation.

6
Parametric Estimation

One big challenge when working with probability distributions is identifying the parameters in the distributions. For example, the exponential distribution has a parameter λ, and you can estimate it to get an idea of the mean and the variance of the distribution.

Parametric estimation is the process of estimating the underlying parameters that govern the distribution of a dataset. Parameters are not limited to those that define the shape of the distribution, but also the locations. For example, if you know that a dataset comes from a uniform distribution but you don't know the lower bound, a, and upper bound, b, of the distribution, you can also estimate the values of a and b as they are also considered legitimate parameters.

Parametric estimation is important because it gives you a good idea of the dataset with a handful of parameters, for example, the distributions and associated descriptive statistics. Although real-life examples won't exactly follow a distribution, parameter estimation does serve as a benchmark for building more complicated models to model the underlying distribution.

After finishing this chapter, you will be able to complete the following
tasks independently:

- Understanding the concepts of parameter estimation and the features of estimators
- Using the method of moments to estimate parameters
- Applying the maximum likelihood approach to estimate parameters with Python

Understanding the concepts of parameter estimation and the features of estimators

A introduction to estimation theory requires a good mathematical understanding and
careful derivation. Here, I am going to use layman's terms to give you a brief but adequate
introduction so that we can move on to concrete examples quickly.

Estimation, in statistics, refers to the process of estimating unknown values from
empirical data that involves random components. Sometimes, people confuse estimation
with **prediction**. Estimation usually deals with hidden parameters that are embodied in a
known dataset: things that already happened, while prediction tries to predict values that
are explicitly not in the dataset: things that haven't happened. For example, estimating
the population of the world 1,000 years ago is an estimation problem. You can use
various kinds of data that may contain information about the population. The population
is a number that will not change but is unknown. On the other hand, predicting the
population in the year 2050 is a prediction problem because the number is essentially
unknown, and we have no data that contains it explicitly.

What parameters can we estimate? In principle, you can estimate any parameter as long
as it is involved in the creation or generation of the random datasets. Let's use the symbol
θ as the set of all unknown parameters and x as the set of data. For example, θ_1 and x_1 will
represent one of the parameters and a single data point, respectively, here indexed by 1. If
$p(x|\theta)$ depends on θ, 'we can estimate that θ exists in the dataset .

> **A note on the exchangeable use of terms**
> Estimation and prediction can sometimes be exchangeable. Often, estimation
> doesn't assert the values of new data, while prediction does, but ambiguity
> always exists.

For example, if you want to know the trajectory of a missile given its current position, the
old positions are indeed unknown *data*, but they can also be treated as hidden *parameters*
that will determine the positions observed later. We will not go down this rabbit hole here.
You are good to go if you understand what's going on.

An **estimator** is required to obtain the estimated values of the parameters that we're interested in. An estimator is also static, and the underlined parameter is called the **estimand**. A particular value that an estimator takes is called an **estimate** (a noun).

Too many concepts? Let's look at a real-world case. Let's take the 2016 US general election as an example. The voting rate is an estimand because it is a parameter to model voting behavior. A valid, straightforward strategy is to take the average voting rates of a sample of counties in the US regardless of their population and other demographic characteristics. This strategy can be treated as an estimator. Let's say that a set of sampled counties gives a value of 0.34, which means 34% of the population vote. Then, the value 0.34 is an estimate, as the realization of our naive estimator. Take another sample of counties; the same estimator may give the value of 0.4 as another estimate.

> **Note: the estimator can be simple**
>
> The estimator is not necessarily complicated or fancy. It is just a way of determining unknown parameters. You can claim the unknown parameter to be a constant regardless of whatever you observe. A constant is a valid estimator, but it is a horribly wrong one. For the same estimand, you can have as many estimators as you want. To determine which one is better, we require more quantitative analysis.

Without further specifications, estimators in this chapter refer to the **point** estimator. The point estimator offers the single best guess of the parameter, while the so-called **interval** estimator gives an interval of the best guesses.

In the next section, let's review the criteria for evaluating estimators.

Evaluation of estimators

For the same estimand, how do we evaluate the qualities of different estimators? Think of the election example; we want the estimation to be as accurate as possible, as robust as possible, and so on. The properties of being accurate and robust have specific mathematical definitions and they are crucial for picking the right estimator for the right tasks.

The following is a list of the criteria:

- Biasness
- Consistency
- Efficiency

Let's look at each of these criteria in detail.

The first criterion – biasness

Recall that an estimator is also a random variable that will take different values depending on the observed sample from the population. Let's use $\hat{\theta}$ to denote the estimator and θ to denote the true value of the parameter (variable), which our estimator tries to estimate. The expected value of the difference between $\hat{\theta}$ and θ is said to be the bias of the estimator, which can be formulated as follows:

$$\text{Bias}\,(\hat{\theta}) \;=\; E(\hat{\theta} - \theta)$$

Note that the expectation is calculated over the distribution $P(x|\theta)$, as varied θ is supposed to change the sampled sets of x.

An estimator is said to be *unbiased* if its bias is 0 for *all* values of parameter θ. Often, we prefer an unbiased estimator over a biased estimator. For example, political analysts want an accurate voting rate, and marketing analysts want a precise customer satisfaction rate for strategy development. If the bias is a constant, we can subtract that constant to obtain an unbiased estimator; if the bias depends on θ, it is not easy to fix in general.

For example, the sample mean from a set using simple random sampling is an unbiased estimator. This is rather intuitive because simple random sampling gives equal opportunity for every member of the set to be selected.

Next, let's move on to the second criterion, which is **consistency** or **asymptotical consistency**.

The second criterion – consistency

As the number of data points increases indefinitely, the resulting sequence of the estimates converges to the true value θ in probability. This is called consistency.

Let's say θ_n is the estimate given n data points, then for any case of $\epsilon > 0$, consistency gives the following formula:

$$\lim_{n \to \infty} P\left(|\theta_n - \theta| > \epsilon\right) = 0$$

For those of you who are not familiar with the language of calculus, think about it this way: no matter how small you choose the infinitesimal threshold (ϵ), you can also choose a number of data points (n) large enough such that the probability that θ_n is different from θ is going to be 0. On the other hand, an inconsistent estimator will fail to estimate the parameter unbiasedly, no matter how much data you use.

> **Note on convergence**
>
> There are two main types of convergence when we talk about probability and distribution. One is called *convergence in probability* and another is called *convergence in distribution*. There are differences if you plan to dig deeper into the mathematical definitions and implications of the two kinds of convergence. All you need to know now is that the convergence in the context of consistency is convergence in probability.

The third criterion – efficiency

The last criterion I want to introduce is relative. If two estimators are both unbiased, which one should we choose? The most commonly used quantity is called **Mean Squared Error (MSE)**. MSE measures the expected value of the square of the difference between the estimator and the true value of the parameter. The formal definition reads as follows:

$$MSE(\hat{\theta}) = E\left(\left(\hat{\theta}(X) - \theta\right)^2\right)$$

Note that the MSE says nothing about the biasness of the estimator. Let's say estimators A and B both have an MSE of 10. It is possible that estimator A is unbiased, but the estimates are scattered around the true value of θ, while estimator B is highly biased but concentrated around a point away from the bull's eye.

What we seek is an unbiased estimator with minimal MSE. This is usually hard to achieve. However, take a step back; among the unbiased estimators, there often exists one estimator with the least MSE. This estimator is called the **Minimum Variance Unbiased Estimator (MVUE)**. Here, we will touch on the concept of variance-bias trade-off. The MSE contains two parts: the *bias* part and the *variance* part. If the bias part is 0, therefore unbiased, then the MSE only contains the variance part. So, we call this estimator the MVUE. We will cover the concepts of bias and variance again in the sense of machine learning, for example, in *Chapter 8, Statistics for Regression*, and *Chapter 9, Statistics for Classification*.

If an estimator has a smaller MSE than another estimator, we say the first estimator is more efficient. **Efficiency** is a relative concept and it is defined in terms of a measuring metric. Here, we use MSE as the measuring metric: the smaller the MSE is, the more efficient the estimator will be.

The concept of estimators beyond statistics

If you extend the concept of estimators beyond the statistical concept to a real-life methodology, the accessibility of data is vitally important. An estimator may have all the advantages but the difficulty of obtaining data becomes a concern. For example, to estimate the temperature of the sun's surface, it is definitely a great idea to send a proxy to do it, but this is probably not a cost-efficient nor time-efficient way. Scientists have used other measurements that can be done on Earth to do the estimation. Some business scenarios share a similar characteristic where unbiasedness is not a big issue, but data accessibility is.

In the next two sections, I will introduce the two most important methods of parameter estimation.

Using the method of moments to estimate parameters

The method of moments associates moments with the estimand. What is a moment?

A moment is a special statistic of a distribution. The most commonly used moment is the nth moment of a real-valued continuous function. Let's use M to denote the moment, and it is defined as follows, where the order of the moment is reflected as the value of the exponent:

$$M_n = \int_{-\infty}^{\infty} (x - c)^n f(x)dx$$

This is said to be the moment about the value c. Often, we set c to be 0:

$$M_n = \int_{-\infty}^{\infty} x^n f(x)dx$$

Some results are immediately available – for example, because the integration of a valid **Probability Density Function (PDF)** always gives 1. Therefore, we have $M_0 = 1$.

Also, M_1 is the expectation value, therefore the mean.

A note on central moments

For high-order moments where c is often set to be the mean, these moments are called **central moments**. In this setting, the second moment, M_2, becomes the variance.

Let's understand how these moments are used to estimate parameters. Let's say you have a set of unknown parameters (θ_K), where K is an integer and θ is our general notation of the unknown parameter defined earlier in this chapter. For example, to estimate a Poisson distribution, which we introduced in *Chapter 5, Common Probability Distributions*, you have $K = 1$ because you have one parameter to estimate.

You then follow these steps to obtain an estimate:

1. Express the ith moment in terms of θ:
    $$M_i = E(X^i) = h_i(\theta_1, \dots, \theta_K)$$

    This is always possible because theoretically, the parameters determine the distribution. Take M_0 and M_1, for example. They have a constant of 1 and the mean of the distribution, respectively.

2. Calculate the moments using the observed data. After that, you obtain K equations with K unknown parameters.

3. Solve the K equations to obtain the unknowns.

The method of moments has several advantages, some of which are listed as follows:

*   The method of moments is easy and quick. The preceding process is guaranteed to work and is usually not computationally expensive.

*   The estimator obtained by the method of moments is usually consistent.

However, the estimator is often biased given the limited amount of data, or even yields unrealistic parameters outside of the parameter space.

You will gain an intuitive understanding through the following two examples.

Example 1 – the number of 911 phone calls in a day

The number 911 is the emergency number for everyone in the United States. Let's assume that the number of 911 calls is independent in a fictious city and we have all the data for 911 calls made in this virtual city every day in a year. Let's also assume that the calling chance for each citizen is the same and unchanged across a year. We know such a discrete distribution, although highly simplified, will follow a Poisson distribution.

Recall that the Poisson distribution takes non-negative integers and has the parameter λ. The **Probability Mass Function (PMF)** reads $\dfrac{\lambda^k e^{-\lambda}}{k!}$.

Let's first generate a set of artificial data using the following code snippet. The true parameter is 20. We will plot the histogram too:

```
np.random.seed(2020)
calls = np.random.poisson(lam=20, size=365)
plt.hist(calls, bins=20);
```

The result looks as follows:

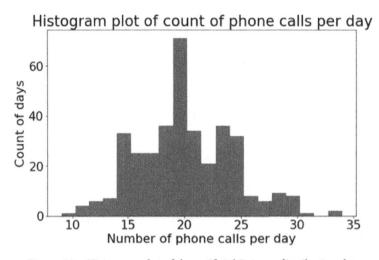

Figure 6.1 – Histogram plot of the artificial Poisson distribution data

Now, let's express the first moment with the unknown parameter. In *Chapter 5, Common Probability Distributions*, we saw that the expectation value is just λ itself.

Next, let's express the first moment with the data, which is just the mean of the data. The np.mean(calls) function call gives the value 19.989. This is our estimation and it is very close to the real parameter, 20.

In short, the logic is the following:

- The np.mean(calls) function call gives the sample mean and we use it to estimate the population mean.

- The population mean is represented by moments. Here, it is just the first moment.

- For a well-defined distribution, the population mean is an expression of unknown parameters.

In this example, the population mean happens to have a very simple expression: the unknown parameter λ itself. But make sure that you understand the whole chain of logic. A more sophisticated example is given next.

Example 2 – the bounds of uniform distribution

Let's see another example of continuous distribution.

We have a set of points that we assume comes from a uniform distribution. However, we don't know the lower bound, α, and upper bound, β. We would love to estimate them. The assumed distribution has a uniform PDF on the legitimate domain. Here is the complete form of the distribution:

$$P(X = x) = \frac{1}{\beta - \alpha}$$

The following code snippet generates artificial data with a true parameter of 0 and 10:

```
np.random.seed(2020)
data = np.random.uniform(0,10,2000)
```

Let's take a look at its distribution. It clearly shows that the 2,000 randomly generated data points are quite uniform. Each bin contains roughly the same amount of data points:

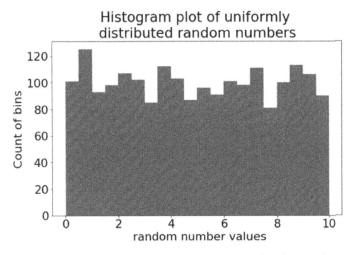

Figure 6.2 – Histogram plot of artificial uniform distribution data

Next, we perform the representation of moments with the unknown parameters:

1. First, let's express the first and second moments with the parameters. The first moment is easy as it is the average of α and β:

$$M_1 = 0.5(\alpha + \beta)$$

The second moment requires some calculation. It is the integration of the product of x^2 and the PDF according to the definition of moments:

$$M_2 = \int_\alpha^\beta \frac{x^2}{\beta - \alpha}\,dx = \frac{1}{3}(\alpha^2 + \alpha\beta + \beta^2)$$

2. Then, we calculate M_1 and M_2 from the data by using the following code snippet:

```
M1 = np.mean(data)
M2 = np.mean(data**2)
```

3. The next step is to express the parameters with the moments. After solving the two equations that represent M_1 and M_2, we obtain the following:

$$\alpha = M_1 - \sqrt{3(M_2 - M_1^2)}$$
$$\beta = 2M_1 - \alpha$$

Substituting the values of the moments, we obtain that α = -0.096 and β = 10.0011. This is a pretty good estimation since the generation of the random variables has a lower bound of 0 and an upper bound of 10.

Wait a second! What will happen if we are unlucky and the data is highly skewed? We may have an unreasonable estimation.

Here is an exercise. You can try to substitute the generated dataset with 1,999 values being 10 and only 1 value being 0. Now, the data is unreasonably unlikely because it is supposed to contain 2,000 data points randomly, uniformly selected from the range 0 to 10. Do the analysis again and you will find that α is unrealistically wrong such that a uniform distribution starting from α cannot generate the dataset we coined itself! How ridiculous!

However, if you observe 1,999 out of 2,000 values aggregated at one single data point, will you still assume the underlying distribution to be uniform? Probably not. This is a good example of why the naked eye should be the first safeguard of your statistical analysis.

You have estimated two sets of parameters in two different problems using the method of moments. Next, we will move on to the maximum likelihood approach.

Applying the maximum likelihood approach with Python

Maximum Likelihood Estimation (**MLE**) is the most widely used estimation method. It estimates the probability parameters by maximizing a likelihood function. The obtained extremum estimator is called the **maximum likelihood estimator**. The MLE approach is both intuitive and flexible. It has the following advantages:

- MLE is consistent. This is guaranteed. In many practices, a good MLE means the job that is left is simply to collect more data.

- MLE is functionally invariant. The likelihood function can take various transformations before maximizing the functional form. We will see examples in the next section.

- MLE is efficient. Efficiency means when the sample size tends to infinity, no other consistent estimator has a lower asymptotic MSE than MLE.

With that power in MLE, I bet you just can't wait to try it. Before maximizing the likelihood, we need to define the likelihood function first.

Likelihood function

A likelihood function is a conditional probability distribution function that conditions upon the hidden parameter. As the name suggests, it measures how likely it is that our observation comes from a distribution with the hidden parameters by assuming the hidden parameters are essentially true. When you change the hidden parameters, the likelihood function changes value. In another words, the likelihood function is a function of hidden parameters.

The difference between a conditional distribution function and a likelihood function is that we focus on different variables. For a conditional distribution, *P(event | parameter)*, we focus on the event and predict how likely it is that an event will happen. So, we are interested in the *f(event) = P(event | parameter = λ)* function, where λ is known.

We treat the likelihood function as a function over the parameter domain where all the events are already observed – *f(parameter) = P(event = E | parameter)*, where the collection of events *E* is known. You can think of it as the opposite of the standard conditional distribution defined in the preceding paragraph.

Let's take coin flipping as an example. Suppose we have a coin, but we are not sure whether it is fair or not. However, what we know is that if it is unfair, getting heads is more likely with a probability of *P(head) = 0.6*.

Now, you toss it 20 times and get 11 heads. Is it more likely to be a fair coin or an unfair coin?

What we want to find is which of the following is more likely to be true: *P(11 out of 20 is head | fair)* or *P(11 out of 20 is head | unfair)*.

Let's calculate the two possibilities. The distribution we are interested in is a binomial distribution.

If the coin is fair, then we have the following likelihood function value:

$$\frac{20!}{11!\,9!}\left(\frac{1}{2}\right)^{20} \approx 0.1602$$

If the coin is biased toward heads, then the likelihood function reads as follows:

$$\frac{20!}{11!\,9!}\left(\frac{3}{5}\right)^{1} 1\left(\frac{2}{5}\right)^{9} = 0.1597$$

It is more likely that the coin is fair. I deliberately picked such a number so that the difference is subtle. *The essence of MLE is to maximize the likelihood function with respect to the unknown parameter.*

A note on the fact that likelihood functions don't sum to 1

You may observe a fact that likelihood functions, even enumerating all possible cases – here, two – do not necessarily sum to unity. This is due to the fact that likelihood functions are essentially not legitimate PDFs.

The likelihood function is a function of *fairness*, where the probability of getting heads can take any value between 0 and 1. What gives a maximal value? Let's do an analytical calculation and then plot it. Let's use p to denote the probability of getting heads and $L(p)$ to denote the likelihood function. You can do a thought experiment here. The value of p changes from 0 to 1, but both $p = 0$ and $p = 1$ make the expression equal to 0. Somewhere in between, there is a p value that maximizes the expression. Let's find it:

$$L(p) = \frac{20!}{11!\,9!}p^{11}(1-p)^{9}$$

Note that the value of p that gives the maximum of this function doesn't depend on the combinatorial factor. We can, therefore, remove it to have the following expression:

$$L(p) = p^{11}(1-p)^{9}$$

You can further take the logarithm of the likelihood function to obtain the famous *log-likelihood function*:

$$logL(p) = 11log(p) + 9log(1-p)$$

The format is much cleaner now. In order to obtain this expression, we used the formulas $log(a^b) = b * log(a)$ and $log(a * b) = log(a) + log(b)$.

Transformation invariance

The transformation suggests that the likelihood function is not fixed nor unique. You can remove the global constant or transform it with a monotonic function such as logarithm to fit your needs.

The next step is to obtain the maximal of the log-likelihood function. The derivative of $log(x)$ is just $\frac{1}{x}$, so the result is simple to obtain by setting the derivative to 0. You can verify that the function only has one extremum by yourself:

$$\frac{dlogL(p)}{dp} = \frac{11}{p} - \frac{9}{1-p} = 0$$

$P = 0.55$ is the right answer. This agrees with our intuition since we observe 11 heads among 20 experiments. The most likely guess is just $\frac{11}{20}$.

For completeness, I will plot the original likelihood distribution before moving to more complex examples. The following code snippet demonstrates this point:

```python
plt.figure(figsize=(10,6))
plt.plot(P, factor*np.power(P,11)*np.power(1-P,9),
         linestyle=":",
         linewidth=4, label="likelihood function")
plt.axvline(0.55,
            linestyle="--",
            linewidth=4,
            label="most likely p",
            color="r")
plt.xlabel("Probability of obtaining head")
plt.ylabel("Likelihood function value")
plt.legend(loc=[0.0,0.6]);
```

The result is as follows. The vertical dashed line indicates the maximum where *p = 0.55*:

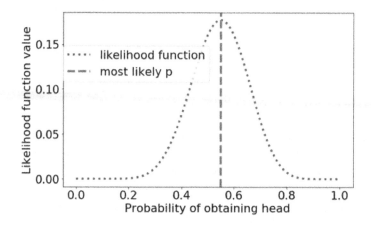

Figure 6.3 – The likelihood function of the coin-tossing experiment

You can verify visually that the likelihood function only has one maximum.

MLE for uniform distribution boundaries

Let's first revisit our previous example, introduced in the *Using the method of moments to estimate parameters* section, where the data is uniformly sampled from the range *[a,b]*, but both *a* and *b* are unknown. We don't need to do any hardcore calculation or computational simulation to obtain the result with MLE.

Suppose the data is denoted as x_1, x_2, up to x_n. *n* is a large number, as we saw in the previous section – 2,000. The likelihood function is therefore as follows:

$$L(a, b) = \left(\frac{1}{b - a}\right)^n$$

The logarithm will bring down the exponent *n*, which is a constant. So, what we want to *maximize* is $log\left(\frac{1}{b - a}\right) = -log(b - a)$, which further means we wish to *minimize* log(b-a).

> **Transformation of logarithm**
>
> Note that $log\left(\frac{1}{x}\right)$ is essentially $log(x^{-1})$. You can pull the *-1* out of the logarithm.

Alright, the result is simple enough such that we don't need derivatives. When b becomes smaller, $log(b-a)$ is smaller. When a is larger but must be smaller than b, $log(b-a)$ is smaller. However, b is the upper bound, so it can't be smaller than the largest value of the dataset, $max(x_i)$, and by the same token, can't be larger than the smallest value of the dataset, $min(x_i)$. Therefore, the result reads as follows:

$A = min(x_i)$

$b = max(x_i)$

This agrees with our intuition and we have fully exploited the information we can get from such a dataset. Also, note that this is much more computationally cheaper than the method of moments approach.

MLE for modeling noise

Let's check another example that is deeply connected with *regression* models, which we are going to see in future chapters. Here, we will approach it from the perspective of estimators.

> **Regression and correlation**
>
> A regression model detects relationships between variables, usually the dependent variables (outcome) and the independent variables (features). The regression model studies the direction of the correlation and the strength of the correlation.

Let's say we anticipate that there is a correlation between random variable X and random variable Y. For simplicity, we anticipate the relationship between them is just proportional, namely $Y \sim k * X$. Here, k is an unknown constant, the *coefficient of proportionality*. However, there is always some noise in a real-world example. The exact relationship between X and Y is, therefore, $Y = k * X + \varepsilon$, where ε stands for the noise random variable.

Let's say we have collected the n **independent** data pairs, x_i and y_i, at our disposal. The following code snippet creates a scatter plot for these data points. For the demonstration, I will choose $n = 100$:

```
plt.figure(figsize=(10,6))
plt.scatter(X,Y)
plt.xlabel("X")
plt.ylabel("Y")
plt.title("Linearly correlated variables with noise");
```

The result looks like the following:

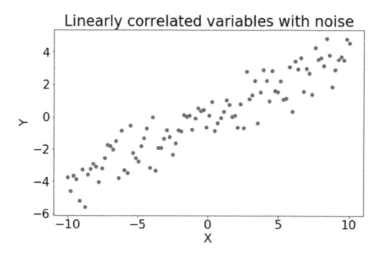

Figure 6.4 – Scatter plot of X and Y

Instead of modeling the distribution of the data, as in the previous example, we are going to model the *noise* since the linear relationship between X and Y is actually known. We will see two cases where the modeling choices change the estimation of the coefficient of proportionality k:

- In the first case, the noise follows a standard normal distribution and can be shown as $N(0,1)$.

- In the second case, the noise follows a standard **Laplace distribution**.

> **A note on the two candidate distributions of noise**
>
> Recall that a standard normal distribution has a PDF that is shown as
> $f(x) = \dfrac{1}{\sqrt{2\pi}} e^{-\frac{x^2}{2}}$. Laplace distribution is very similar to the standard normal
> distribution. It has a PDF that can be presented as $f(x) = \dfrac{1}{2} e^{-|x|}$. The big
> difference is that one decays faster while the other decays slower. The positive
> half of the standard Laplace distribution is just half of the exponential
> distribution, with $\lambda = 1$.

The following code snippet plots the two distributions in one graph:

```
xs = np.linspace(-5,5,100)
normal_variables = 1/np.sqrt(2*np.pi)*np.exp(-0.5*xs**2)
laplace_variables = 0.5*np.exp(-np.abs(xs))

plt.figure(figsize=(10,8))
plt.plot(xs,normal_variables,label="standard
normal",linestyle="--",linewidth=4)
plt.plot(xs,laplace_variables,label="standard
Laplace",linestyle=":",linewidth=4)
plt.legend();
```

The result looks as in the following figure. The dashed line is the standard normal PDF and the dotted line is the standard Laplace PDF:

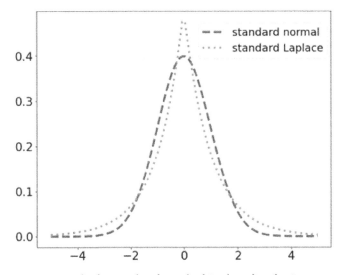

Figure 6.5 – Standard normal and standard Laplace distribution around 0

I will model the noises according to the two distributions. However, the noise is indeed generated from a standard normal distribution.

Let's first examine case 1. Suppose the noise, ϵ, follows the standard normal distribution. This means $\epsilon_i = y_i - kx_i$, as you use other variables to represent ϵ_i follows the given distribution. Therefore, we have $f(\epsilon_i|k) = \dfrac{1}{\sqrt{2\pi}} e^{-\frac{(y_i - kx_i)^2}{2}}$ for every such random noise data point.

Now, think of k is the hidden parameter. We just obtained our likelihood function for one data point. As each data point is *independent*, the likelihood function can therefore be aggregated to obtain the overall likelihood function, as shown in the following formula:

$$L(k) = f(\epsilon_0, \dots, \epsilon_n|k) = \prod_i f(\epsilon_i|k)$$

What we want to find is k such that it maximizes the likelihood function. Let's introduce the mathematical way to express this idea:

$$k_{\text{MLE}} = \text{argmax}_k L(k)$$

Let's take the logarithm of the likelihood function and make use of the rule that the logarithm of a product is the sum of each term's logarithm.

Note on simplifying the logarithm of a sum

The rule of simplifying the likelihood function's expression is called the product rule of logarithm. It is shown as $ln\left(\prod f_i\right) = \sum (ln f_i)$.

Therefore, using the product rule to decompose the log-likelihood function, we have $logL(k) = \sum_i log(f(\epsilon_i|k))$. For each term, we have the following:

$$log(f(\epsilon_i|k)) = -0.5 log(2\pi) - \frac{(y_i - k\,x_i)^2}{2}$$

Substitute the expression into the log-likelihood function:

$$logL(k) = -\frac{n}{2} log(2\pi) - \frac{1}{2} \sum (y_i - k\,x_i)^2$$

Note that the optimal k won't depend on the first term, which is a constant. So, we can drop it and focus on the second part.

Now, let's calculate the derivative with respect to k:

$$\frac{dlogL(k)}{dk} = \sum_i (y_i - k\,x_i)x_i$$

At the maximum of the function, the expression of the derivative will become 0. Equating this to 0, we find the optimal value of k:

$$k^\star = \frac{\sum x_i y_i}{\sum x_i x_i}$$

> **On verifying maximality**
>
> If you are familiar with calculus, you may wonder why I didn't calculate the second derivative to verify that the value is indeed a maximum, rather than a possible minimum. You are right that in principle, such a calculation is needed. However, in our examples in this chapter, the functional forms are quite simple: like a simple quadratic form with only one maximum. The calculation is therefore omitted.

The following code snippet does the calculation. Note that if a variable is a NumPy array, you can perform element-wise calculation directly:

```python
np.sum(X*Y)/np.sum(X*X)
```

The result is 0.40105608977245294.

Let's visualize it to check how well this estimation does. The following code snippet adds the estimated y values to the original scatter plot as a dashed bold line:

```python
plt.figure(figsize=(10,6))
plt.scatter(X,Y,alpha = 0.4)
plt.xlabel("X")
plt.ylabel("Y")
plt.plot(X,X*k_1,linewidth=4,linestyle="--",c="r",
label="fitted line")
plt.legend();
```

The result looks as follows:

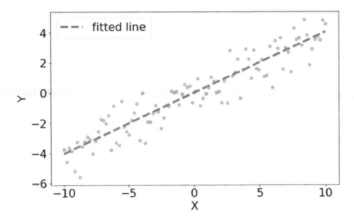

Figure 6.6 – Estimated Y value according to normal noise assumption

The result looks quite reasonable.

Now, let's try the other case. The logic of MLE remains the same until we take the exact form of the likelihood function, $f(\epsilon_i|k)$. The likelihood function for the second Laplace-distributed noise case is the following:

$$L(k) = \prod f(\epsilon_i|k) = \prod \frac{1}{2} e^{-|y_i - kx_i|}.$$

Taking the logarithm, the log-likelihood has a form as follows. I have removed the irrelevant constant 0.5 as I did in the coin-tossing example to simplify the calculation:

$$\log L(k) = -\sum |y_i - kx_i|$$

In order to maximize the log-likelihood function, we need to **minimize** the summation $\sum |y_i - kx_i|$.

This summation involves absolute values, and the sign of each term depends on the value of k. Put the book down and think for a while about the minimization.

Let's define a function, *sign(x)*, which gives us the sign of *x*. If *x* is positive, *sign(x) = 1*, if *x* is negative, *sign(x) = -1*; otherwise, it is *0*. Then, the derivative of the preceding summation with respect to *k* is essentially the following:

$$\frac{dlogL(k)}{dk} = \sum x_i \, sign(y_i - kx_i) = 0$$

Because the *sign(x)* function jumps, it is still not easy to get a hint. Let's do a computational experiment. I will pick *k* between 0 and 1, then create a graph of the log-likelihood function values and the derivatives so that you can have a visual impression. The following code snippet creates the data I needed:

```
Ks = np.linspace(0.2,0.6,100)
```

```
def cal_log_likelihood(X, Y, k):
    return -np.sum(np.abs(Y-k*X))
def cal_derivative(X,Y,k):
    return np.sum(X*np.sign(Y-k*X))
```

```
Likelihoods = [cal_log_likelihood(X,Y,k) for k in Ks]
Derivatives = [cal_derivative(X,Y,k) for k in Ks]
```

I picked the range *[0.2,0.6]* and selected *k* values for a 0.04 increment. Why did I pick this range? This is just a first guess from the scatter plot.

The following code snippet plots the results:

```
plt.figure(figsize=(10,8))
plt.plot(Ks,Likelihoods,label="Likelihood
function",linestyle="--",linewidth=4)
plt.plot(Ks,Derivatives,label=
"Derivative",linestyle=":",linewidth=4)
plt.legend()
plt.xlabel("K");
```

The dashed line is the likelihood function value and the dotted line is the derivative of the likelihood function:

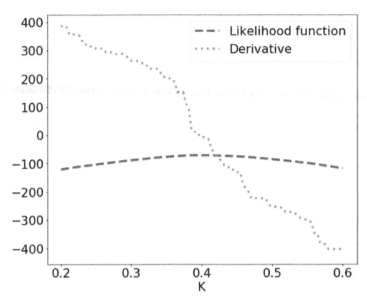

Figure 6.7 – Searching for the optimal k point through computational experimentation

You may notice that there seems to be a plateau for the functions. This is true. Let's zoom in to the range where *k* takes the value *[0.38,0.42]*. The following code snippet does the job:

```
Ks = np.linspace(0.38,0.42,100)
Likelihoods = [cal_log_likelihood(X,Y,k) for k in Ks]
Derivatives = [cal_derivative(X,Y,k) for k in Ks]
plt.figure(figsize=(10,8))
plt.plot(Ks,Likelihoods,label="Likelihood
function",linestyle="--",linewidth=4)
plt.plot(Ks,Derivatives,label=
"Derivative",linestyle=":",linewidth=4)
plt.legend()
plt.xlabel("K");
```

The result looks like the following:

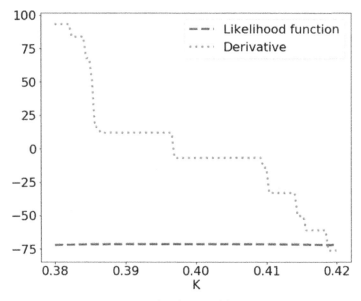

Figure 6.8 – The plateau of derivatives

This strange behavior comes from the fact that taking the derivative of the absolute value function lost information about the value itself. We only have information about the sign of the value left. However, we can still obtain an estimation of the optimal value by using the `numpy.argmax` function. This function returns the index of the maximal value in an array. We can then use this index to index the array for our *k* values. The following one-line code snippet does the job:

```
Ks[np.argmax(Likelihoods)]
```

The result is about 0.397. Then, we know the real *k* values are in the range *[0.397 – 0.0004, 0.397 + 0.0004]*, which is smaller than our result from case 1. Why 0.0004? We divide a range of 0.04 into 100 parts equally, so each grid is 0.0004.

Let's plot both results together. They are almost indistinguishable. The following code snippet plots them together:

```
plt.figure(figsize=(10,8))
plt.scatter(X,Y,alpha = 0.4)
plt.xlabel("X")
plt.ylabel("Y")
plt.plot(X,X*k_1,linewidth=4,linestyle="--",c="r",
label="estimation from \nnormal noise assumption")
plt.plot(X,X*k_2,linewidth=4,linestyle=":",c="g",
label="estimation from \nLaplace noise assumption")
plt.legend();
```

The result looks as follows:

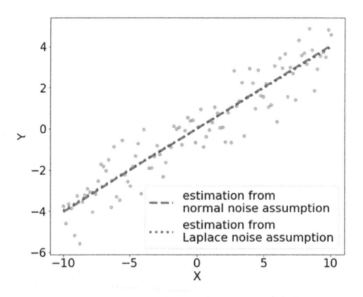

Figure 6.9 – Estimations of the coefficient of proportionality

Alright, we are almost done. Let's find out how the data is generated. The following code snippet tells you that it is indeed generated from the normal distribution:

```
random.seed(2020)
X = np.linspace(-10,10,100)
Y = X * 0.4 + np.array([random.normalvariate(0,1) for _ in
range(100)])
```

In this example, we modeled the random noise with two different distributions. However, rather than a simple unknown parameter, our unknown parameter now carries correlation information between data points. This is a common technique to use MLE to estimate unknown parameters in a model, by assuming a distribution.

We used two different distributions to model the noise. However, the results are not very different. This is *not* always the case. Sometimes, poorly modeled noise will lead to the wrong parameter estimation.

MLE and the Bayesian theorem

Another important question remaining in a real-world case is how to build comprehensive modeling with simply the raw data. The likelihood function is important, but it may miss another important factor: the prior distribution of the parameter itself, which may be independent of the observed data. To have a solid discussion on this extended topic, let me first introduce the **Bayesian theorem** for general events A and B.

The Bayesian theorem builds the connection between $P(A|B)$ and $P(B|A)$ through the following rule:

$$P(A|B) = \frac{P(B|A) * P(A)}{P(B)}$$

This mathematical equation is derived from the definition of the conditional distribution. $P(A|B) = \frac{P(A \cap B)}{P(B)}$ and $P(B|A) = \frac{P(A \cap B)}{P(A)}$ are both true statements, therefore $P(A|B)P(B) = P(B|A)P(A)$, which gives the Bayesian's rule.

Why is the Bayesian rule important? To answer this question, let's replace A with observation O and B with the hidden, unknown parameter λ:

$$P(O|\lambda) = \frac{P(\lambda|O) * P(O)}{P(\lambda)}$$

Now, let's assign real-life meaning to parts of the equation:

- $P(O|\lambda)$ is the likelihood function we wish to maximize.

- $P(\lambda|O)$ is a posterior probability of λ.

- $P(\lambda)$ is a prior probability of λ.

- $P(O)$ is essentially 1 because it is observed, therefore determined.

If you have forgotten the concepts of posterior probability and prior probability, please refer to the *Understanding the important concepts* section in *Chapter 5, Common Probability Distributions*. The Bayesian theorem basically says that the likelihood probability is just the ratio of posterior probability and prior probability. Recall that the posterior distribution is a corrected or adjusted probability of the unknown parameter. The stronger our observation O suggests a particular value of λ, the bigger the ratio of $\frac{P(\lambda|O)}{P(\lambda)}$ is. In both of our previous cases, $P(\lambda)$ is invisible because we don't have any prior knowledge about λ.

Why is prior knowledge of the unknown parameter important? Let's again use the coin-tossing game, not an experiment anymore, as an example. Suppose the game can be done by one of two persons, Bob or Curry. Bob is a serious guy, who is not so playful.

Bob prefers using a fair coin over an unfair coin. *80% of the time, Bob uses the fair coin.* Curry is a naughty boy. He randomly picks a fair coin or unfair coin for the game, fifty-fifty. Will you take the fact of who you are playing the game with into consideration? Of course, you will!

If you play with Curry, you will end up with the same analysis of solving MLE problems as coin tossing and noise modeling. Earlier, we didn't assume anything about the prior information of p. However, if you play with Bob, you know that he is more serious and honest, therefore he is unlikely to use an unfair coin. You need to factor this into your decision.

One common mistake that data scientists make is the ignorance of prior distribution of the unknown parameter, which leads to the wrong likelihood function. The calculation of the modified coin tossing is left to you as an exercise.

The Bayesian theorem is often utilized together with the **law of total probability**. It has an expression as follows:

$$P(A) = \sum_i P(A \cap B_i) = \sum_i P(A|B_i)P(B_i)$$

We won't prove it mathematically here, but you may think of it in the following way:

1. For the first equals sign, for the enumeration of all mutually exclusive events, B_i, each B_i overlaps with event A to some extent; therefore, the aggregation of the events B_i will complete the whole set of A.

2. For the second equals sign, we apply the definition of conditional probability to each term of the summation.

> **Example of the law of total probability**
>
> Suppose you want to know the probability that a baby's name is Adrian in the US. Since Adrian is a gender-neutral baby name, you can calculate it using the law of total probability as *P(Adrian) = P(Adrian|boy) * P(boy) + P(Adrian|girl) * P(girl)*.

The last example in this chapter is the famous Monty Hall question. It will deepen your understanding of the Bayesian rule.

You are on a show to win a prize. There is a huge prize behind one of three doors. Now, you pick door *A*: the host opens door *B* and finds it empty. You are offered a second chance to switch to door *C* or stick to door *A*, what should you do? The prior probability for each door, *A*, *B*, or *C*, is $P(A) = P(B) = P(C) = \frac{1}{3}$. The host will always try to open an empty door after you select: if you selected a door without the prize, the host will open another empty door. If you select the door with the prize, the host will open one of the remaining doors randomly.

Let's use E_B to denote the event that door *B* is opened by the host, which is already observed. Which pair of the following probabilities should you calculate and compare?

*   The likelihood of $P(E_B|A)$ and $P(E_B|C)$
*   The posterior probability $P(A|E_B)$ and $P(C|E_B)$

The answer is the posterior probability. Without calculation, you know $P(E_B|A)$ is $\frac{1}{2}$. Why? Because if the prize is in fact behind door *A*, door *B* is simply selected randomly by the host. However, this information alone will not give us guidance on the next action. The posterior probability is what we want because it instructs us what to do after the observation.

Let's calculate $P(A|E_B)$ first. According to the Bayesian rule and the law of total probability, we have the following equation:

$$P(A|E_B) = \frac{P(E_B|A)P(A)}{P(E_B)} = \frac{P(E_B|A)P(A)}{P(E_B|A)P(A) + P(E_B|B)P(B) + P(E_B|C)P(C)}$$

Now, what is $P(E_B|C)$? It is 1 because the host is sure to pick the empty door to confuse you:

$$P(A|E_B) = \frac{\frac{1}{2} * \frac{1}{3}}{\frac{1}{2} * \frac{1}{3} + 0 * \frac{1}{3} + 1 * \frac{1}{3}} = \frac{1}{3}$$

Let's go over the several conditional probabilities together:

- $P(E_B|A)$: The prize is behind door A, so the host has an equal chance of randomly selecting from door B and door C. This probability is $\frac{1}{2}$.

- $P(E_B|B)$: The prize is behind door B, so the host will **not** open door B at all. This probability is 0.

- $P(E_B|C)$: The prize is behind door C, so the host will **definitely** open door B. Otherwise, opening door C will reveal the prize. This probability is essentially 1.

By the same token, $P(C|E_B) = \frac{2}{3}$. The calculation is left to you as a small exercise.

This is counter-intuitive. You should switch, rather than sticking to your original choice! From the first impression, since the door the host opens is empty, there should be an equal chance that the prize will be in one of the two remaining two doors equally. The devil is in the details. The host has to open a door that is empty. You will see from a computational sense about the **breaking of symmetry** in terms of choices.

First, let's ask the question of whether we can do a computational experiment to verify the results. The answer is yes, but the setup is a little tricky. The following code does the job, and I will explain it in detail:

```python
import random
random.seed(2020)
doors = ["A","B","C"]
count, stick, switch = 0, 0, 0
trials = []
for i in range(10000):
    prize = random.choice(doors)
    pick = random.choice(doors)
    reveal = random.choice(doors)
    trial = 1
    while reveal == prize or reveal == pick:
```

```
        reveal = random.choice(doors)
        trial+=1
    trials.append(trial)
    if reveal != pick and reveal != prize:
        count += 1
        if pick== prize:
            stick +=1
        else:
            switch += 1
print("total experiment: {}".format(count))
print("times of switch: {}".format(switch))
print("times of stick: {}".format(stick))
```

Run it and you will see the following results:

```
total experiment: 10000
times of switch: 6597
times of stick: 3403
```

Indeed, you should switch. The code follows the following logic:

1. For 10,000 experiments, the **prize** is pre-selected randomly. The user's **pick** is also randomly selected. The user may or may not pick the prize.

2. Then, the host **reveals** one of the doors. However, we know that the host will reveal one empty door from the remaining two doors for sure. We use the `trial` variable to keep track of the times that we try to generate a random selection to meet this condition. This variable is also appended to a list object whose name is `trials`.

3. At last, we decide whether to switch or not.

The symmetry is broken when the host tries to pick the empty door. Let's use the following code to show the distribution of trials:

```
plt.figure(figsize=(10,6))
plt.hist(trials,bins = 40);
```

The plot looks like the following:

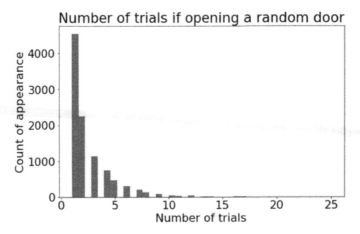

Figure 6.10 – Number of trials in the computer simulation

In our plain simulation, in order to meet the condition that the host wants to satisfy, we must do random selection more than one time, and sometimes even more than 10 times. This is where the bizarreness hides.

Enough said on the Bayesian theorem; you have grasped the foundation of MLE. MLE is a simplified scenario of the Bayesian approach to estimation by assuming the prior distribution of the unknown parameter is uniform.

Summary

In this chapter, we covered two important methods of parameter estimation: the method of moments and MLE. You then learned the background of MLE, the Bayesian way of modeling the likelihood function, and so on. However, we don't know how well our estimators perform, yet. In general, it requires a pipeline of hypothesis testing with a quantitative argument to verify a claim. We will explore the rich world of hypothesis testing in the next chapter, where we will put our hypotheses/assumptions to the test.

7
Statistical Hypothesis Testing

In *Chapter 6, Parametric Estimation*, you learned two important parameter estimation methods, namely, the method of moments and MLE. The underlying assumption for parameter estimation is that we know that the data follows a specific distribution, but we do not know the details of the parameters, and so we estimate the parameters.

Parametric estimation offers an estimation, but most of the time we also want a quantitative argument of confidence. For example, if the sample mean from one population is larger than the sample mean from another population, is it enough to say the mean of the first population is larger than that of the second one? To obtain an answer to this question, you need statistical hypothesis testing, which is another method of statistical inference of massive power.

In this chapter, you are going to learn about the following topics:

- An overview of hypothesis testing
- Making sense of confidence intervals and P values from visual examples
- Using the `SciPy` Python library to do common hypothesis testing

- Understanding the ANOVA model and corresponding testing

- Applying hypothesis testing to time series problems

- Appreciating A/B testing with real-world examples

Some concepts in this chapter are going to be subtle. Buckle up and let's get started!

An overview of hypothesis testing

To begin with the overview, I would like to share an ongoing example from while I was writing this book. As the coronavirus spread throughout the world, pharmaceutical and biotechnology companies worked around the clock to develop drugs and vaccines. Scientists estimated that it would take at least a year for a vaccine to be available. To verify the effectiveness and safety of a vaccine or drug, clinical trials needed to be done cautiously and thoroughly at different stages. It is a well-known fact that most drugs and vaccines won't reach the later trial stages and only a handful of them ultimately reach the market. How do clinical trials work? In short, the process of screening medicines is a process of **hypothesis testing**.

A hypothesis is just a statement or claim about the statistics or parameters describing a studied population. In clinical trials, the hypothesis that a medicine is effective or safe is being tested. The simplest scenario includes two groups of patients selected randomly. You treat one group with the drug and another without the drug and control the rest of the factors. Then, the trial conductors will measure specific signals to compare the differences, for example, the concentration of the virus in the respiratory system or the number of days to full recovery. The trial conductors then decide whether the differences or the statistics calculated are significant enough. You can pre-select a *significance level*, α, to check whether the trial results meet the expected level of significance.

Now, imagine you observe the average math course scores for 9th grade students in a school. You naturally assume that the distribution of each year's math course scores follows a normal distribution. However, you find this year's sample average score, μ_{2020}, is slightly below last year's population average score, 75. Do you think this finding just comes from the randomness of sampling, or is the fundamental level of math skills of *all* students deteriorating?

You can use MLE or the methods of the moment to fit this year's data to a normal distribution and compare the fitted mean. However, this still doesn't give you a quantitative argument of confidence. In a score-based (a score out of 100) grading system, let's say last year's average score for all students is 75 and the average score for your 2020 class, a 900-student sample, is 73. Is the decrease real? How small or big is the two-point difference?

To answer these questions, we first need to clarify what constitutes a valid hypothesis. Here are two conditions:

- The statement must be expressed mathematically. For example, *this year's average score is the same as last year's* is a valid statement. This statement can be expressed as $H_0: \mu_{2020} = 75$ with no ambiguity. However, *this year's average score is roughly the same as last year's* is not a valid statement because different people have different assessments of what is roughly the same.

- The statement should be testable. A valid statement is about the statistics of observed data. If the statement requires data other than the observed data, the statement is not testable. For example, you can't test the differences in students' English scores if only math scores are given.

This famous saying by the statistician Fisher summarizes the requirements for a hypothesis well, although he was talking about the null hypothesis specifically:

> *The null hypothesis must be exact, that is, free of vagueness and ambiguity, because it must supply the basis of the "problem of distribution," of which the test of significance is the solution.*

Now we are ready to proceed more mathematically. Let's rephrase the math score problem as follows.

The average math score for the previous year's 9th grade students is 75. This year, you randomly sample 900 students and find the sample mean is 73. You want to know whether the average score for this year's students is lower than last year's.

To begin hypothesis testing, the following three steps are required:

1. Formulate a **null hypothesis**. A null hypothesis basically says *there is nothing special going on*. In our math score example, it means there is no difference between this year's score and last year's score. A null hypothesis is denoted by H_0. On the other hand, the corresponding **alternative hypothesis** states the opposite of the null hypothesis. It is denoted by H_1 or H_a. In our example, you can use $H_1: \mu_{2020} \neq 75$. Note that different choices of null hypothesis and alternative hypothesis will lead to different results in terms of accepting or rejecting the null hypothesis.

2. Pick a **test statistic** that can be used to assess how well the null hypothesis holds and calculate it. A test statistic is a random variable that you will calculate from the sampled data under the assumption that the null hypothesis is true. Then, you calculate the P-value according to the known distribution of this test statistic.

3. Compute the P-value from the test statistic and compare it with an acceptable **significance level**, α.

Gosh! So many new terms! Don't worry, let's go back to our examples and you will see this unfold gradually. After that, you will be able to understand these concepts in a coherent way. You will be able to follow these three steps to approach various kinds of hypothesis testing problems in a unified setting.

Understanding P-values, test statistics, and significance levels

To explain the concepts with the math example, let's first get a visual impression of the data. I will be using two sample math scores for 900 students in 2019 and sample math scores for 900 students in 2020.

> **Note on given facts**
>
> The dataset for 2019 is not necessary for hypothesis testing because we are given the *fact* that the average score for 2019 is exactly 75. I will generate the datasets to provide you with a clear comparable visualization.

At this point, I am not going to tell you how I generated the 2020 data; otherwise, the *ground truth* would be revealed to you beforehand. I do assure you that the data for 2019 is generated from sampling a normal distribution with a mean of 75 and a variance of 25.

The two datasets are called `math2020` and `math2019`. Each of them contains 900 data points. Let me plot them with histogram plots so you know roughly what they look like. The following code snippet does the job:

```
plt.figure(figsize=(10,6))
plt.hist(math2020,bins=np.
linspace(50,100,50),alpha=0.5,label="math2020")
plt.hist(math2019,bins=np.
linspace(50,100,50),alpha=0.5,label="math2019")
plt.legend();
```

Note that I explicitly set the bins to make sure the bin boundaries are fully determined. The result looks as follows:

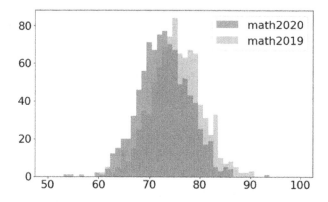

Figure 7.1 – Histogram plot of math scores from 2020 and 2019

Note that the scores from 2020 do seem to have a smaller mean than the scores from 2019, which is supposed to be very close to 75. Instead of calling the corresponding `numpy` functions, I will just use the following `describe()` function from the `scipy` library's `stats` module:

```
from scipy import stats
stats.describe(math2020)
```

The result is the following:

```
DescribeResult(nobs=900, minmax=(53.61680120097629,
93.29408158813376), mean=72.89645796453996,
variance=24.81446705891462, skewness=0.007960630504578523,
kurtosis=0.3444548003252992)
```

Do the same thing for the year 2019. I find that the mean for the year 2019 is around 75.

In *Chapter 4, Sampling and Inferential Statistics*, we discussed the issue of sampling, which itself involves randomness. Is the difference in means an artifact of randomness or is it real? To answer this question, let's first embed some definitions into our example, starting with the null hypothesis.

A null hypothesis basically says *YES: everything is due to randomness.* An alternative hypothesis says *NO* to randomness and claims that there are fundamental differences. A hypothesis test is tested against the null hypothesis to see whether there is evidence to reject it or not.

Back to the math score problem. We can pick the null hypothesis $H_0: \mu_{2020} = 75$ and set the alternative hypothesis $H_1: \mu_{2020} \neq 75$. Or, we can choose $H_0: \mu_{2020} \geq 75$ and set $H_1: \mu_{2020} < 75$. Note that the combination of the null hypothesis and the alternative hypothesis must cover all possible cases. The first case is called a **two-tailed hypothesis** because either $\mu_{2020} < 75$ or $\mu_{2020} > 75$ will be a rebuttal of our null hypothesis. The alternative is a **one-tailed hypothesis**. Since we only want to test whether our mean score is less than or equal to 75, we choose the one-tailed hypothesis for our example. Even in the null hypothesis, the mean can be larger than 75, but we know this is going to have a negligible likelihood.

> **On the choice of one-tailed or two-tailed hypotheses**
>
> Whether to use a one-tailed hypothesis or a two-tailed hypothesis depends on the task at hand. One big difference is that choosing a two-tailed alternative hypothesis requires an equal split of the significance level on both sides.

What we have now is a dataset, a null hypothesis, and an alternative hypothesis. The next step is to find evidence to test the null hypothesis. The null hypothesis reads $H_0: \mu_{2020} \geq 75$, whereas the alternative hypothesis reads $H_1: \mu_{2020} < 75$.

After setting up the hypothesis, the next step is to find a rule to measure the strength of the evidence, or in other words, to quantify the risk of making mistakes that reject a true null hypothesis. The significance level, α, is essentially an index of the likelihood of making the mistake of rejecting a true null hypothesis.

For example, if a medicine under trial is useless, $\alpha = 0.05$ means that we set a threshold that at the chance of less than or equal to 5%, we may incorrectly conclude that the medicine is useful. If we set the bar way lower, at $\alpha = 0.001$, it means that we are very picky about the evidence. In other words, we want to minimize the cases where we are so unlucky that randomness leads us to the wrong conclusion.

As we continue to talk about significance, all hypothesis testing to be discussed in this chapter will be done with **statistical significance tests**. A statistical significance test assumes the null hypothesis is correct until evidence that contradicts the null hypothesis shows up.

Another perspective of hypothesis testing treats the null hypothesis and the alternative hypothesis equally and tests which one fits the statistical model better. I only mention it here for completeness.

To summarize, if the evidence and test statistics show contradictions against the null hypothesis with high statistical significance (smaller α values), we reject the null hypothesis. Otherwise, we fail to reject the hypothesis. Whether you reject the null hypothesis or not, there is a chance that you will make mistakes.

> **Note**
>
> Hypothesis testing includes the test of correlation or independence. In this chapter, we mainly focus on the test of differences. However, claiming two variables are correlated or independent is a legitimate statement/hypothesis that can be tested.

Making sense of confidence intervals and P-values from visual examples

P-values determine whether a research proposal will be funded, whether a publication will be accepted, or at least whether an experiment is interesting or not. To start with, let me give you some bullet points about P-values' properties:

- *The P-value is a magical probability, but it is not the probability that the null hypothesis will be accepted.* Statisticians tend to search for supportive evidence for the alternative hypothesis because the null hypothesis is boring. Nobody wants to hear that there is nothing interesting going on.

- *The P-value is the probability of making mistakes if you reject the null hypothesis.* If the P-value is very small, it means that you can safely reject the null hypothesis without worrying too much that you made mistakes because randomness tricked you. If the P-value is 1, it means that you have absolutely no reason to reject the null hypothesis, because what you get from the test statistic is the most typical results under the null hypothesis.

- *The P-value is defined in the way it is so that it can be comparable to the significance level, α.* If we obtain a P-value smaller than the significance level, we say the result is significant at significance level α. The risk of making a mistake that rejects the null hypothesis wrongly is acceptable. If the P-value is not smaller than α, the result is not significant.

- *From first principles, the P-value of an event is also the summed probability of observing the event and all events with equal or smaller probability.* This definition doesn't contradict the point about contradicting the null hypothesis. Note that under the assumption of a true null hypothesis, the cumulative probability of observing our test statistics and all other equal or rarer values of test statistics is the probability of mistakenly rejecting the null hypothesis.

The importance of first-principles thinking

First-principles thinking is very important in studying statistics and programming. It is advised that you resist the temptation to use rules and procedures to get things done quickly but instead learn the definitions and concepts, so you have a foundation in terms of first principles.

Please read the definition of the P-value carefully to make sure you fully understand it. Before moving on to a concrete example of test statistics, let's have a look at the P-value from two examples from first principles. The importance of correctly understanding the P-value cannot be stressed enough.

Calculating the P-value from discrete events

In our first example, we will study the *probability* and the *P-value* of events in coin-tossing experiments. Let's toss a fair coin 6 times and count the total number of heads. There are 7 possibilities, from 0 heads to 6 heads. We can calculate the probability either theoretically or computationally. I will just do a quick experiment with the following lines of code and compare the results with the theoretical values.

The following code snippet generates the experiment results for 1 million tosses and stores the results in the `results` variable:

```
random.seed(2020)
results = []
for _ in range(1000000):
    results.append(sum([random.random() < 0.5 for i in range(6)]))
```

The following code snippet normalizes the results and lists them alongside the theoretical results:

```
from collections import Counter
from math import factorial as factorial
counter = Counter(results)
```

```
for head in sorted(counter.keys()):
    comput = counter[head]/1000000
    theory = 0.5**6*factorial(6)/factorial(head)/factorial(6-
head)
    print("heads: {}; Computational: {}; Theoretical: {}".
format(head,comput, theory))
```

The results look as follows. The computational results agree with the theoretical results pretty well:

```
heads: 0; Computational: 0.015913; Theoretical: 0.015625
heads: 1; Computational: 0.093367; Theoretical: 0.09375
heads: 2; Computational: 0.234098; Theoretical: 0.234375
heads: 3; Computational: 0.312343; Theoretical: 0.3125
heads: 4; Computational: 0.234654; Theoretical: 0.234375
heads: 5; Computational: 0.093995; Theoretical: 0.09375
heads: 6; Computational: 0.01563; Theoretical: 0.015625
```

Let's answer the following questions to help us clarify the definition of the P-value. The answers should be based on theoretical results:

1. What is the probability of getting 5 heads, what about P-value?

   The probability is 0.09375. However, the P-value is the sum of 0.09375 + 0.09375 + 0.015625 + 0.015625 = 0.21875. The P-value is the probability of you seeing such events with equal probability or rarer probability. Getting 1 head is equally likely as getting 5 heads. Getting 6 heads or 0 heads is more extreme. With a P-value of roughly 0, we say that the event of observing 5 heads is quite typical. The P-value for observing 6 heads is about 0.031. The calculation is left to you as an exercise.

2. What is the P-value of getting 3 heads?

   The surprising answer here is 1. Among all 7 kinds of possibilities, getting 3 heads is the most likely outcome; therefore, the rest of the outcomes are all rarer than getting 3 heads. Another implication is that there are no other events that are more **typical** than observing 3 heads.

Now, you should have a better understanding of the P-value by having treated it as a measurement of typicalness.

In the next section, let's move on to a case involving the continuous **Probability Density Function (PDF)** case, where we need some integration.

Calculating the P-value from the continuous PDF

We just calculated P-values from discrete events. Now let's examine a continuous distribution. The distribution I am going to use is the **F-distribution**. The F-distribution is the distribution we are going to use in the analysis of the variance test later, so it is good to have a first impression here. The analytical form of the F-distribution is parameterized by two degrees of freedom, d_1 and $d_2 \sim F(d1, d2)$. If x is greater than 0, the PDF is as follows.

$$f(x, d_1, d_2) = \frac{1}{B\left(\frac{d_1}{2}, \frac{d_2}{2}\right)} \left(\frac{d_1}{d_2}\right)^{\frac{d_1}{2}} x^{\frac{d_1}{2}-1} \left(1 + \frac{d_1}{d_2}x\right)^{-\frac{d_1+d_2}{2}}$$

The $B(x,y)$ function is called the **beta function**, and it's a special kind of function. If you are familiar with calculus, it has the following definition as an integration:

$$B(x, y) = \int_0^1 t^{x-1}(1 - t)^{y-1}dt$$

Fortunately, we don't need to write our own function to generate these samples. The `scipy` library provides another handy function, f, for us to use.

The following code snippet generates the PDFs with four pairs of parameters and plots them:

```python
from scipy.stats import f


plt.figure(figsize=(10,8))
styles = ["-",":","--","-."]
for i, [dfn, dfd] in
enumerate([[20,30],[20,60],[50,30],[50,60]]):
    x = np.linspace(f.ppf(0.001, dfn, dfd), f.ppf(0.999, dfn,
dfd), 100)
    plt.plot(x, f.pdf(x, dfn, dfd), linestyle= styles[i],
            lw=4, alpha=0.6,
            label='{} {}'.format(dfn,dfd))
plt.legend();
```

The plotted graph looks like this:

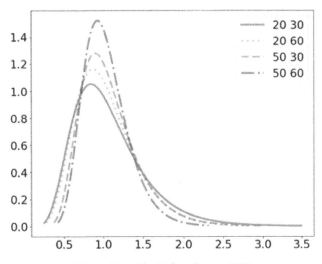

Figure 7.2 – The F-distribution PDF

The probability distribution function of the F-distribution is not symmetrical; it is right-skewed with a long tail. Let's say you have a random variable, x, following the distribution $F(20,60)$. If you observe x to be 1.5, what is the P-value for this observation?

The following code snippet highlights the region where the equal or rare events are highlighted in red. I generated 100 linearly spaced data points and stored them in the x variable and selected those rarer observations on the right and those on the left:

```
plt.figure(figsize=(10,8))
[dfn, dfd] =[20,60]
x = np.linspace(f.ppf(0.001, dfn, dfd), f.ppf(0.999, dfn, dfd),
100)
plt.plot(x,
        f.pdf(x, dfn, dfd),
        linestyle= "--",
        lw=4, alpha=0.6,
        label='{} {}'.format(dfn,dfd))
right = x[x>1.5]
left = x[f.pdf(x, dfn, dfd) < f.pdf(right,dfn,dfd)[0]][0:8]
plt.fill_between(right,f.
pdf(right,dfn,dfd),alpha=0.4,color="r")
plt.fill_between(left,f.pdf(left,dfn,dfd),alpha=0.4,color="r")
plt.legend();
```

There is a little bit of hardcoding here where I manually selected the left part of the shaded area. You are free to inspect the expression of the left variable. The result looks as follows:

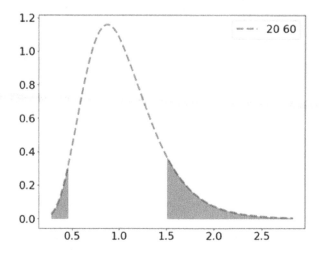

Figure 7.3 – A rarer observation than 1.5 in F(20,60)

The integration of the shaded area gives us the P-value for observing the value 1.5. The following code snippet uses the **Cumulative Distribution Function (CDF)** to calculate the value:

```
f.cdf(left[-1],dfn,dfd) + (1-f.cdf(right[0],dfn,dfd))
```

The P-value is about 0.138, so not very bad. It is somewhat typical to observe a 1.5 from such an F-distribution. If your pre-selected significance level is $\alpha = 0.05$, then this observation is not significant enough.

By now, you should understand the definition and implication of the P-value from first principles. The remaining question is, what exactly is the P-value in a hypothesis test? The answer involves test statistics.

In the second step of hypothesis testing, we calculate the best kind of statistic and check its P-value against a pre-selected significance level.

In the math score example, we want to compare a sample mean against a constant; this is a **one-sample, one-tailed** test. The statistic we want to use is the *t-statistic*. The specific hypothesis test we want to apply is *Student's t-test*. Please bear with me on the new concepts. The t-statistic is nothing special; it's just another random variable that follows a specific distribution, which follows Student's t-distribution. We will cover both specific and Student's t-distribution shortly, with clear definitions and visualizations.

> **Tests and test statistics**
>
> Different problems require different test statistics. If you want to test the differences in samples across several categories or groups, you should use the **Analysis of Variance (ANOVA)** F-test. If you want to test the independence of two variables in a population, you should use the Chi-square test, which we will cover very soon.

Under the null hypothesis, the t-statistic *t* is calculated as follows:

$$t = \frac{\mu_{2020} - 75}{s/\sqrt{n}}$$

n is the sample size and *s* is the sample standard deviation. The random variable *t* follows Student's t-distribution with a degree of freedom of *n-1*.

> **Student's t-distribution**
>
> **Student's t-distribution** is a continuous probability distribution used when estimating the mean of a normally distributed distribution with an unknown population standard deviation and a small sample size. It has a complicated PDF with a parameter called the **Degree of Freedom (DOF)**. We won't go into the formula of the PDF as it's convoluted, but I will show you the relationship between the DOF and the shape of the t-distribution PDF.

The following code snippet plots the t-distributions with various DOFs alongside the standard normal distribution functions. Here I use the `scipy.stats` module:

```
from scipy.stats import t, norm
plt.figure(figsize=(12,6))
DOFs = [2,4,8]
linestyles= [":","--","-."]
for i, df in enumerate(DOFs):
    x = np.linspace(-4, 4, 100)
    rv = t(df)
    plt.plot(x, rv.pdf(x), 'k-', lw=2, label= "DOF = " +
str(df),linestyle=linestyles[i]);

plt.plot(x,norm(0,1).pdf(x),'k-', lw=2, label="Standard
Normal")
plt.legend();
```

The result looks like the following. Pay attention to the line styles. As you see, when the DOF increases, the t-distribution PDF tends to approach the standard normal distribution with larger and larger centrality:

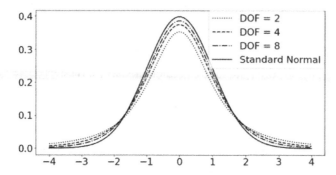

Figure 7.4 – The Student's t-distribution PDF and a standard normal PDF

Alright, our statistic $t = \dfrac{\mu_{2020} - 75}{s/\sqrt{n}}$ follows the t-distribution with a DOF of 899. By substituting the numbers, we can get the value of our t-statistic using the following code:

```
(np.mean(math2020)-75)/(np.std(math2020)/30)
```

The result is about `-12.6758`.

> **Replacing the t-distribution with a normal distribution**
>
> With a large DOF (899 in our case), the t-distribution will be completely indistinguishable from a normal distribution. In practice, you can use a normal distribution to do the test safely.

Significance levels in t-distribution

Let's say we selected a significance level of $\alpha = 0.01$. Is our result significant enough? We need to find out whether our result exceeds the threshold of the significance level 0.01.

The t-distribution doesn't have an easy-to-calculate PDF, so given a significance level of $\alpha = 0.01$, how do we easily find the threshold(s)?

Before the advent of easy-to-use libraries or programs, people used to build t-statistics tables to solve this issue. For a given significance level, you can basically look up the table and find the corresponding t-statistic value.

As the t-distribution is symmetric, the importance of whether you are doing a one-tail test or a two-tailed test increases. Let's first check a t-distribution table for a one-tail test. For example, with a DOF of 5, to be significant at the 0.05 level, the t-statistic needs to be 2.015:

DOF	$\alpha = 0.1$	0.05	0.025	0.01	0.005	0.001	0.0005
1	3.078	6.314	12.706	31.821	63.656	318.289	636.578
2	1.886	2.920	4.303	6.965	9.925	22.328	31.600
3	1.638	2.353	3.182	4.541	5.841	10.214	12.924
4	1.533	2.132	2.776	3.747	4.604	7.173	8.610
5	1.476	2.015	2.571	3.365	4.032	5.894	6.869

Figure 7.5 – The t-distribution table for one-tailed significance levels

For a more intuitive impression, the following code snippet plots the different thresholds of the t-distribution PDF:

```
plt.figure(figsize=(10,6))
df = 5
x = np.linspace(-8, 8, 200)
rv = t(df)
plt.plot(x, rv.pdf(x), 'k-', lw=4,linestyle="--");
alphas = [0.1,0.05,0.025,0.01,0.005,0.001,0.0005]
thresholds = [1.476,2.015,2.571,3.365,4.032,5.894,6.869]
for thre, alpha in zip(thresholds,alphas):
    plt.plot([thre,thre],[0,rv.pdf(thre)] ,label = "{}".
format(str(alpha)),linewidth=4)
plt.legend();
```

The result looks as follows:

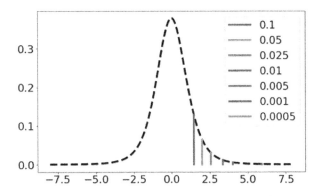

Figure 7.6 – The significance levels for a t-statistics distribution with DOF=5

Adding the following two lines will zoom into the range that we are interested in:

```
plt.xlim(-2,8)
plt.ylim(0,0.15)
```

The result looks as follows. If you can't distinguish the colors, just remember that the smaller the significance level is, the further away the threshold is from the origin:

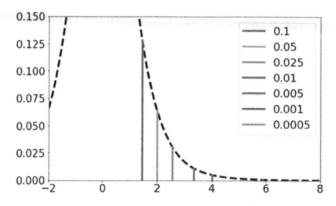

Figure 7.7 – A zoomed-in t-distribution showing different significance levels

As the significance level decreases (that is, as α decreases), we tend toward keeping the null hypothesis because it becomes increasingly harder to observe a sample with such low probability.

Next, let's check the two-tailed t-distribution table. The two-tailed case means that we must consider both ends of the symmetric distribution. The summation of both gives us the significance level:

DOF	$\alpha = 0.2$	0.10	0.05	0.02	0.01	0.002	0.001
1	3.078	6.314	12.706	31.821	63.656	318.289	636.578
2	1.886	2.920	4.303	6.965	9.925	22.328	31.600
3	1.638	2.353	3.182	4.541	5.841	10.214	12.924
4	1.533	2.132	2.776	3.747	4.604	7.173	8.610
5	1.476	2.015	2.571	3.365	4.032	5.894	6.869

Figure 7.8 – The t-distribution table for two-tailed significance levels

Notice that for *α = 0.2*, the t-statistic is the same as *α = 0.1* for a one-tailed test. The following code snippet illustrates the relationship between t-statistic and one-tailed test, using *α = 0.01* as an example. I picked the most important region to show:

```
plt.figure(figsize=(10,6))
df = 5
x = np.linspace(-8, 8, 200)
rv = t(df)
plt.plot(x, rv.pdf(x), 'k-', lw=4,linestyle="--");
alpha=0.01
one_tail = 3.365
two_tail = 4.032
plt.plot([one_tail,one_tail],[0,rv.pdf(one_tail)] ,
        label = "one_tail",linewidth=4,linestyle="--")
plt.plot([two_tail,two_tail],[0,rv.pdf(two_tail)] ,
        label = "two
tail",linewidth=4,color="r",linestyle=":")
plt.plot([-two_tail,-two_tail],[0,rv.pdf(two_tail)] ,
        label = "two
tail",linewidth=4,color="r",linestyle=":")

plt.fill_between(np.linspace(-8,-two_tail,200),
                rv.pdf(np.linspace(-8,-two_
tail,200)),color="g")
plt.fill_between(np.linspace(one_tail,two_tail,200),
                rv.pdf(np.linspace(one_tail,two_
tail,200)),color="g")
plt.ylim(0,0.02)
plt.legend();
```

The result looks as follows:

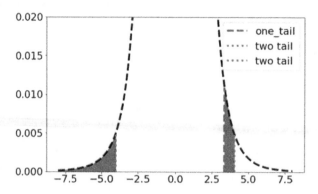

Figure 7.9 – A comparison of two-tailed and one-tailed results for the same significance level

You need to trust me that the shaded parts have the same area. The one-tailed case only covers the region to the right of the vertical dashed line (the left edge of the right shaded area), but the two-tailed case covers both sides symmetrically (the outer portion of the two dotted vertical lines). Since the significance levels are the same, they should both cover the same **area under the curve** (**AUC**), which leads to the equal area of the two shaded regions.

For our one-sided test, our t-statistic is less than -10. It is equivalent to the threshold for the positive value because of the symmetry of the problem. If you look up the t-distribution table, with such a large DOF of 899, the difference between large DOFs is quite small. For example, the following two rows are found at the end of the t-distribution table:

DOF	$\alpha = 0.1$	0.05	0.025	0.01	0.005	0.001	0.0005
120	1.289	1.658	1.980	2.358	2.617	3.160	3.373
1000	1.282	1.646	1.962	2.330	2.581	3.098	3.300

Figure 7.10 – A t-distribution table with very large DOFs

In the math score example, the absolute value 12.67 for our t-statistic is far away from both 2.358 and 2.330. We have enough confidence to reject the null hypothesis, which means that the alternative hypothesis is true: indeed, students' math skills have declined.

The following code snippet reveals how I generated the score data:

```
random.seed(2020)
math2019 = [random.normalvariate(75,5) for _ in range(900)]
math2020 = [random.normalvariate(73,5) for _ in range(900)]
```

Feel free to reproduce the random data generated to visualize it yourself. Next, let's examine another concept in hypothesis testing: power.

The power of a hypothesis test

I will briefly mention another concept you may see from other materials: **the power of a hypothesis test**. The power of hypothesis testing is the probability of making the correct decision if the alternative hypothesis is true.

It is easier to approach this concept from its complementary part. The opposite side of this is the probability of failing to reject the null hypothesis H_0 while the alternative hypothesis H_1 is true. This is called a **type II error**. The smaller the type II error is, the greater the power will be. Intuitively speaking, greater power means the test is more likely to detect something interesting going on.

On the other hand, everything comes with a cost. If the type II error is low, then we will inevitably reject the null hypothesis based on some observations that indeed originate from pure randomness. This is an error that's called a **type I error**. The type I error is the mistake of rejecting the null hypothesis H_0 while H_0 is indeed true. Does this definition ring a bell?

When you choose a significance level α, you are choosing your highest acceptable type I error rate.

As you can imagine, the type I error and type II error will compensate for each other in most cases. We will come back to this topic again and again when we talk about machine learning.

Examples of type I and type II errors

A classic example of type I and type II errors has to do with radar detection. Say that a radar system is reporting no incoming enemy aircraft: the null hypothesis is that there are no incoming enemy aircraft and the alternative hypothesis is that there actually are incoming enemy aircraft. A type I error is reporting the enemy aircraft when there are no aircraft in the area. A type II error would be when there are indeed incoming enemy aircraft, but none were reported.

In the next section, we are going to use the SciPy library to apply what we have learned so far to various kinds of hypothesis testing problems. You will be amazed at how much you can do.

Using SciPy for common hypothesis testing

The previous section went over a t-test and the basic concepts in general hypothesis testing. In this section, we are going to fully embrace the powerful idea of the paradigm of hypothesis testing and use the `SciPy` library to solve various hypothesis testing problems.

The paradigm

The powerful idea behind the hypothesis testing paradigm is that if you know that your assumption when hypothesis testing is (roughly) satisfied, you can just invoke a well-written function and examine the P-value to interpret the results.

> **Tip**
>
> I encourage you to understand why a test statistic is built in a specific way and why it follows a specific distribution. For example, for the t-distribution, you should understand what the DOF is. However, this will require a deeper understanding of mathematical statistics. If you just want to use hypothesis testing to gain insights, knowing the paradigm is enough.

If you want to apply hypothesis testing to your dataset, follow this paradigm:

1. Identify the problems you are interested in exploring. What are you going to test? A difference, correlation, or independence?

2. Find the correct hypothesis test and assumption. Examine whether the assumption is satisfied carefully.

3. Choose a significance level and perform the hypothesis test with a software package. Recall that in the previous section, we did this part manually, but now it is all left to the software.

In this section, I will follow the paradigm and do three different examples in SciPy.

T-test

First, I will redo the t-test with SciPy.

The default API for a single sample t-test from `scipy.stats` only provides for two-tailed tests. We have already seen an example of interpreting and connecting two-tailed and one-tailed significance levels, so this isn't an issue anymore.

The function we are going to use is called `scipy.stats.ttest_1samp`. The following code snippet applies this function to our math score data:

```
from scipy import stats
stats.ttest_1samp(math2020,75.0)
```

The result reads as follows:

```
Ttest_1sampResult(statistic=-12.668347669098846,
pvalue=5.842470780196407e-34)
```

The first value, `statistic`, is the t-statistic, which agrees with our calculation. The second term is the P-value; it is so small that if the null hypothesis is true and you drew a 900-student sample every second, it would take longer than the amount of time the universe has existed for you to observe a sample as rare as we have here.

Let's do a two-sample t-test. The two-sample t-test will test whether the means of two samples are the same. For a two-sample test, the significance level is two-tailed as our hypothesis is $H_0: \mu_1 = \mu_2$.

There are two cases for the two-sample t-test, depending on the variance in each sample. If the two variances are the same, it is called a **standard independent two-sample t-test**; if the variances are unequal, the test is called **Welch's t-test**.

Let's first examine the standard t-test. The following code snippet generates and plots two normally distributed samples: one at mean 2, and another at 2.1, with an equal population variance of 1:

```
np.random.seed(2020)
sample1 = np.random.normal(2,1,400)
sample2 = np.random.normal(2.1,1,400)
plt.figure(figsize=(10,6))
plt.hist(sample1,bins=np.linspace(-1,5,10),alpha=0.5,label="sa
mple1")
```

```
plt.hist(sample2,bins=np.linspace(-1,5,10),alpha=0.5,label="sa
mple2")
```

```
plt.legend();
```

The result looks as follows:

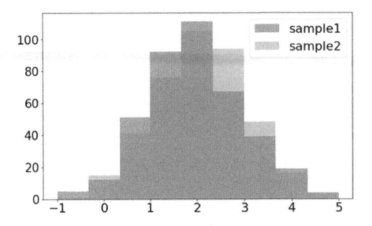

Figure 7.11 – Two samples with unequal means

Let's call the `ttest_ind` t-test function directly with the following line of code:

```
stats.ttest_ind(sample1,sample2)
```

The result looks as follows:

```
Ttest_indResult(statistic=-1.7765855804956159,
pvalue=0.07601736167057595)
```

Our t-statistic is about -1.8. If our significance level is set to 0.05, we will fail to reject our null hypothesis.

How about increasing the number of samples? Will it help? Intuitively, we know that more data contains more information about the population; therefore, it is expected that we'll see a smaller P-value. The following code snippet does the job:

```
np.random.seed(2020)
```

```
sample1 = np.random.normal(2,1,900)
```

```
sample2 = np.random.normal(2.1,1,900)
```

```
stats.ttest_ind(sample1,sample2)
```

The result shows a smaller P-value:

```
Ttest_indResult(statistic=-3.211755683955914,
pvalue=0.0013425868478419776)
```

Note that P-values can vary significantly from sample to sample. In the following code snippet, I sampled the two distributions and conducted the two-sample t-test 100 times:

```
np.random.seed(2020)
p_values = []
for _ in range(100):
    sample1 = np.random.normal(2,1,900)
    sample2 = np.random.normal(2.1,1,900)
    p_values.append(stats.ttest_ind(sample1,sample2)[1])
```

Let's see how the P-value itself distributes in a boxplot:

```
plt.figure(figsize=(10,6))
plt.boxplot(p_values);
```

The boxplot of the P-values will look as follows:

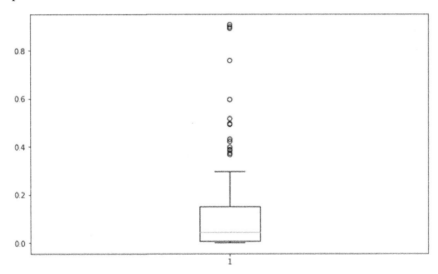

Figure 7.12 – A boxplot of P-values for 100 standard two-sample t-tests

The majority of the P-values do fall into the region of [0, 0.2], but there are a handful of outliers as well.

Next, if you don't know whether the two samples have the same variance, you can use Welch's t-test. First, let's use the following code snippet to generate two samples from two different uniform distributions with different sample sizes as well:

> **Note**
>
> Our null hypothesis remains unchanged, which means that the two-sample means are the same.

```
np.random.seed(2020)
sample1 = np.random.uniform(2,10,400)
sample2 = np.random.uniform(1,12,900)
plt.figure(figsize=(10,6))
plt.hist(sample1,bins=np..
linspace(0,15,20),alpha=0.5,label="sample1")
plt.hist(sample2,bins=np.
linspace(0,15,20),alpha=0.5,label="sample2")
plt.legend();
```

The result looks as follows:

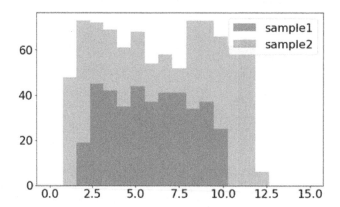

Figure 7.13 – Two uniformly distributed samples with different means, variances, and sample sizes

Let's call the same `SciPy` function, but this time, we'll tell it that the variances are not equal by setting the `equal_var` parameter to `False`:

```
stats.ttest_ind(sample1,sample2,equal_var=False)
```

The result shows quite a small P-value:

```
Ttest_indResult(statistic=-3.1364786834852163,
pvalue=0.0017579405400172416)
```

With a significance level of 0.01, we will have enough confidence to reject the null hypothesis. You don't have to know what Welch's t-statistic distributes; this is the gift that the Python community gives to you.

The normality hypothesis test

Our next test is a normality test. In a normality test, the null hypothesis H_0 is that *the sample comes from a normal distribution*. The alternative hypothesis H_1 is that *the sample doesn't come from a normal distribution*.

There are several ways to do normality tests (not a hypothesis test). You can visually examine the data's histogram plot or check its boxplot or Q-Q plot. However, we will refer to the statisticians' toolsets in this section.

A note on Q-Q plots

Q-Q plots are not covered in this book. They are used to compare two distributions. You can plot data from a distribution against data from an ideal normal distribution and compare distributions.

There are several major tests for normality. The most important ones are the **Shapiro-Wilk test** and the **Anderson-Darling test**. Again, we won't have time or space to go over the mathematical foundation of either test; all we need to do is check their assumptions and call the right function in a given scenario.

How large should a random sample be to suit a normality test? As you may have guessed, if the size of the sample is small, it really doesn't make much sense to say whether it comes from a normal distribution or not. The extreme case is the sample size being 1. It is possible that it comes from any distribution. There is no exact rule on how big is big enough. The literature mentions that 50 is a good threshold beyond which the normality test is applicable.

I will first generate a set of data from Chi-squared distributions with different parameters and use the two tests from SciPy to obtain the P-values.

> **A note on Chi-square distributions**
>
> The Chi-squared distribution or $x2$ distribution is a very important distribution in statistics. The sum of the square of k independent standard normal random variables follows a Chi-squared distribution with a DOF of k.

The following code snippet plots the real PDFs of Chi-squared distributions, so that you get an idea about the DOF's influence over the shape of the PDF:

```
from scipy.stats import chi2
plt.figure(figsize=(10,6))
DOFs = [4,8,16,32]
linestyles= [":","--","-.","-"]
for i, df in enumerate(DOFs):
    x = np.linspace(chi2.ppf(0.01, df),chi2.ppf(0.99, df), 100)
    rv = chi2(df)
    plt.plot(x, rv.pdf(x), 'k-', lw=4,
            label= "DOF = " +
str(df),linestyle=linestyles[i]);
plt.legend();
```

The result looks as follows:

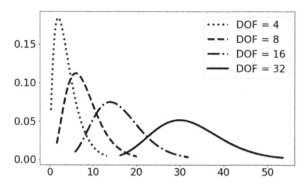

Figure 7.14 – Chi-squared distributions with different DOFs

Next, let's generate two sets of data of sample size 400 and plot them:

```
np.random.seed(2020)
sample1= np.random.chisquare(8,400)
sample2 = np.random.chisquare(32,400)
plt.figure(figsize=(10,6))
```

```
plt.hist(sample1,bins=np.
linspace(0,60,20),alpha=0.5,label="sample1")
```
```
plt.hist(sample2,bins=np.
linspace(0,60,20),alpha=0.5,label="sample2")
```
```
plt.legend();
```

The histogram plot looks as follows. Sample one has a DOF of 8 while sample two has a DOF of 32:

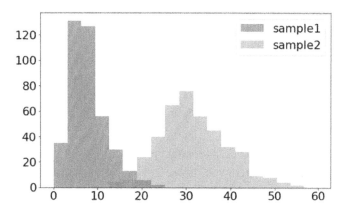

Figure 7.15 – The Chi-squared distributions with different DOFs

Now, let's call the `shapiro()` and `anderson()` test functions in `SciPy.Stats` to test the normality. The following code snippet prints out the results. The `anderson()` function can be used to test fitness to other distributions but defaults to a normal distribution:

```
print("Results for Shapiro-Wilk Test: ")
print("Sample 1:", shapiro(sample1))
print("Sample 2:", shapiro(sample2))
print()
print("Results for Anderson-Darling Test:")
print("Sample 1:", anderson(sample1))
print("Sample 2:", anderson(sample2))
```

The results for the Shapiro-Wilk test read as follows:

```
Sample 1: (0.9361660480499268, 4.538336286635802e-12)
Sample 2: (0.9820653796195984, 7.246905443025753e-05)
```

The results for the Anderson-Darling Test read as follows:

```
Sample 1: AndersonResult(statistic=6.007815329566711,
critical_values=array([0.57 , 0.65 , 0.779, 0.909, 1.081]),
significance_level=array([15. , 10. , 5. , 2.5, 1. ]))
Sample 2: AndersonResult(statistic=1.8332323421475962,
critical_values=array([0.57 , 0.65 , 0.779, 0.909, 1.081]),
significance_level=array([15. , 10. , 5. , 2.5, 1. ]))
```

The results for Shapiro-Wilk follow the format of (statistic, P-value), so it is easy to see that for both sample one and sample two, the null hypothesis should be rejected.

The results for the Anderson-Darling test gives the statistic, but you need to determine the corresponding critical value. The significance level list is in percentages, so 1 means 1%. The corresponding critical value is 1.081. For both cases, the statistic is larger than the critical value, which also leads to rejection of the null hypothesis.

> **Different test statistics can't be compared directly**
>
> For the same hypothesis test, if you choose a different test statistic, you cannot compare the P-values from different methods directly. As you can see from the preceding example, the Shapiro-Wilk test has a much smaller P-value than the Anderson-Darling test for both samples.

Before moving on to the next test, let's generate a sample from a normal distribution and test the normality. The following code snippet uses a sample from a standard normal distribution with a sample size of 400:

```
sample3 = np.random.normal(0,1,400)
print("Results for Shapiro-Wilk Test: ")
print("Sample 3:", shapiro(sample3))
print()
print("Results for Anderson-Darling Test:")
print("Sample 3:", anderson(sample3))
```

The results read as follows. Note that the function call may have a different output from the provided Jupyter notebook, which is normal:

```
Results for Shapiro-Wilk Test:
Sample 3: (0.995371401309967, 0.2820892035961151)


Results for Anderson-Darling Test:
```

```
Sample 3: AndersonResult(statistic=0.46812258253402206,
critical_values=array([0.57 , 0.65 , 0.779, 0.909, 1.081]),
significance_level=array([15. , 10. ,  5. ,  2.5,  1. ]))
```

It is true that we can't reject the null hypothesis even with a significance level as high as $\alpha = 0.15$.

The goodness-of-fit test

In a normality test, we tested whether a sample comes from a *continuous* normal distribution or not. It is a fitness test, which means we want to know how well our observation agrees with a pre-selected distribution.

Let's examine another goodness-of-fit test for a *discrete* case, the **Chi-squared goodness-of-fit test**.

Suppose you go to a casino and encounter a new game. The new game involves drawing cards from a deck of cards three times (the deck doesn't contain jokers). You will win the game if two or three of the cards drawn belong to the suit of hearts; otherwise, you lose your bet. You are a cautious gambler, so you sit there, watch, and count. After a whole day of walking around the casino and memorizing, you observe the following results of card draws. There are four cases in total. I've tabulated the outcomes here:

Number of Hearts	Number of Observations
0	460
1	451
2	102
3	10
All cases	1023

Figure 7.16 – Counting the number of hearts

> **Tip**
> Note that in real life, casinos will not allow you to count cards like this. It is not in their interests and you will most likely be asked to leave if you are caught.

First, let's calculate—given a 52-card deck where there are 13 hearts – what the expected observation look like.

For example, picking 2 hearts would mean picking 2 hearts from the 13 hearts of the deck and pick 1 card from the remaining 39 cards, which yields a total number of $\frac{13!}{11!\,2!}\frac{39!}{38!\,1!}$. So, the total combination of choosing 3 hearts out of 52 cards is $\frac{52!}{3!\,39!}$. Taking the ratio of those two instances, we have the probability of obtaining 2 hearts being about 13.8%.

The number of all observations is 1,023, so in a fair-game scenario, we should observe roughly 1,023*13.80%, which gives 141 observations of 2 hearts cards being picked.

Based on this calculation, you probably have enough evidence to question the casino owner. The following code snippet calculates the fair-game probability and expected observations. I used the `comb` function from the `SciPy` library:

```
from scipy.special import comb
P = [comb(39,3-i)*comb(13,i)/comb(52,3) for i in range(4)]
expected = [1023*p for p in P]
observed = [460,451,102,10]
```

The index in the P and `expected` arrays means the number of observed hearts. For example, P[0] represents the probability of observing 0 hearts.

Let's use a bar plot to see the differences between the expected values and the observed values. The following code snippet plots the expected values and the observed values back to back:

```
x = np.array([0,1,2,3])
plt.figure(figsize=(10,6))
plt.bar(x-0.2,expected,width=0.4,label="Expected")
plt.bar(x+0.2,observed,width=0.4, label= "Observed")
plt.legend()
plt.xticks(ticks=[0,1,2,3]);
```

The output of the code is as shown in the following graph:

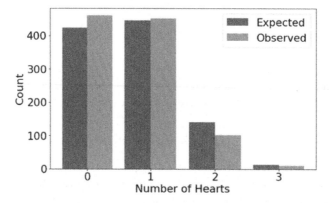

Figure 7.17 – The expected number of hearts and the observed number of hearts

We do see that it is somewhat more probable to get fewer hearts than other cards. Is this result significant? Say we have a null hypothesis, H_0, that the game is fair. How likely is it that our observation is consistent with the null hypothesis? The Chi-square goodness-of-fit test answers this question.

> **Tip**
>
> Chi-square and Chi-squared are often used interchangeably.

In this case, the x^2 statistic is calculated as $\sum_i^4 \frac{(O_i - E_i)^2}{E_i}$, where O_i is the number of observations for category i, and E_i is the number of expected observations for category i. We have four categories and the DOF for this x^2 distribution is $4 - 1 = 3$.

Think about the expressive meaning of the summation. If the deviation from the expectation and the observation is large, the corresponding term will also be large. If the expectation is small, the ratio will become large, which puts more weight on the small-expectation terms. Since the deviation for 2-heart and 3-heart cases is somewhat large, we do expect that the statistic will be largely intuitive.

The following code snippet calls the `chisquare` function in SciPy to test the goodness of the fit:

```
from scipy.stats import chisquare
chisquare(observed,expected)
```

The result reads as follows:

```
Power_divergenceResult(statistic=14.777716323788255,
pvalue=0.002016803916729754)
```

With a significance level of 0.01, we reject the null hypothesis that the game can't be fair.

The following PDF of the x^2 distribution with a DOF of 3 can give you a visual idea of how unfair the game is:

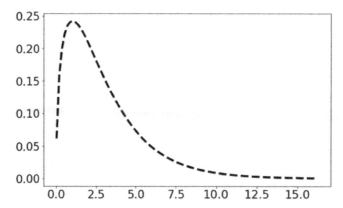

Figure 7.18 – A Chi-squared distribution with and DOF of 3

The code for generating the distribution is as follows:

```
plt.figure(figsize=(10,6))
x = np.linspace(chi2.ppf(0.001, 3),chi2.ppf(0.999, 3), 100)
rv = chi2(3)
plt.plot(x, rv.pdf(x), 'k-', lw=4,
        label= "DOF = " + str(3),linestyle="--");
```

Next, let's move on to the next topic: ANOVA.

A simple ANOVA model

The **ANOVA** model is actually a collection of models. We will cover the basics of ANOVA in this section.

ANOVA was invented by British statistician R.A. Fisher. It is widely used to test the statistical significance of the *difference between means of two or more samples.* In the previous t-test, you saw the two-sample t-test, which is a generalized ANOVA test.

Before moving on, let me clarify some terms. In ANOVA, you may often see the terms factor, group, and treatment. Factor, group, and treatment basically mean the same thing. For example, if you want to study the average income of four cities, then city is the factor or group. It defines the criteria how you would love to classify your datasets. You can also classify the data with the highest degree earned; therefore you can get another factor/group: degree. The term treatment originates from clinical trials, which have a similar concept of factors and groups. You may also hear the word level. Level means the realizations that a factor can be. For example, San Francisco, Los Angeles, Boston, and New York are four levels for the factor/group city. Some literature doesn't distinguish between groups or levels when it is clear that there is only one facet to a whole dataset.

When the total number of samples extends beyond two – let's say g groups, with group i having n_i data points – the null hypothesis can be formulated as follows:

$$H_0: \mu_1 = \mu_2 = \cdots = \mu_g$$

In general, you can do a sequence of t-tests to test each pair of samples. You will have $g(g-1)/2$ t-tests to do. For two different groups, group i and group j, you have the null hypothesis $H_0: \mu_1 = \mu_2 = \cdots = \mu_g$. This approach has two problems:

- You need to do more than one hypothesis test and the number of tests needed doesn't scale well.

- The results require additional analysis.

Now, let's examine the principles of ANOVA and see how it approaches these problems. I will use the average income question as an example. The sample data is as follows:

Index	City	Income (Year)							
1	SF	120,000	110,300	127,800	68,900	79,040	208,000	159,000	89,000
2	LA	65,700	88,340	240,000	190,000	45,080	25,900	69,000	120,300
3	BO	87,999	86,340	98,000	124,000	113,800	98,000	108,000	78,080
4	NY	300,000	62,010	45,000	130,000	238,000	56,000	89,000	123,000

Figure 7.19 – Income data samples from four cities

Assumptions for ANOVA

ANOVA has three assumptions. The first assumption is that the data from each group must be distributed normally. The second assumption is that samples from each group must have the same variance. The third assumption is that each sample should be randomly selected. In our example, I assume that these three conditions are met. However, the imbalance of income does violate normality in real life. Just to let you know.

The ANOVA test relies on the fact that the summation of variances is decomposable. The total variance of all the data can be partitioned into variance between groups and variance within groups:

$$VAR_{total} = VAR_{betwee} + VAR_{within}$$

Here's that again but using notation common in the literature:

$$S_T^2 = S_B^2 + S_W^2$$

Now, we define the three terms. Let me use X_{ij} to denote the j - th data point from the j - th group, μ to denote the mean of the whole dataset (in our example, the mean of all the income data from all four groups), and μ_i to denote the mean from group i. For example, μ_1 is the average income for people living in San Francisco:

The total variance S_T^2 can be defined as follows:

$$S_T^2 = \sum_{i=1}^{g} \sum_{j=1}^{n_i} (X_{ij} - \mu)^2$$

The variance within groups S_W^2 is defined as follows:

$$S_W^2 = \sum_{i=1}^{g} \sum_{j=1}^{n_i} (X_{ij} - \mu_i)^2$$

The only difference is that the data point in each group now subtracts the group mean, rather than the total mean.

The variance between groups is defined as follows:

$$S_A^2 = \sum_{i=1}^{g} n_i (\mu_i - \mu)^2$$

The square of the difference between the group mean and the total mean is weighted by the number of group members.

The reason why this partition holds comes from the fact that a data point X_{ij} can be decomposed as follows:

$$X_{ij} = \mu + (\mu_i - \mu) + (X_{ij} - \mu_i)$$

The first term on the right-hand side of the equation is the total mean. The second term is the difference of means across the group, and the third term is the difference within the group. I encourage you to substitute this expression into the formula of S_T^2 and collect terms to rediscover it as the sum of S_B^2 and S_W^2. It is a good algebraic exercise.

The following code snippet does the calculation to verify the equation. First, I create the following four numpy arrays:

```
SF = np.array([120000,110300,127800,68900,79040,208000,
159000,89000])
```

```
LA =
np.array([65700,88340,240000,190000,45080,25900,69000,120300])
```

```
BO =
np.array([87999,86340,98000,124000,113800,98000,108000,78080])
```

```
NY =
np.array([300000,62010,45000,130000,238000,56000,89000,123000])
```

Next, the following code snippet calculates S_T^2, S_B^2, and S_W^2:

```
mu = np.mean(np.concatenate((SF,LA,BO,NY)))
```

```
ST = np.sum((np.concatenate((SF,LA,BO,NY)) - mu)**2)
```

```
SW = np.sum((SF-np.mean(SF))**2) +np.sum((LA-np.mean(LA))**2) +
\
```

```
np.sum((BO-np.mean(BO))**2)+ np.sum((NY-np.mean(NY))**2)
```

```
SB = 8*(np.mean(SF)-mu)**2 + 8*(np.mean(LA)-mu)**2 + \
8*(np.mean(BO)-mu)**2 + 8*(np.mean(NY)-mu)**2
```

Now, let's verify that ST = SW + SB:

```
ST == SW+SB
```

The answer is True.

So, indeed, we have this relationship.

How is this relationship useful? Let me first denote the variance for each group with σ^2 (they are the same because this is one of the assumptions) and then check each term carefully.

The question is, what is the distribution of the statistic $\frac{S_W^2}{\sigma^2}$? Recall that for group i, the sum of the squared differences is just a Chi-square distribution with a DOF of ni - 1:

$$\sum_j^{n_i} \left(X_{ij} - \mu_i\right)^2 / \sigma^2 \sim \chi_{n_i-1}^2$$

When the null hypothesis holds, namely, $\mu_i = \mu_j$ for arbitrary i and j, $\frac{S_W^2}{\sigma^2}$ is just the summation of the statistic. Because each group is independent, we have $\frac{S_W^2}{\sigma^2} \sim \chi_{n-g}^2$, where n is the total number of the samples and g is the number of groups.

How about $\frac{S_B^2}{\sigma^2}$? When the null hypothesis holds, each observation, no matter which group it comes from, can be treated as a realization of $N(\mu, \sigma^2)$; therefore, S_T^2 will follow a Chi-square distribution with a DOF of n - 1. However, we have the equation $S_T^2 = S_B^2 + S_W^2$, so $\frac{S_B^2}{\sigma^2}$ must follow an x^2 distribution with a DOF of g - 1, where $g - 1 = (n - 1) - (n - g)$.

The test statistic F is further defined as the ratio of the two equations, where σ^2 is canceled:

$$F = \frac{S_B^2/(g - 1)}{S_W^2/(n - g)}$$

The statistic F follows an F-distribution of $F(g - 1, n - g)$.

If the null hypothesis doesn't hold, the variance between groups S_B^2 will be large, so F will be large. If the null hypothesis is true, S_B^2 will be small, so F will also be small.

Let's manually calculate our test statistic for the income problem and compare it with the functionality provided by SciPy. The following code snippet computes the F statistic:

```
F = SB/(4-1)/(SW/(4*8-4))
F
```

The result is about 0.388.

Before we do the F-test, let's also look at the PDF of the F-distribution. The following code snippet plots the F-distribution with DOFs of 3 and 28:

```
plt.figure(figsize=(10,6))
x = np.linspace(f.ppf(0.001, 3, 28),f.ppf(0.999, 3, 28), 100)
rv = f(dfn=3, dfd=28)
plt.plot(x, rv.pdf(x), 'k-', lw=4,linestyle="--");
```

The plot looks as follows:

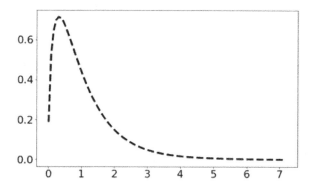

Figure 7.20 – The F-distribution with DOFs of 3 and 28

You can estimate that such a small statistic, 0.388, will probably have a very large P-value. Now, let's use the `f_oneway()` function from `sciPy.stats` to do the F-test. The following code snippet gives us the statistic and the P-value:

```
from scipy.stats import f_oneway
f_oneway(LA,NY,SF,BO)
```

Here is the result:

```
F_onewayResult(statistic=0.38810442907126874,
pvalue=0.7624301696455358)
```

The statistic agrees with our own calculation and the P-value suggests that we can't reject the null hypothesis even at a very high significance value.

Beyond simple ANOVA

After the F-test, when the means are different, various versions of ANOVA can be used further to analyze the factors behind the difference and even their interactions. But due to the limitations of space and time, we won't cover this.

Stationarity tests for time series

In this section, we are going to discuss how to test the *stationarity* of an *auto-regression time series*.

First, let's understand what a time series is.

A **time series** is a series of data points indexed in time order. A typical time series is obtained by measuring the underlying quantities at equally spaced time intervals. Examples include the opening value of a stock market index, the monthly GDP of a country, or your weekly expenditure.

Time series data introduces an ordered structure into a dataset, which can lead to many interesting problems. For example, a time series may have an upward or downward trend. It may also have seasonal/periodical behavior. For time series data such as stock market data, stochastic behavior will introduce randomness. Finding correlations and forecasting futures are key focuses of economists and financial analysts who work on economic or financial time series.

Now, let's understand what stationarity is.

Some notation needs to be introduced. Suppose a time series $\{X_t\}$ is generated from a random process, which means for every timestamp $t = 1, 2, 3, \ldots, X_t$ is randomly sampled from a probability distribution. In general, we don't know much about the relationship between the distribution and time. The distribution itself may have a shifted value inclusive of the expected value and variance, and so on.

For a stationary time series, the following properties will be met:

- The expectation $E(X_t)$ is independent of t.
- The variance $Var(X_t)$ is also independent of t.
- The covariance $Cov(X_t, X_t+k)$ only depends on the time index difference k.

Let's look at a few examples of stationary and non-stationary time series in the next subsection.

Examples of stationary and non-stationary time series

Let's look at one stationary time series example first. The so-called **white noise** time series is a simple classical stationary time series whose value at time t is given by the following formula:

$$X_t = \epsilon_t$$

Here, $\epsilon_t \sim N(0, \sigma^2)$.

A note on the name of white noise

The name of white noise actually comes from white light. White light is a mixture of lights of all colors. White noise is a mixture of sounds with different frequencies. White noise is an important sound because the ideal white noise will have equal power, or energy, throughout the frequency spectrum. Due to the limitation of space, we won't go deep into this topic.

The following code snippet generates a white noise time series. You can verify that there is no time dependence between X_t and X_t+k. The covariance is 0 for arbitrary k:

```
np.random.seed(2020)
plt.figure(figsize=(10,6))
white_noise = [np.random.normal() for _ in range(100)]
plt.xlabel("Time step")
plt.ylabel("Value")
plt.plot(white_noise);
```

The results look as follows. You can see that it is *stationary*:

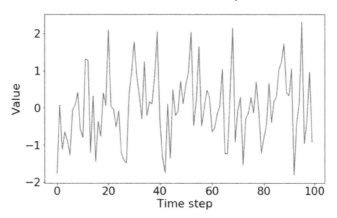

Figure 7.21 – The white noise time series

Another simple time series is **random walk**. It is defined as the addition of the previous term in a sequence and a white noise term, $\epsilon_t \sim N(0, \sigma^2)$. You can define X_0 to be a constant or another white noise term:

$$X_t = X_{t-1} + \epsilon_t$$

Just as for white noise time series, the random walk time series has a consistent expectation. However, the variance is different. Because of the addition of independent normally distributed white noises, the variance will keep increasing:

$$X_t = X_0 + \epsilon_1 + \epsilon_2 + \cdots + \epsilon_t$$

Therefore, you have the variance expressed as follows:

$$Var(X_t) = \sum_i Var(\epsilon_i) = t\sigma^2$$

This is a little bit surprising, because you might have expected the white noises to cancel each other out because they essentially symmetrical around 0. The white noises do cancel each other out in the mean sense but not in the variance sense.

The following code snippet uses the same set of random variables to show the differences between white noise time series and random walk time series:

```
plt.figure(figsize=(10,6))
np.random.seed(2020)
white_noise = [np.random.normal() for _ in range(1000)]
random_walk = np.cumsum(white_noise)
plt.plot(white_noise, label = "white noise")
plt.plot(random_walk, label = "standard random walk")
plt.legend();
```

Here, I used the cumsum() function from numpy to calculate a cumulative sum of a numpy array or list. The result looks as follows:

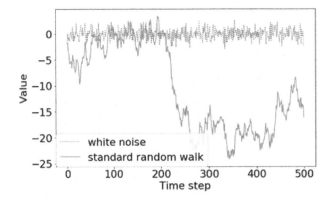

Figure 7.22 – Stationary white noise and non-stationary random walk

Say you took the difference to define a new time series $\{\delta X_t\}$:

$$\delta X_t = X_t - X_{t-1} = \epsilon_t$$

Then the new time series would become stationary. In general, a non-stationary time series can be reduced to a stationary time series by (continuously) taking differences.

Now, let's talk about the concept of autoregression.

Autoregression describes the property of a model where future observations can be predicted or modeled with earlier observations plus some noise. For example, the random walk can be treated as a sequence of observations from a first-order autoregressive process, as shown in the following equation:

$$X_t = X_{t-1} + \epsilon_t$$

The observation at timestamp t can be constructed from its one-step-back value X_{t-1}. Generally, you can define an autoregressive time series with order n as follows, where instances of Φi are real numbers:

$$X_t = \phi_1 X_{t-1} + \phi_2 X_{t-2} + \cdots + \phi_n X_{t-n} + \epsilon_t$$

Without formal mathematical proof, I would like to show you the following results. The autoregressive process given previously has a characteristic equation as follows:

$$f(s) = 1 - \phi_1 s - \phi_2 s^2 - \cdots - \phi_n s^n = 0$$

In the domain of complex numbers, this equation will surely have n roots. Here is the theorem about these roots:

- If all the roots have an *absolute value larger than 1*, then the time series is stationary.

Let me show that to you with two examples.

Our random walk model has the following characteristic function, $f(s) = 1 - s = 0$, which has a root equal to 0, so it is not stationary. How about the following modified random walk? Let's see:

$$X_t = 0.8 X_{t-1} + \epsilon_t$$

It has a characteristic function of $f(s) = 1 - 0.8s = 0$, which has a root of 1.25. By our theorem, this time series should be stationary.

The influence of `X_{t-1}` is reduced by a ratio of `0.8`, and this effect will be compounding and fading away. The following code snippet uses the exact same data we have for white noise and random walk to demonstrate this fading behavior. I picked the first `500` data points so linestyles can be distinguishable for different lines:

```
plt.figure(figsize=(10,6))
np.random.seed(2020)
white_noise = [np.random.normal() for _ in range(500)]
random_walk_modified = [white_noise[0]]
for i in range(1,500):
    random_walk_modified.append(random_walk_modified[-1]*0.8 \
                                + white_noise[i])
random_walk = np.cumsum(white_noise)
plt.plot(white_noise, label = "white noise",linestyle=":")
plt.plot(random_walk, label = "standard random walk")
plt.plot(random_walk_modified, label = "modified random
walk",linestyle="-.")
plt.legend();
```

The graph looks as follows:

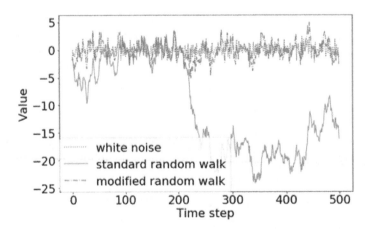

Figure 7.23 – A comparison of a modified random walk and a standard random walk

Let's try a more complicated example. Is the time series obeying the following the autoregressive relationship?

$$X_t = 0.6X_{t-1} - 1.2X_{t-2} + \epsilon_t$$

The characteristic equation reads $f(s) = 1 - 0.6s + 1.2s^2$. It has two roots. Both roots are complex numbers with non-zero imaginary parts. The roots' absolute values are also smaller than 1 on the complex plane. The following code snippet plots the two roots on the complex plane. You can see that they are just inside the unit circle, as shown in *Figure 7.24*:

```
for root in np.roots([1.2,-0.6,1]):
    plt.polar([0,np.angle(root)],[0,abs(root)],marker='o')
```

The graph looks as follows:

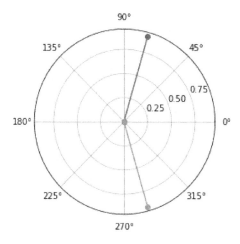

Figure 7.24 – A polar plot of roots inside a unit circle

You should expect the time series to be non-stationary because both roots have absolute values smaller than 1. Let's take a look at it with the following code snippet:

```
plt.figure(figsize=(10,6))
np.random.seed(2020)
white_noise = [np.random.normal() for _ in range(200)]
series = [white_noise[0],white_noise[1]]
for i in range(2,200):
    series.append(series[i-1]*0.6-series[i-2]*1.2 + white_noise[i])
plt.plot(series, label = "oscillating")
plt.xlabel("Time step")
plt.ylabel("Value")
plt.legend();
```

The result looks as follows:

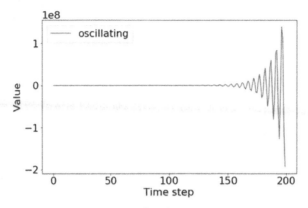

Figure 7.25 – A non-stationary second-order autoregressive time series example

Check the scales on the y-axis and you will be surprised. The oscillation seems to come from nowhere. The exercise of visualizing this time series in the log scale is left to you as an exercise.

In most cases, given a time series, the **Augmented Dickey-Fuller (ADF)** unit root test in the `statsmodels` library can be used to test whether a unit root is present or not. The null hypothesis is that there exists a unit root, which means the time series is *not* stationary.

The following code snippet applies the ADF unit root test on the white noise time series, the random walk, and the modified random walk. You can leave the optional arguments of this function as their defaults:

```
from statsmodels.tsa.stattools import adfuller
adfuller(white_noise)
```

The result is as follows:

```
(-13.456517599662801,
 3.598405967794306e-25,
 0,
 199,
 {'1%': -3.4636447617687436,
  '5%': -2.8761761179270766,
  '10%': -2.57457158581854},
 516.1905447452475)
```

You need to focus on the first two highlighted values terms in the result, the statistic and the P-value. The dictionary contains the significance levels. In this case, the P-value is very small, and we can safely reject the null hypothesis. There is no unit root, so the time series is stationary.

For the random walk time series, the result of `adfuller(random_walk_modified)` is as follows:

```
(-1.4609492394159564,
 0.5527332285592418,
 0,
 499,
 {'1%': -3.4435228622952065,
  '5%': -2.867349510566146,
  '10%': -2.569864247011056},
 1374.4481241324318)
```

The P-value is very large; therefore, we can't reject the null hypothesis: a unit root might exist. The time series is not stationary.

The result for the modified random walk is shown in the following code block. The P-value is also very small. It is a stationary time series:

```
(-7.700113158114325,
 1.3463404483644221e-11,
 0,
 499,
 {'1%': -3.4435228622952065,
  '5%': -2.867349510566146,
  '10%': -2.569864247011056},
 1375.6034107373926)
```

> **Forcefully applying a test is dangerous**
>
> How about our wildly jumping time series? If you try to use the `adfuller()` function on it, you will find a wild statistic and a P-value of 0! The ADF test simply fails because the underlying assumptions are violated. Because of the limitations of space and the complexity of it, I omitted coverage of this. You are encouraged to explore the roots of the cause and the mechanism of ADF tests from first principles by yourself.

We have covered enough hypothesis tests; it is time to move on to A/B testing, where we will introduce cool concepts such as randomization and blocking.

Appreciating A/B testing with a real-world example

In the last section of this chapter, let's talk about A/B testing. Unlike previous topics, A/B testing is a very general concept. A/B testing is something of a geeky engineer's word for statistical hypothesis testing. At the most basic level, it simply means a way of finding out which setting or treatment performs better in a single-variable experiment. Most A/B testing can be classified as a simple **Randomized Controlled Trial (RCT)**. What randomized control means will be clear soon.

Let's take a real-world example: a consulting company proposes a new working-hours schedule for a factory, claiming that the new schedule will improve the workers' efficiency as well as their satisfaction. The cost of abruptly shifting the working-hours schedule may be big and the factory does not want the risk involved. Therefore, the consulting company proposes an A/B test. Consultants propose selecting two groups of workers, group A and group B. These groups have controlled variables, such as worker's wages, occupations, and so on, such that the two groups are as similar as possible in terms of those variables. The only difference is that one group follows the old working-hours schedule and the other group follows the new schedule. After a certain amount of time, the consultants measure the efficiency and level of satisfaction through counting outputs, handing out quantitative questionnaires, or taking other surveys.

If you are preparing for a data scientist interview, the A/B test you will likely encounter would be about the users of your website, application, or product. For example, landing-page optimization is a typical A/B test scenario. What kind of front page will increase users' click rates and conversion? The content, the UI, the loading time, and many other factors may influence users' behavior.

Now that we have understood the importance of A/B testing, let's dive into the details of its steps.

Conducting an A/B test

To conduct an A/B test, you should know the variables that fall into the following three categories:

- **The metric**: This is a dependent variable that you want to measure. In an experiment, you can choose one or more such variables. In the previous example, workers' efficiency is a metric.

- **The control variables**: These are variables that you can control. A control variable is independent. For example, the font and color scheme of a landing page are controllable. You want to find out how such variables influence your metric.

- **Other factors**: These are variables that may influence the metric, but you have no direct control over them. For example, the wages of workers are not under your control. The devices that users use to load your landing page are also not under your control. However, wages surely influence the level of satisfaction of workers and device screen sizes influence users' clicking behavior. Those factors must be identified and handled properly.

Let's look at an experiment on landing page optimization. Let's say we want to find out about the color scheme's influence on users' clicking behavior. We have two choices, a warm color scheme and a cold color scheme. We also want group A to have the same size as group B. Here is a short list of variables that will influence the users' clicking rate. You are free to brainstorm more such variables:

- The device the user is using – for example, mobile versus desktop

- The time at which the user opens the landing page

- The browser type and version – for example, Chrome versus **Internet Explorer** (**IE**)

- The battery level or Wi-Fi signal level

How do we deal with such variables? To understand their influence on users' click rates, we need to first eliminate the influence of other factors so that if there is a difference in click rates, we can confidently attribute the difference to the four variables we selected. This is why we introduce randomization and blocking.

Randomization and blocking

The most common way to eliminate or minimize the effect of unwanted variables is through blocking and randomization.

In a completely randomized experiment, the individual test case will be assigned a treatment/control variable value randomly. In the landing page scenario, this means that regardless of the device, browser, or the time a user opens the page, a random choice of a warm color scheme or a cold color scheme is made for the user.

Imagine the scenario that the number of participants of the experiment is very large; the effect of those unwanted variables would diminish as the sample size approaches infinity. This is true because in a completely randomized experiment, the larger the sample size is, the smaller the effect that randomness has on our choices. When the sample size is large enough, we expect the number of IE users who see the warm color scheme to be close to the number of IE users who see the cold scheme.

The following computational experiment will give you a better idea of how randomization works. I chose three variables in this computational experiment: device, browser, and Wi-Fi signal. First, let's assume that 60% of the users use mobile, 90% of them use Chrome, and 80% of them visit the website using a strong WiFi signal. We also assume that there are no interactions among those variables; for instance, we do not assume that Chrome users have a strong preference to stick to a strong WiFi connection.

The following code snippet will assign a color scheme to a random combination of our three variables:

```
def build_sample():
    device = "mobile" if np.random.random() < 0.6 else
"desktop"
    browser = "chrome" if np.random.random() < 0.9 else "IE"
    wifi = "strong" if np.random.random() < 0.8 else "weak"
    scheme = "warm" if np.random.random() < 0.5 else "cold"
return (device, browser, wifi, scheme)
```

Let's first generate 100 sample points and sort the results by the number of appearances:

```
from collections import Counter
results = [build_sample() for _ in range(100)]
counter = Counter(results)
for key in sorted(counter, key = lambda x: counter[x]):
    print(key, counter[key])
```

The result looks as follows. You can see that some combinations don't show up:

```
('desktop', 'IE', 'strong', 'warm') 1
('mobile', 'IE', 'weak', 'cold') 1
('mobile', 'IE', 'strong', 'cold') 2
('mobile', 'chrome', 'weak', 'warm') 3
('mobile', 'chrome', 'weak', 'cold') 4
('desktop', 'chrome', 'weak', 'warm') 4
```

```
('desktop', 'chrome', 'weak', 'cold') 5
('desktop', 'IE', 'strong', 'cold') 6
('desktop', 'chrome', 'strong', 'warm') 10
('desktop', 'chrome', 'strong', 'cold') 19
('mobile', 'chrome', 'strong', 'warm') 20
('mobile', 'chrome', 'strong', 'cold') 25
```

If you check each pair with the same setting, for example, users who use the mobile Chrome browser with strong WiFi signal, have a roughly 50-50% chance of getting the cold or warm color scheme landing page.

Let's try another 10,000 samples. The only change in the code snippet is changing 100 to 10000. The result looks like this:

```
('desktop', 'IE', 'weak', 'cold') 41
('desktop', 'IE', 'weak', 'warm') 45
('mobile', 'IE', 'weak', 'warm') 55
('mobile', 'IE', 'weak', 'cold') 66
('desktop', 'IE', 'strong', 'warm') 152
('desktop', 'IE', 'strong', 'cold') 189
('mobile', 'IE', 'strong', 'cold') 200
('mobile', 'IE', 'strong', 'warm') 228
('desktop', 'chrome', 'weak', 'cold') 359
('desktop', 'chrome', 'weak', 'warm') 370
('mobile', 'chrome', 'weak', 'cold') 511
('mobile', 'chrome', 'weak', 'warm') 578
('desktop', 'chrome', 'strong', 'warm') 1442
('desktop', 'chrome', 'strong', 'cold') 1489
('mobile', 'chrome', 'strong', 'warm') 2115
('mobile', 'chrome', 'strong', 'cold') 2160
```

Now, you see even with the two most unlikely combinations, we have about 30 to 40 data points. There is (although we tried to mitigate it) an imbalance between the highlighted two combinations; we have more cold scheme users than warm scheme users.

This is the benefit that randomization brings to us. However, this usually comes at a high cost. It is not easy to obtain such large data samples in most cases. There is also a risk that if the warm color scheme or cold color scheme is very bad for the users' conversion rates, such a large-scale A/B test will be regrettable.

With a small sample size, issues of being unlucky can arise. For example, it is possible that IE desktop users with weak WiFi signals are all assigned the warm color scheme. Given how A/B testing is done, there is no easy way to reverse such bad luck.

Blocking, on the other hand, arranges samples into blocks according to the unwanted variables first, then randomly assigns block members to different control variable values.

Let's look at the landing page optimization example. Instead of grouping users after providing them with random color schemes, we group the users according to the device, browser, or WiFi signal before making the decision as to which color scheme to show to them.

Inside the block of desktop IE users, we can intervene such that, randomly, half of them will see the warm color scheme and the other half will see the cold scheme. Since all the unwanted variables are the same in each block, the effect of the unwanted variables will be limited, or **homogeneous**. Further comparisons can also be done across blocks, just like for complete randomization.

You may think of blocking as a kind of **restricted randomization**. We want to utilize the benefit of randomization, but we don't want to fall into a trap such as a specific group of candidates purely being associated with one control variable value. Another example is that in a clinical trial, you don't want complete randomization to lead to all aged people using a placebo, which may happen. You must force randomization somehow by grouping candidates first.

Common test statistics

So an A/B test has given you some data – what's next? You can do the following, for a start:

- Use visualization to demonstrate differences. This is also called *testing by visualization*. The deviation of the results can be obtained by running A/B tests for several rounds and calculating the variance.

- Apply a statistical hypothesis test.

Many of the statistical hypothesis tests we have covered can be used. For example, we have covered t-tests, a test for testing differences of means between two groups – it is indeed one of the most important A/B test statistics. When the sizes of group A and group B are different or the variances are different, we can use Welch's t-test, which has the fewest assumptions involved.

For the clicking behavior of users, **Fisher's exact test** is good to use. It is based on the binomial distribution. I will provide you with an exercise on it in *Chapter 13, Exercises and Projects*. For the work efficiency question we mentioned at the very beginning of this section, ANOVA or a t-test can be used.

For a summary of when to use which hypothesis test, here is a good resource: `https://www.scribbr.com/statistics/statistical-tests/`.

> **Tip**
>
> Try to include both informative visualizations and statistical hypothesis tests in your reports. This way, you have visual elements to show your results intuitively as well as solid statistical analysis to justify your claims. Make sure you blend them coherently to tell a complete story.

Common mistakes in A/B tests

In my opinion, several common mistakes can lead to misleading A/B test data collection or interpretations:

- Firstly, a careless A/B test may miss important hidden variables. For example, say you want to randomly select users in the United States to do an A/B test and you decide to do the randomization by partitioning the names. For example, people whose first name starts with the letters A-F are grouped into a group, those with G-P go into another, and so on. What can go wrong?

  Although this choice seems to be OK, there are some pitfalls. For example, popular American names have changed significantly throughout the years. The most popular female names in the 1960s and 1970s are Lisa, Mary, and Jennifer. In the 2000s and 2010s, the most popular female names become Emily, Isabella, Emma, and Ava. You may think that you are selecting random names, but you are actually introducing biases to do with age. Also, different states have different popular names as well.

- Another common mistake is making decisions too quickly. Different from academic research, where rigorousness is above all, managers in the corporate world prefer to jump to conclusions and move on to the next sales goals. If you only have half or even one-third of the tested data available, you should hold on and wait until all the data is collected.

- The last mistake is focusing on too many metrics or control variables at the same time. It is true that several metrics can depend on common control variables and a metric can depend on several control variables. Introducing too many metrics and control variables will include **higher-order interactions** and make the analysis less robust with low confidence. If possible, you should avoid tracking too many variables at the same time.

Higher-order interaction

Higher-order interaction refers to the joint effect of three or more independent variables on the dependent variable. For example, obesity, smoking, and high blood pressure may contribute to heart issues much more severely if all three of them happen together. When people refer to the main effect of something, they often mean the effect of one independent variable, and the interaction effect refers to the joint effect of two variables.

Let's summarize what we have learned in this chapter.

Summary

This chapter was an intense one. Congratulations on finishing it!

First, we covered the concept of the hypothesis, including the basic concepts of hypotheses, such as the null hypothesis, the alternative hypothesis, and the P-value. I spent quite a bit of time going over example content to ensure that you understood the concept of the P-value and significance levels correctly.

Next, we looked at the paradigm of hypothesis testing and used corresponding library functions to do testing on various scenarios. We also covered the ANOVA test and testing on time series.

Toward the end, we briefly covered A/B testing. We demonstrated the idea with a classic click rate example and also pointed out some common mistakes.

One additional takeaway for this chapter is that in many cases, new knowledge is needed to understand how a task is done in unfamiliar fields. For example, if you were not familiar with time series before reading this chapter, now you should know how to use the unit root test to test whether an autoregressive time series is stationary or not. Isn't this amazing?

In the next chapter, we will begin our analysis of regression models.

Section 3: Statistics for Machine Learning

Section 3 introduces two statistical learning categories: regression and classification. Concepts in machine learning are introduced. Statistics with respect to learning models are developed and examined. Methods such as boosting and bagging are explained.

This section consists of the following chapters:

- *Chapter 8, Statistics for Regression*
- *Chapter 9, Statistics for Classification*
- *Chapter 10, Statistics for Tree-Based Methods*
- *Chapter 11, Statistics for Ensemble Methods*

8
Statistics for Regression

In this chapter, we are going to cover one of the most important techniques—and likely the most frequently used technique – in data science, which is **regression**.

Regression, in layman's terms, is to build or find relationships between variables, features, or any other entities. The word regression originates from the Latin *regressus*, which means *a return*. Usually, in a regression problem, you have two kinds of variables:

- Independent variables, also referred to as features or predictors
- Dependent variables, also known as response variables or outcome variables

Our goal is to try to find a relationship between dependent and independent variables.

> **Note**
> It is quite helpful to understand word origins or how the scientific community chose a name for a concept. It may not help you understand the concept directly, but it will help you memorize the concepts more vividly.

Regression can be used to explain phenomena or to predict unknown values. In *Chapter 7, Statistical Hypothesis Testing*, we saw examples in the *Stationarity test for time series* section of time series data, to which regression models generally fit well. If you are predicting the stock price of a company, you can use various independent variables such as the fundamentals of the company and macro-economic indexes to do a regression analysis against the stock price, then use the regression model you obtained to predict the future stock price of that company if you assume the relationship you found will persist.

Of course, such simple regression models were used decades ago and likely will not make you rich. In this chapter, you are still going to learn a lot from those classical models, which are the baselines of more sophisticated models. Understanding basic models will grant you the intuition to understand more complicated ones.

The following topics will be covered in this chapter:

- Understanding a simple linear regression model and its rich content
- Connecting the relationship between regression and estimators
- Having hands-on experience with multivariate linear regression and collinearity analysis
- Learning regularization from logistic regression examples

In this chapter, we are going to use real financial data, so prepare to get your hands dirty!

Understanding a simple linear regression model and its rich content

Simple linear regression is the simplest regression model. You only have two variables: one dependent variable, usually denoted by y, and an independent variable, usually denoted by x. The relationship is linear, so the model only contains two parameters. The relationship can be formulated with the following formula:

$$y = kx + b + \epsilon$$

k is the slope and b is the intercept. ϵ is the noise term.

> **Note**
>
> Proportionality is different from linearity. Proportionality implies linearity and it is a stronger requirement that b must be 0 in the formula. Linearity, graphically, means that the relationship between two variables can be represented as a straight, but strict mathematical requirement of **additivity** and **homogeneity**. If a relationship (function f) is linear, then for any input x_1 and x_2 and scaler k, we must have the following equations:
> $f(x_1 + x_2) = f(x_1) + f(x_2)$ and $f(kx_1) = kf(x_1)$.

Here is the code snippet that utilizes the `yfinance` library to obtain Netflix's stock price data between 2016 and 2018. You can use `pip3 install yfinance` to install the library. If you are using Google Colab, use `!pip3 install yfinance` to run a shell command. Pay attention to the `!` symbol at the beginning.

The following code snippet imports the libraries:

```
import numpy as np
import matplotlib.pyplot as plt
import random
import yfinance as yf
```

The following code snippet creates a `Ticker` instance and retrieves the daily stock price information. The `Ticker` is a symbol for the stock; Netflix's ticker is `NFLX`:

```
import yfinance as yf
netflix = yf.Ticker("NFLX")
start = "2016-01-01"
end = "2018-01-01"
df = netflix.history(interval="1d",start = start,end = end)
df
```

The result is a Pandas DataFrame, as shown in the following figure:

Date	Open	High	Low	Close	Volume	Dividends	Stock Splits
2016-01-04	109.00	110.00	105.21	109.96	20794800	0	0
2016-01-05	110.45	110.58	105.85	107.66	17664600	0	0
2016-01-06	105.29	117.91	104.96	117.68	33045700	0	0
2016-01-07	116.36	122.18	112.29	114.56	33636700	0	0
2016-01-08	116.33	117.72	111.10	111.39	18067100	0	0
...	...	...	...	...	...	...	...
2017-12-22	188.33	190.95	186.80	189.94	3878900	0	0
2017-12-26	189.78	189.94	186.40	187.76	3045700	0	0
2017-12-27	187.80	188.10	185.22	186.24	4002100	0	0
2017-12-28	187.18	194.49	186.85	192.71	10107400	0	0
2017-12-29	192.51	193.95	191.22	191.96	5187600	0	0

503 rows × 7 columns

Figure 8.1 – Historical data for Netflix stock in 2016 and 2017

The next step for our analysis is to get an idea of what the data looks like. The common visualization for the two-variable relationship is a scatter plot. We are not particularly interested in picking the open price or the close price of the stock. I will just pick the opening price as the price we are going to run regression against the **Date** column.

Date is not a normal column as other columns, it is the *index* of the DataFrame. You can use df.index to access it. When you convert a date to numerical values, Matplotlib may throw a warning. You can use the following instructions to suppress the warning.

The following code snippet suppresses the warning and plots the data:

```
from pandas.plotting import import register_matplotlib_converters
register_matplotlib_converters()
plt.figure(figsize=(10,8))
plt.scatter(df.index, df["Open"]);
```

The result looks as shown in the following figure:

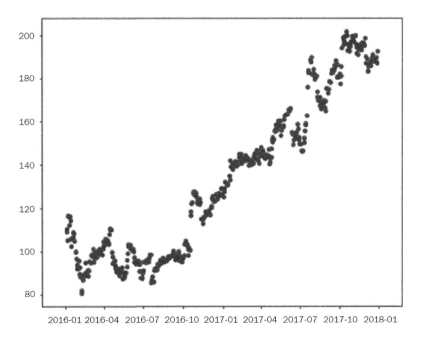

Figure 8.2 – Scatter plot of Netflix stock price data

Note that there are some jumps in the stock prices, which may indicate stock price surges driven by good news. Also, note that the graph scales will significantly change how you perceive the data. You are welcome to change the figure size to *(10,3)* and you may be less impressed by the performance of the stock price!

For this time period, the stock price of Netflix seems to be linear with respect to time. We shall investigate the relationship using our two-parameter simple linear regression model. However, before that, we must do some transformation. The first transformation is to convert a sequence of date objects, the DataFrame index, to a list of integers. I redefined two variables, x and y, which represent the number of days since January 4, 2016, and the opening stock price of that day.

The following code snippet creates two such variables. I first created a `timedelta` object by subtracting the first element in the index, January 4, 2016, and then converted it to the number of days:

```
x= (df.index - df.index[0]).days.to_numpy()
y = df.Open.to_numpy()
```

> **Note**
>
> If you checked the Netflix stock prices in the past 2 years, you would surely agree with me that simple linear regression would be likely to fail. We will try to use more sophisticated regression models in later chapters on such data.

Why don't we use standardization? The reason is that in simple linear regression, the slope k and intercept b, when data is at its original scale, have meanings. For example, k is the daily average stock price change. Adding one more day to variable x, the stock price will change accordingly. Such meanings would be lost if we standardized the data.

Next, let's take a look at how to use the SciPy library to perform the simplest linear regression based on least squared error minimization.

Least squared error linear regression and variance decomposition

Let's first run the `scipy.stats.linregress()` function to gain some intuition and I will then explain linear regression from the perspective of ANOVA, specifically, variance decomposition.

The following code snippet runs the regression:

```
from scipy.stats import linregress
linregress(x,y)
```

The result looks as follows:

```
LinregressResult(slope=0.1621439447698934,
intercept=74.83816138860539, rvalue=0.9447803151619397,
pvalue=6.807230675594974e-245, stderr=0.002512657375708363)
```

The result contains the *slope* and the *intercept*. It also contains an *R-value*, a *P-value*, and a *standard error*. Based on our knowledge from *Chapter 7, Statistical Hypothesis Testing*, even without knowing the underlined hypothesis test, such a small P-value tells you that you can reject whatever the null hypothesis is. The R value is called the **correlation coefficient**, whose squared value R^2 is more well-known, **the coefficient of determination**.

There are two major things that the `linregress()` function offers:

- A correlation coefficient is calculated to quantitatively present the relationship between dependent and independent variables.

- A hypothesis is conducted, and a P-value is calculated.

In this section, we focus on the calculation of the correlation coefficient and briefly talk about the hypothesis testing at the end.

Regression uses independent variables to explain dependent variables. In the most boring case, if the stock price of Netflix is a horizontal line, no more explanation from the independent variable is needed. The slope *k* can take value 0 and the intercept *b* can take the value of the motionless stock price. If the relationship between the stock price and the date is perfectly linear, then the independent variable *fully* explains the dependent variable in a linear sense. What we want to explain quantitatively is the variance of the dependent variable.

`np.var(y)*len(y)` calculates the **sum of squares total (SST)** of the stock prices. The result is about *653922*. The following code snippet adds the horizontal line that represents the mean of the stock prices and the differences between stock prices and their mean as vertical segments. This is equivalent to estimating the stock prices using the mean stock price. *This is the best we can do with the dependent variable only.*

```
plt.figure(figsize=(20,8))
plt.scatter(x, y)
y_mean = np.mean(y)
plt.hlines(y_mean, np.min(x), np.max(x),color="r")
sst = 0
for x_, y_ in zip(x,y):
    plt.plot([x_,x_],[y_mean,y_],color="black",linestyle="-")
    sst += (y_ - y_mean)**2
print(sst)
```

The total variance, intuitively, is the summed square of the differences between the stock price of the mean following the following formula. You can verify that the `SST` variable is indeed about 6,53,922:

$$\sum_i (y_i - \bar{y})^2$$

As you may expect, the differences between the stock price and the mean are not symmetrically distributed along time due to the increase in Netflix stock. The difference has a name: **residuals**. The result looks as shown in the following figure:

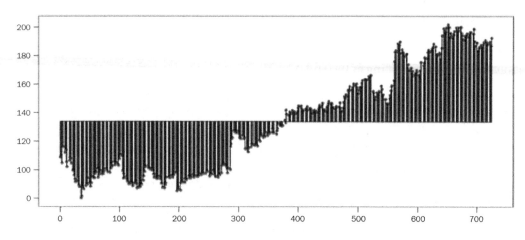

Figure 8.3 – Visualization of SST and residuals

If we have a known independent variable x – in our case, the number of days since the first data point, we prefer a sloped line to estimate the stock price rather than the naïve horizontal line now. Will the variance change? Can we decrease the summed square of residuals? Regardless of the nature of the additional independent variable, we can first approach this case from a *pure error-minimizing perspective.*

I am going to rotate the line around the point (np.mean(x),np.mean(y)). Let's say now we have a slope of 0.10. The following code snippet re-calculates the variance and re-plots the residuals. Note that I used the variable sse, **sum of squared errors** (SSE), to denote the total squared errors as shown in the following example:

```
plt.figure(figsize=(20,8))
plt.scatter(x, y)
y_mean = np.mean(y)
x_mean = np.mean(x)
plt.plot([np.min(x),np.max(x)],
        [x_2_y(0.1,x_mean,y_mean,np.min(x)),x_2_y(0.1,x_
mean,y_mean,np.max(x)),],
        color="r")
sse = 0
for x_, y_ in zip(x,y):
    y_on_line = x_2_y(0.1,x_mean,y_mean,x_)
```

```
      plt.plot([x_,x_],[y_on_
line,y_],color="black",linestyle="-")
      sse += (y_on_line - y_)**2
print(sse)
```

The SSE is about 155964 – much smaller than the SST. Let's check the plot generated from the preceding code snippet:

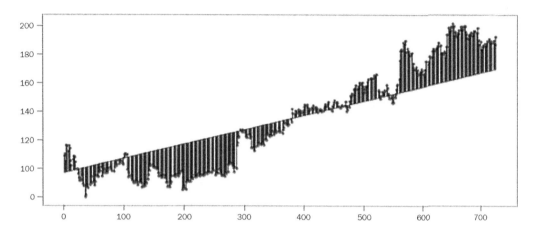

Figure 8.4 – Visualization of SSE and residuals

It is visually clear that the differences for the data points shrink in general. Is there a minimal value for `SSE` with respect to the slope k? The following code snippet loops through the slope from 0 to 0.3 and plots it against `SSE`:

```
y_mean = np.mean(y)
x_mean = np.mean(x)
slopes = np.linspace(0,0.3,20)
sses = [0 for i in range(len(slopes))]
for x_, y_ in zip(x,y):
    for i in range(len(sses)):
        y_on_line = x_2_y(slopes[i],x_mean,y_mean,x_)
        sses[i] += (y_on_line - y_)**2

plt.figure(figsize=(20,8))
plt.rc('xtick',labelsize=18)
plt.rc('ytick',labelsize=18)
plt.plot(slopes,sses);
```

The result looks as shown in the following graph:

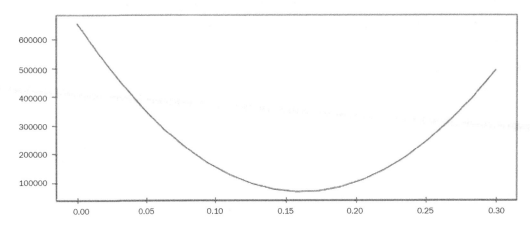

Figure 8.5 – Slope versus the SSE

This visualization demonstrates the exact idea of **Least Square Error** (**LSE**). When we change the slope, the SSE changes, and at some point, it reaches its minimum. In linear regression, the sum of the squared error is parabolic, which guarantees the existence of such a unique minimum.

> **Note**
>
> The intercept is also an undetermined parameter. However, the intercept is usually of less interest, because it is just a shift along the y axis, which doesn't reflect how strongly the independent variable correlates with the dependent variable.

The following code snippet considers the influence of the intercept. To find the minimum with respect to the two parameters, we need a 3D plot. You are free to skip this code snippet and it won't block you from learning further materials in this chapter.

The following code snippet prepares the data for the visualization:

```
def cal_sse(slope,intercept, x, y):
    sse = 0
    for x_, y_ in zip(x,y):
        y_on_line = x_2_y(slope,0,intercept,x_)
        sse += (y_on_line - y_)**2
    return sse


slopes = np.linspace(-1,1,20)
intercepts = np.linspace(-200,400,20)
slopes, intercepts = np.meshgrid(slopes,intercepts)
sses = np.zeros(intercepts.shape)
for i in range(sses.shape[0]):
    for j in range(sses.shape[1]):
        sses[i][j] = cal_sse(slopes[i][j],intercepts[i][j],x,y)
```

The following code snippet plots the 3D surface, namely SSE versus slope and intercept:

```
from mpl_toolkits.mplot3d import Axes3D
from matplotlib import cm
fig = plt.figure(figsize=(14,10))
ax = fig.gca(projection='3d')
ax.view_init(40, -30)
ax.set_xlabel("slope")
ax.set_ylabel("intercept")
ax.set_zlabel("sse")
plt.rc('xtick',labelsize=8)
plt.rc('ytick',labelsize=8)
surf = ax.plot_surface(slopes, intercepts, sses, cmap=cm.coolwarm,
                       linewidth=0, antialiased=True)
fig.colorbar(surf, shrink=0.5, aspect=5)


plt.show()
```

The result looks as shown in the following figure:

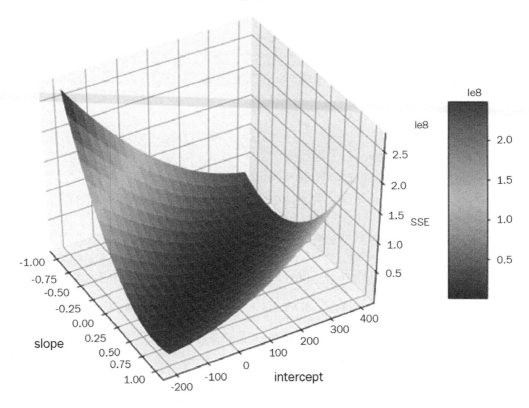

Figure 8.6 – SSE as a function of slope and intercept

The combination of the optimal values of slope and intercept gives us the minimal SSE.

It is a good time to answer a natural question: how much of the variance in the independent variable can be attributed to the independent variable? The answer is given by the R^2 value. It is defined as follows:

$$R^2 = \frac{SST - SSE}{SST}$$

It can also be defined as shown in the following equation:

$$R^2 = \frac{SSR}{SST}$$

where $SSR = SST - SSE$ is called the sum of squared regression or regression sum of squares. Do a thought experiment with me: if $R^2 = 0$, it means we have no error after regression. All the changes of our dependent variable can be attributed to the change of the independent variable, up to a proportionality coefficient k and a shift value b. This is too good to be true in general and it is also the best that simple linear regression can do.

The slope and intercept given by the `linregress()` function gives us an R^2 value of $0.89(0.9447^2)$. The verification of this value is left to you as an exercise.

In the next section, we are going to learn about the limitations of R^2.

The coefficient of determination

R^2 is a key indicator of the quality of the regression model. If SSR is large, it means we captured enough information in the change of the dependent variable with the change of the independent variable. If you have a very large R^2 and your model is simple, the story can end here.

However, beyond simple linear regression, sometimes R^2 can be *misleading*. Let's take multivariable, polynomial regression as an example. Let's say we have two independent variables, x_1 and x_2, and we are free to use variables such as x'_2 as new predictors. The expected expression of the dependent variable y will look like the following:

$$y = \beta + \alpha_{11}x_1 + \alpha_{21}x_2 + \alpha_{12}x_1^2 + \cdots + \alpha_{kj}x_k^j$$

In the stock price example, you can pick an additional independent variable such as the unemployment rate of the United States. Although there is little meaning in taking the square of the number of days or the unemployment rate, nothing stops you from doing it anyway.

> **Note**
>
> In a simple linear model, you often see r^2 rather than R^2 to indicate the coefficient of determination. r^2 is only used in the context of simple linear regression.

R^2 will always increase when you add additional $\alpha_{kj}x_k^j$ terms. Given a dataset, R^2 represents the power of explainability on this dataset. You can even regress the stock price on your weight if you measure it daily during that time period, and you are going to find a better R^2. An increased R^2 alone doesn't necessarily indicate a better model.

A large R^2 doesn't indicate any **cause-effect relationship**. For example, the change of time doesn't drive the stock price of Netflix high as it is not the cause of change of the dependent variable. This is a common logic fault and a large R^2 just magnifies it in many cases. It is always risky to conclude cause-effect relationships without thorough experiments.

R^2 is very sensitive to a single data point. For example, I created a set of data to demonstrate this point. The following code snippet does the job:

```
np.random.seed(2020)
x = np.linspace(0,2,20)
y = 3*x + np.random.normal(size=len(x))
x_new = np.append(x,np.array([0]))
y_new = np.append(y,np.array([10]))
plt.scatter(x,y)
plt.scatter([0],[10])
linregress(x_new,y_new)
```

The plot looks as shown in the following figure. Pay attention to the one outlier at the top left:

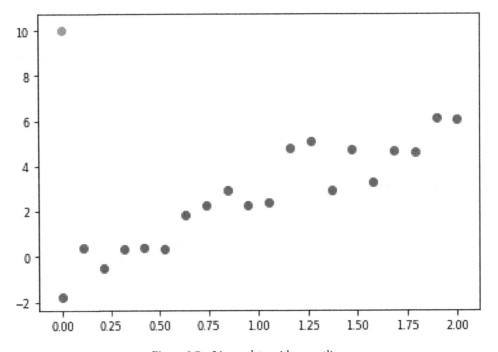

Figure 8.7 – Linear data with an outlier

The R^2 value is less than 0.3. However, removing the outlier updates the R^2 value to around 0.88.

A small R^2 may indicate that you are using the wrong model in the first place. Take the following as an example. Simple linear regression is not suitable to fit the parabolic data:

```
np.random.seed(2020)
x = np.linspace(0,2,20)
y = 4*x**2-8*x + np.random.normal(scale=0.5,size=len(x))
plt.scatter(x,y)
linregress(x,y)
```

The R^2 is less than 0.01. It is not correct to apply simple linear regression on such a dataset where nonlinearity is obvious. You can see the failure of such a dataset where simple linear regression is applied in the following figure. This is also why exploratory data analysis should be carried out before building models. We discussed related techniques in *Chapter 2, Essential Statistics for Data Assessment*, and *Chapter 3, Visualization with Statistical Graphs*.

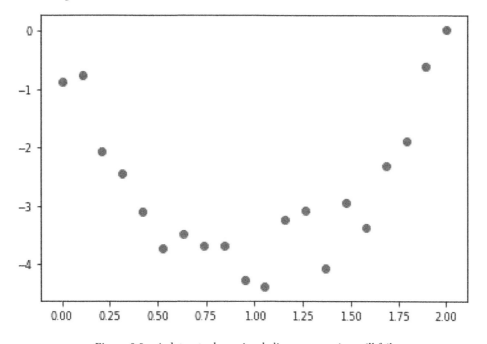

Figure 8.8 – A dataset where simple linear regression will fail

Hypothesis testing

Let's briefly talk about hypothesis testing in simple linear regression. The P-value in the `linregress` function is a P-value for the t-test. The t-test is a two-tailed test with the following null hypothesis:

$$H_0: k = 0$$

A small P-value indicates that we have enough confidence to reject the null hypothesis. The details of the calculation are cumbersome with matrix algebra therefore omitted.

Connecting the relationship between regression and estimators

Recall that in *Chapter 6, Parametric Estimation*, we studied an example where we used **Maximal Likelihood Estimation (MLE)** to estimate the slope in a 0-intercept linear equation, which was formulated in the following form:

$$Y = kX + \epsilon$$

> **Note on MLE**
>
> Please review the MLE for modeling noise example in *Chapter 6, Parametric Estimation*. It is an example with rich content.

In the example, we assumed the distribution of the noise ϵ was normal $N(0, 1)$ and showed that the log-likelihood takes the following form:

$$logL(k) = \sum_i log\big(f(\epsilon_i|k)\big) = \sum_i \left(-0.5log(2\pi) - \frac{(y_i - k\, x_i)^2}{2}\right)$$

Note, if we add another parameter b, the derivation is still legitimate:

$$logL(k, b) = \sum_i log\big(f(\epsilon_i|k, b)\big) = \sum_i \left(-0.5log(2\pi) - \frac{(y_i - k\, x_i - b)^2}{2}\right)$$

Taking the derivative with respective to k and b, respectively, we obtain:

$$\frac{dlogL(k, b)}{dk} = \sum_i (y_i - k\, x_i - b)x_i$$

We also obtain the following equation:

$$\frac{dlogL(k,b)}{db} = \sum_{i}(y_i - k\,x_i)$$

> **Note**
>
> The log-likelihood function only depends on each data point through $(y_i - kx_i - b)^2$, whose sum is exactly SSE. Maximizing the log-likelihood is equivalent to minimizing the squared error.

Now, we have two unknowns (k and b) and two equations. We can solve it algebraically. Indeed, we have already solved the problem graphically through the 3D visualization, but it is nice to have an algebraic solution. We have the following formula for the algebraic solution:

$$k = \frac{\Sigma_i(x_i - \bar{x})(y_i - \bar{y})}{\Sigma_i(x_i - \bar{x})^2}$$

and $b = \bar{y} - k\bar{x}$

Now, let's calculate the slope and intercept for the Netflix data with this formula and check them against the *linregress* results. The following code does the job:

```
x= (df.index - df.index[0]).days.to_numpy()
y = df.Open.to_numpy()
x_mean = np.mean(x)
y_mean = np.mean(y)
k = np.sum((x-x_mean)*(y-y_mean))/np.sum((x-x_mean)**2)
b = y_mean - k * x_mean
print(k,b)
```

The results are about *0.16214* and *74.838*, which agree with the *linregress* results perfectly.

A computational approach is not illuminating in the sense of mathematical intuition. Next, let's try to understand simple linear regression from the estimation perspective.

Simple linear regression as an estimator

At this moment, we have covered the simple linear regression model from several perspectives. As you may notice, the following three perspectives can be unified now:

- Simple linear regression is a process of decomposing the SST into SSR and SSE, where the SSR is explained by an independent variable.

- Simple linear regression is a pure error minimizing process that minimizes the MSE. This is also called **Ordinary Least Squares (OLS)**.

- Simple linear regression is an estimation of unknown parameters under the assumption that the noise is independently and normally distributed.

All three perspectives are correct. When you apply simple linear regression, you already implicitly assume the noise in your dataset is normally distributed. This is likely true because of CLT's universality.

Before moving on to multivariate linear regression, let me briefly talk about the correlation coefficient R itself and the standard error in the *linregress* output.

The expression of k can be decomposed into the following form:

$$k = \frac{\sum_i (x_i - \bar{x})(y_i - \bar{y})}{\sum_i (x_i - \bar{x})^2} = r_{xy} \frac{s_y}{s_x}$$

where s_x and s_y are **uncorrelated sample standard deviation**. They are defined as shown in the following equations:

$$s_x = \sqrt{\frac{1}{N} \sum_i (x_i - \bar{x})}$$

and

$$s_y = \sqrt{\frac{1}{N} \sum_i (y_i - \bar{y})}$$

r_{xy} is called the **sample correlation coefficient**. It is defined as shown in the following equation:

$$r_{xy} = \frac{\sum_i (x_i - \bar{x})(y_i - \bar{y})}{\sqrt{\sum_i (x_i - \bar{x})^2 \sum_i (y_i - \bar{y})^2}}$$

You might have noticed that the expression does give you k. In the linear model, r_{xy} connects the standard deviations of dependent and independent variables. Due to an inequality restriction, r_{xy} can only take values between *-1* and *1*, and equality is reached when x and y are perfectly correlated, negatively or positively. The square of r_{xy} gives us R^2. r_{xy} can be either positive or negative but R^2 doesn't contain the directional information but the strength of explanation.

The standard error is associated with the estimated value of k. Due to space limitations, we can't go over the mathematics here. However, knowing that an estimator is also a random variable with variance is enough to continue this chapter. A smaller variance of estimator means it is more robust and stable. A corresponding concept is the **efficiency of an estimator**. Two unbiased estimators may have different efficiencies. A more efficient estimator has a smaller variance for all possible values of the estimated parameters. In general, the variance can't be infinitely small. The so-called *Cramér–Rao lower bound* restricts the minimal variance that could be achieved by an unbiased estimator.

> **Note**
>
> I would like to suggest an interesting read on this cross-validated `question`, which you will find here: `https://stats.stackexchange.com/questions/64195/how-do-i-calculate-the-variance-of-the-ols-estimator-beta-0-conditional-on`

Having hands-on experience with multivariate linear regression and collinearity analysis

Simple linear regression is rarely useful because, in reality, many factors will contribute to certain outcomes. We want to increase the complexity of our model to capture more sophisticated one-to-many relationships. In this section, we'll study multivariate linear regression and collinearity analysis.

First, we want to add more terms into the equation as follows:

$$y = k_1 x_1 + k_2 x_2 + \cdots + k_n x_n + \epsilon$$

There is no non-linear term and there are independent variables that contribute to the dependent variable collectively. For example, people's wages can be a dependent variable and their age and number of employment years can be good explanatory/independent variables.

> **Note on multiple regression and multivariate regression**
>
> You may see interchangeable usage of *multiple* linear regression and *multivariate* linear regression. Strictly speaking, they are different. Multiple linear regression means that there are multiple independent variables while multivariate linear regression means the response/dependent variable is a vector (multiple), which means you must do regression on each element of it.

I will be using an exam dataset for demonstration purposes in this section. The dataset is provided in the official GitHub repository of this book. The following code snippet reads the data:

```python
import pandas as pd
exam = pd.read_csv("exams.csv")
exam
```

Let's inspect the data:

	EXAM1	EXAM2	EXAM3	FINAL
0	73	80	75	152
1	93	88	93	185
2	89	91	90	180
3	96	98	100	196
4	73	66	70	142
5	53	46	55	101
6	69	74	77	149
7	47	56	60	115
8	87	79	90	175
9	79	70	88	164
10	69	70	73	141
11	70	65	74	141
12	93	95	91	184
13	79	80	73	152
14	70	73	78	148
15	93	89	96	192
16	78	75	68	147
17	81	90	93	183
18	88	92	86	177
19	78	83	77	159
20	82	86	90	177
21	86	82	89	175
22	78	83	85	175
23	76	83	71	149
24	96	93	95	192

Figure 8.9 – Exam data for multivariate linear regression

The dataset contains three in-semester exams (the independent variable) and one final exam (the dependent variable). Let's first do some exploratory graphing.

Here, I introduce a new kind of plot, a violin plot. It is like a boxplot, but it gives a better idea of how the data is distributed inside the first and third quartiles. Don't hesitate to try something new when you are learning with Python!

First, we need to transform our exam DataFrame to the long format such that it only contains two columns, the *score* column and the *exam_name* column. We covered a similar example for the boxplot in *Chapter 2*, *Essential Statistics for Data Assessment*. Feel free to review that part. The following code snippet does the transformation:

```
exam["index"] = exam.index
exam_long = pd.melt(exam,id_vars=["index"],value_vars = exam.
columns[:-1])[["variable","value"]]
exam_long.columns = ["exam_name","score"]
```

I will sample 10 rows with `exam_long.sample(10)` from the new DataFrame for a peek:

	exam_name	score
64	EXAM3	78
34	EXAM2	70
98	FINAL	149
83	FINAL	175
89	FINAL	148
57	EXAM3	60
68	EXAM3	86
1	EXAM1	93
53	EXAM3	100
52	EXAM3	90

Figure 8.10 – The exam DataFrame in long format

The following code snippet displays the violin plot. You will see why it is called a violin plot:

```
import seaborn as sns
sns.set(style="whitegrid")
plt.figure(figsize=(8,6))
sns.violinplot(x="exam_name", y="score", data=exam_long);
```

The result looks as shown in the following figure:

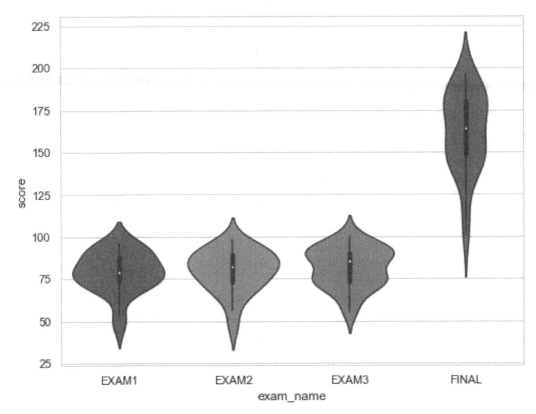

Figure 8.11 – Violin plot of the exam scores

We see that the score distributions are somewhat alike for the first three exams, whereas the final exam has a longer tail.

Next, let's do a set of scatter plots for pairs of exams with the following code snippet:

```
fig, ax = plt.subplots(1,3,figsize=(12,6))
ax[0].scatter(exam.EXAM1,exam.FINAL,color="green")
ax[1].scatter(exam.EXAM2,exam.FINAL,color="red")
ax[2].scatter(exam.EXAM3,exam.FINAL)
ax[0].set_xlabel("Exam 1 score")
ax[1].set_xlabel("Exam 2 score")
ax[2].set_xlabel("Exam 3 score")
ax[0].set_ylabel("Final exam score");
```

The result looks as shown in the following figure:

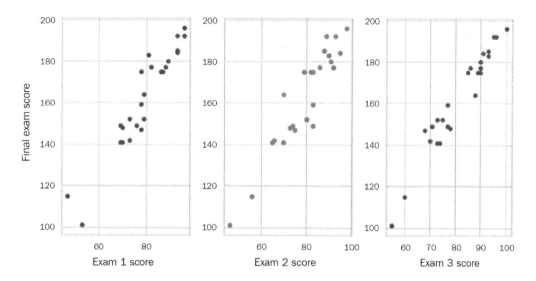

Figure 8.12 – Final exams versus the other three exams

The linear model seems to be a great choice for our dataset because, visually, the numbered exam scores are strongly, linearly correlated with the final exam score.

From simple linear regression to multivariate regression, the idea is the same: we would like to minimize the sum of squared errors. Let me use the `statsmodels` library to run ordinary least square (OLS) regression. The following code snippet does the job:

```
import statsmodels.api as sm
X = exam[["EXAM1","EXAM2","EXAM3"]].to_numpy()
X = sm.add_constant(X)
y = exam["FINAL"].to_numpy()
sm.OLS(y,X).fit().summary()
```

The result looks as shown in the following figures. Although there is a lot of information here, we will be covering only the essential parts.

First, the regression result, or summary, is listed in the following figure:

OLS Regression Results			
Dep. Variable:	y	R-squared:	0.99
Model:	OLS	Adj. R-squared:	0.988
Method:	Least Squares	F-statistic:	670.1
Date:	Wed, 20 May 2020	Prob (F-statistic):	5.34E-21

Figure 8.13 – OLS regression result

Secondly, the characteristics of the dataset and the model are also provided in the following figure:

Time:	14:53:12	Log-Likelihood:	-57.312
No. Observations:	25	AIC:	122.6
Df Residuals:	21	BIC:	127.5
Df Model:	3		
Covariance Type:	nonrobust		

Figure 8.14 – OLS model characterization

Lastly, the coefficients and statistics for each predictor feature (the numbered exam scores) are provided in the following table:

	coef	std err	t	P>|t|	[0.025	0.975]
const	-4.3361	3.764	-1.152	0.262	-12.164	3.492
x1	0.3559	0.121	2.932	0.008	0.103	0.608
x2	0.5425	0.101	5.379	0	0.333	0.752
x3	1.1674	0.103	11.333	0	0.953	1.382

Figure 8.15 – Coefficients and statistics for each predictor feature

First, R^2 is close to 1, which is a good sign that the regression on independent variables successfully captured almost all the variance of the dependent variable. Then we have an adjusted R^2. The adjusted R^2 is defined as shown in the following equation:

$$R_{adj}^2 = 1 - \frac{(1 - R^2)(n - 1)}{n - df - 1}$$

df is the degree of freedom (here, it is 3 because we have 3 independent variables) and n is the number of points in the data.

Note on the sign of adjusted R^2

The adjusted R^2 penalizes the performance when adding more independent variables. The adjusted R^2 can be negative if the original R^2 is not large and you try to add meaningless independent variables.

Collinearity

The linear model we just built seems to be good, but the warning message says that there are multicollinearity issues. From the scatter plot, we see that the final exam score seems to be predictable from either of the exams. Let's check the correlation coefficients between the exams:

```
exam[["EXAM1","EXAM2","EXAM3"]].corr()
```

The result looks as shown in the following figure:

	EXAM1	EXAM2	EXAM3
EXAM1	1	0.901363	0.892743
EXAM2	0.901363	1	0.846359
EXAM3	0.892743	0.846359	1

Figure 8.16 – Correlation between numbered exams

EXAM 1 and *EXAM 2* have a correlation coefficient of more than 0.90 and the smallest coefficient is around 0.85!

Strong collinearity between independent variables becomes a problem because it tends to inflate the variance of the estimated regression coefficient. This will become clearer if we just regress the final score on *EXAM 1*:

```
linregress(exam.EXAM1, exam.FINAL)
```

The result is as follows:

```
LinregressResult(slope=1.8524548489068682,
intercept=15.621968742401123, rvalue=0.9460708318102032,
pvalue=9.543660489160869e-13, stderr=0.13226692073027208)
```

Note that with a slightly smaller R^2 value, the standard error of the slope is less than 10% of the estimated value. However, if you check the output for the three-independent-variables case, the standard error for the coefficients of *EXAM 1* and *EXAM 2* is about one-third and one-fifth of the values, respectively. How so?

An intuitive and vivid argument is that the model is *confused* about which independent variable it should pick to attribute the variance to. The *EXAM 1* score alone explains 94% of the total variance and the *EXAM 2* score can explain almost 93% of the total variance, too. The model can either assign a more deterministic slope to either the *EXAM 1* score or *EXAM 2*, but when they exist simultaneously, the model is confused, which numerically inflates the standard error of the regression coefficients.

In some numerical algorithms where randomness plays a role, running the same program twice might give different sets of coefficients. Sometimes the coefficient can even be negative when you already know it should be a positive value.

Are their quantitative ways to detect collinearity? There are two common methods. They are listed here. The first one pre-examines variables and the second one checks the **Variance Inflation Factor (VIF)**:

- You can check the correlation coefficient between pairs of independent variables as we just did in the example. A large absolute value for the correlation coefficient is usually a bad sign.

- The second method of calculating the VIF is more systematic and unbiased in general. To calculate the VIF of a coefficient, we run a regression against its corresponding independent variable x_i using the rest of the corresponding variables, obtain the R^2 and calculate VIF_i using the following equation:

$$VIF_i = \frac{1}{1 - R_i^2}$$

Let's do an example. I will use the *EXAM 2* score and the *EXAM 3* score as dependent variables and the *EXAM 1* score as an independent variable:

```
X = exam[["EXAM2","EXAM3"]].to_numpy()
X = sm.add_constant(X)
y = exam["EXAM1"].to_numpy()
sm.OLS(y,X).fit().rsquared
```

The result is around *0.872*. Therefore, the VIF is about 7.8. This is already a big value. A VIF greater than 10 suggests serious collinearity.

Is collinearity an issue? The answer is yes and no. It depends on our goals. If our goal is to predict the independent variable as *accurately* as possible, then it is not an issue. However, in most cases, we don't want to carry unnecessary complexity and redundancy in the model. There are several ways to get rid of collinearity. Some of those are as follows:

- Select independent variables and drop the rest. This may lose information.

- Obtain more data. More data brings diversity into the model and will reduce the variance.

- Use **Principle Component Analysis** (**PCA**) to transform the independent variables into fewer new variables. We will not cover it here because of space limitations. The idea is to bundle the variance explainability of independent variables together, in a new variable.

- Use **lasso regression**. Lasso regression is regression with regularization of L1- norm.

In the next section, we will see how it is done and what exactly L1-norm means.

Learning regularization from logistic regression examples

L-1 norm regularization, which penalizes the complexity of a model, is also called **lasso** regularization. The basic idea of regularization in a linear model is that parameters in a model can't be too large such that too many factors contribute to the predicted outcomes. However, lasso does one more thing. It not only penalizes the magnitude but also the parameters' existence. We will see how it works soon.

The name lasso comes from **least absolute shrinkage and selection operator**. It will shrink the values of parameters in a model. Because it uses the absolute value form, it also helps with selecting explanatory variables. We will see how it works soon.

Lasso regression is just like linear regression but instead of minimizing the sum of squared errors, it minimizes the following function. The index *i* loops over all data points where *j* loops over all coefficients:

$$\sum_i (y - k_j x_{1i} - k_2 x_{2i} - \cdots - k_v x_{vi} - \beta)^2 + \lambda \sum_j |k_j|$$

Unlike standard OLS, this function no longer has an intuitive graphic representation. It is an **objective function**. An objective function is a term from optimization. We choose input values to maximize or minimize the value of an objective function.

The squared term on the left in the objective function is the OLS sum of squared error. The term on the right is the **regularization term**. λ, a positive number, is called the **regularization coefficient**. It controls the strength of the penalization. The regularization term is artificial. For example, the regression coefficients/slopes share the same coefficient, but it is perfectly okay if you assign a different regularization coefficient to different regression coefficients.

When $\lambda = 0$, we get back OLS. As λ increases more and more, the coefficient will shrink and eventually reach 0.

If you change the regularization term from $\lambda \sum_j |k_j|$ to $\lambda \sum_j k_j^2$ just like the OLS term, you will get **ridge regression**. Ridge regression also helps control the complexity of a model, but it doesn't help with selecting explanatory variables. We will compare the effects with examples.

We will run the lasso regression, ridge regression, and normal linear regression (again) with modules from the `sklearn` library.

> **Note**
>
> It is a good habit to check the same function offered from different libraries so you can compare them meaningfully. For example, in the `sklearn` library, the objective function is defined such that the sum of squared error is reduced by $\frac{1}{2n}$. If you don't check the document and simply compare results from your own calculation, you may end up with confusing conclusions about regularization coefficient choice. This is also why in the code that follows, the regularization coefficient for the ridge model multiplies *2n*. The APIs for two models are not consistent in the `sklearn` library.

The following code snippet prepares the data like earlier:

```
from sklearn import linear_model
X = exam[["EXAM1","EXAM2","EXAM3"]].to_numpy()
y = exam["FINAL"].to_numpy()
```

In `sklearn`, the regularization coefficient is defined as α, so I am going to use α instead of λ. First, I choose α to be `0.1`:

```
alpha = 0.1
linear_regressor = linear_model.LinearRegression()
linear_regressor.fit(X,y)
lasso_regressor = linear_model.Lasso(alpha=alpha)
lasso_regressor.fit(X,y)
```

```
ridge_regressor = linear_model.Ridge(alpha=alpha*len(y)*2)
ridge_regressor.fit(X,y)
print("linear model coefficient: ", linear_regressor.coef_)
print("lasso model coefficient: ", lasso_regressor.coef_)
print("ridge model coefficient: ", ridge_regressor.coef_)
```

The result reads as follows:

```
linear model coefficient:  [0.35593822 0.54251876 1.16744422]
lasso model coefficient:  [0.35537305 0.54236992 1.16735218]
ridge model coefficient:  [0.3609811  0.54233219 1.16116573]
```

Note that there isn't much difference in the values. Our regularization term is still too small compared to the sum of squared error term.

Next, I will generate a set of data varying α. I will plot the scale of the three coefficients with respect to increasing α:

```
linear_regressor = linear_model.LinearRegression()
linear_regressor.fit(X,y)
linear_coefficient = np.array([linear_regressor.coef_] * 20).T
lasso_coefficient = []
ridge_coefficient = []
alphas = np.linspace(1,400,20)
for alpha in alphas:
    lasso_regressor = linear_model.Lasso(alpha=alpha)
    lasso_regressor.fit(X,y)
    ridge_regressor = linear_model.Ridge(alpha=alpha*len(y)*2)
    ridge_regressor.fit(X,y)
    lasso_coefficient.append(lasso_regressor.coef_)
    ridge_coefficient.append(ridge_regressor.coef_)
lasso_coefficient = np.array(lasso_coefficient).T
ridge_coefficient = np.array(ridge_coefficient).T
```

Note that the `.T` method is very handy – it transposes a two-dimensional NumPy array. The following code snippet plots all the coefficients against the regularization coefficient. Note how I use the `loc` parameter to position the legends:

```
plt.figure(figsize=(12,8))
for i in range(3):
    plt.plot(alphas, linear_coefficient[i], label = "linear
coefficient {}".format(i),
            c="r", linestyle=":",linewidth=6)
    plt.plot(alphas, lasso_coefficient[i], label = "lasso
coefficient {}".format(i),
            c= "b",linestyle="--",linewidth=6)
    plt.plot(alphas, ridge_coefficient[i], label = "ridge
coefficient {}".format(i),
            c="g",linestyle="-.",linewidth=6)
plt.legend(loc=(0.7,0.5),fontsize=14)
plt.xlabel("Alpha")
plt.ylabel("Coefficient magnitude");
```

The result looks as shown in the following figure. Note that different line styles indicate different regression models.

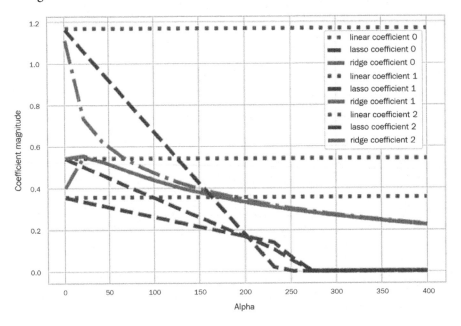

Figure 8.17 – Coefficient magnitudes versus the regularization coefficient

Note that the dotted line doesn't change with respect to the regularization coefficient because it is not regularized. The lasso regression coefficients and the ridge regression coefficients start roughly at the same levels of their corresponding multiple linear counterparts.

The ridge regression coefficients decrease toward roughly the same scale and reach about 0.2 when $\alpha = 400$. The lasso regression coefficients, on the other hand, decrease to 0 one by one around $\alpha = 250$.

When the coefficient is smaller than 1, the squared value is smaller than the absolute value. This is true to the fact that lasso regression coefficients decreasing to 0 doesn't depend on this. You can do an experiment by multiplying all independent variables by 0.1 to amplify the coefficients, and you will find similar behavior. This is left to you as an exercise.

So, when α is large, why does lasso regression tend to penalize the number of coefficients while ridge regression tends to drive coefficients at roughly the same magnitude?

Let's do one last thought experiment to end this chapter. Consider the scenario that we have two positive coefficients, k_1 and k_2, where k_1 is larger than k_2. Under the lasso penalization, decreasing either coefficient by a small value δ will decrease the objective function by δ. No secret there.

However, in ridge regression, decreasing the larger value k_1 will always decrease the objective function more as shown in the following equation:

$$\Delta_{k_1} = k_1^2 - (k_1 - \delta)^2 = 2k_1\delta - \delta^2$$

For k_2, you can do the same calculation as the following:

$$\Delta_{k_2} = k_2^2 - (k_2 - \delta)^2 = 2k_2\delta - \delta^2$$

Because k_1 is greater than k_2, decreasing the larger value benefits the minimization more. The ridge regression discourages the elimination of smaller coefficients but prefers decreasing larger coefficients. The lasso regression, on the other hand, is capable of generating a sparse model with fewer coefficients. These regularizations, especially the ridge regression, are particularly useful to handle multicollinearity.

For readers interested in exploring this further, I recommend you check out the corresponding chapter in the classical book *Elements of Statistical Learning* by Jerome H. Friedman, Robert Tibshirani, and Trevor Hastie.

Summary

In this chapter, we thoroughly went through basic simple linear regression, demystified some core concepts in linear regression, and inspected the linear regression model from several perspectives. We also studied the problem of collinearity in multiple linear regression and proposed solutions. At the end of the chapter, we covered two more advanced and widely used regression models, lasso regression and ridge regression. The concepts introduced in this chapter will be helpful for our future endeavors. In the next chapter, we are going to study another important family of machine learning algorithms and the statistics behind it: classification problems.

9
Statistics for Classification

In the previous chapter, we covered regression problems where correlations, in the form of a numerical relationship between independent variables and dependent variables, are established.

Different from regression problems, classification problems aim to predict the categorical dependent variable from independent variables. For example, with the same Netflix stock price data and other potential data, we can build a model to use historical data that predicts whether the stock price will rise or fall after a fixed amount of time. In this case, the dependent variable is binary: rise or fall (let's ignore the possibility of having the same value for simplicity). Therefore, this is a typical *binary classification* problem. We will look at similar problems in this chapter.

In this chapter, we will cover the following topics:

- Understanding how a logistic regression classifier works
- Learning how to evaluate the performance of a classifier
- Building a naïve Bayesian classification model from scratch
- Learning the mechanisms of a support vector classifier
- Applying cross-validation to avoid classification model overfitting

We have a lot of concepts and coding to cover. So, let's get started!

Understanding how a logistic regression classifier works

Although this section name sounds a bit unheard, it is correct. Logistic regression is indeed a regression model, but it is mostly used for classification tasks. A classifier is a model that contains sets of rules or formulas (sometimes millions or more) to perform the classification task. In a simple logistic regression classifier, we only need one rule built on a single feature to perform the classification.

Logistic regression is very popular in both traditional statistics as well as machine learning.

The name logistic originates from the name of the function used in logistic regression: logistic function. Logistic regression is the **Generalized Linear Model (GLM)**. The GLM is not a single model, but an extended group of models of **Ordinary Least Squares (OLS)** models. Roughly speaking, the linear part of the model in GLM is similar to OLS, but various kinds of transformation and interpretations are introduced, so GLM models can be applied to problems that simple OLS models can't be used for directly. You will see what this means in logistic regression in the following section.

The logistic function and the logit function

It's easier to look at the logit function first because it has a more intuitive *physical* meaning. The logit function has another name: the log-odds function, which makes much more sense. The standard logit function takes the form $\log\left(\frac{p}{1-p}\right)$, where p is between 0 and 1, indicating the probability of one possibility happening in a binary outcome. *The logistic function is the inverse of the logit function.* A standard logistic function takes the form $\frac{1}{1+e^{-x}}$, where x can take a value from $-\infty$ to $+\infty$ and the function takes a value between 0 and 1.

The task for this section is to predict whether a stock index such as SPX will rise or fall from another index called the **fear and greedy index**. The fear and greedy index is an artificial index that represents the sentiment of the stock market. When most people are greedy, the index is high and the overall stock index is likely to rise. On the other hand, when most people are fearful, the index is low and the stock index is likely to fall. There are various kinds of fear and greedy indexes. The one composed by *CNN Money* is a 100-point scale and contains influences from seven other economic and financial indicators. 50 represents neutral, whereas larger values display the greediness of the market.

We are not going to use real data, though. Instead, I will use a set of artificial data as shown in the following code snippet. As we did in *Chapter 7, Statistical Hypothesis Testing*, I will hide the generation of the data from you until the end of the section. The following code snippet creates the scatter plot of the fear and greedy index and the stock index change of the corresponding day:

```
plt.figure(figsize=(10,6))
plt.scatter(fg_index[stock_index_change > 0],
            stock_index_change[stock_index_change > 0],
            s=200,
            marker=6,
            label="Up")
plt.scatter(fg_index[stock_index_change < 0],
            stock_index_change[stock_index_change < 0],
            s=200,
            marker=7,
            label="Down")
plt.hlines(0,0,100,label="Neutral line")
plt.xlabel("Fear & Greedy Index",fontsize=20)
plt.ylabel("Stock Index Change",fontsize=20)
plt.legend(ncol=3);
```

The graph looks as in the following figure:

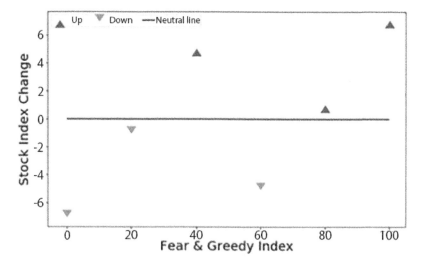

Figure 9.1 – Fear and greedy index versus stock index change

This might be suitable for simple linear regression, but this time, we are not interested in the exact values of stock index change, but rather the direction of the market. The horizontal neutral line bisects the data into two categories: the stock index either goes up or goes down. Our goal is to predict whether a stock index will rise or fall given a fear and greedy index value.

The formulation of a classification problem

The goal of the classification task is to predict the binary outcome from a single numerical independent variable. If we use the OLS model directly, the outcome of a classification is binary but the normal OLS model offers continuous numerical outcomes.

This problem leads to the core of logistic regression. Instead of predicting the probability, we predict the odds. Instead of predicting the hard-cut binary outcome, we can predict the probability of one of the outcomes. We can predict the probability that the stock index will rise as *p*, therefore *1 - p* becomes the probability that the stock price will fall, no matter how small the scale is.

> **Notes on the term odds**
>
> The odds of an event out of possible outcomes is the ratio of the event's probability and the rest. You might have heard the phrase *against all odds*, which means doing something when the odds of success are slim to none. Although probability is limited to [0,1], the odds can take an arbitrary value from 0 to infinity. By applying a shift to the odds, we get negative values to suit our needs.

By running a regression against the odds, we have an intermediate dependent variable, which is numerical and unbounded. However, there is one final question:

How do we choose the parameter of the regression equation?

We want to **maximize our likelihood function**. Given a set of parameters and corresponding predicted probabilities, we want the predictions to maximize our likelihood function. In our stock price example, it means the data points from the up group have probabilities of being up that are as large as possible, and data points from the down group have probabilities of being down that are as large as possible too. You can review *Chapter 6, Parametric Estimation*, to refresh your memory of the maximal likelihood estimator.

Implementing logistic regression from scratch

Make sure you understand the chain of logic before we start from a regression line to go over the process. Then, we talk about how to find the optimal values of this regression line's parameters. Due to the limit of space, I will omit some code and you can find them in this book's official GitHub repository: https://github.com/PacktPublishing/Essential-Statistics-for-Non-STEM-Data-Analysts.

The following is the step-by-step implementation and corresponding implementation of logistic regression. We used our stock price prediction example. We start by predicting the odds as a numerical outcome:

1. First, l will draw a sloped line to be our first guess of the regression against the odds of the stock index rising.

2. Then, I will project the corresponding data points on this regressed line.

3. Let's look at the results. The following graph has two y axes. The left axis represents the odds value and the right axis represents the original stock index change. I plotted one arrow to indicate how the projection is done. The smaller markers, as shown in the following figure, are for the right axis and the large markers on the inclined line indicate the regressed odds:

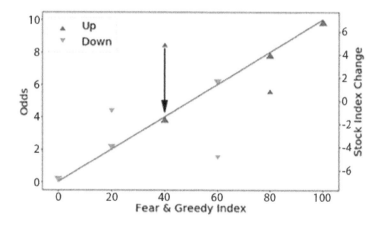

Figure 9.2 – Fear and greedy index versus odds

The regression parameters I chose are very simple—no intercept and only a slope of 0.1. Notice that one of the *up* data points has smaller odds than one of the *down* data points.

4. Now, we transform the odds into probability. This is where the logistic function comes into play:

$$\text{Probability} = \frac{1}{1 + e^{-k\,odds}}$$

Note that the k parameter can be absorbed into the slope and intercept, so we still have two parameters. However, since the odds are always positive, the probability will only be larger than $\frac{1}{2}$. We need to apply a shift to the odds, whose value can be observed into the parameter intercept. I apply an intercept of -5 and we get the following:

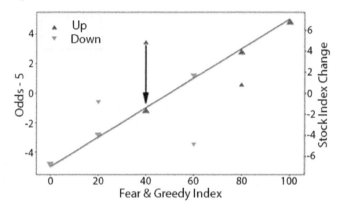

Figure 9.3 – Fear and greedy index versus shifted odds

Note that the shifted values lose the meaning of the odds, because negative odds don't make sense.

Next, we need to use the logistic function to transform the regressed *shifted odds* into probability. The following code snippet defines a handy logistic function. You may also see the name *sigmoid function* used in other materials, which is the same thing. The word sigmoid means shaped like the character S. The following code block defines the `logistic()` function:

```
def logistic(x):
    return 1 / (1 + np.exp(-x))
```

The following two code snippets plot the shifted odds and transformed probability on the same graph. I also defined a new function called `cal_shifted_odds` for clarity. We plot the odds with the first code snippet:

```
def cal_shifted_odds(val, slope, intercept):
    return val*slope + intercept
```

```
slope, intercept = 0.1, -5
fig, ax1 = plt.subplots(figsize=(10,6))


shifted_odds = cal_shifted_odds(fg_index,slope,intercept)


ax1.scatter(fg_index[stock_index_change > 0],
            shifted_odds[stock_index_change > 0],
            s=200,
            marker=6,
            label = "Up")


ax1.scatter(fg_index[stock_index_change < 0],
            shifted_odds[stock_index_change < 0],
            s=200,
            marker=7,
            label = "Down")


ax1.plot(fg_index, shifted_odds,
         linewidth=2,
         c="red")
```

The following code snippet continues to plot the probability:

```
ax2 = ax1.twinx()


ax2.scatter(fg_index[stock_index_change > 0],
            logistic(shifted_odds)[stock_index_change >
0],
            s=100,
            marker=6,
            label="Up")
ax2.scatter(fg_index[stock_index_change < 0],
            logistic(shifted_odds)[stock_index_change <
0],
            s=100,
            marker=7,
            label="Down")
```

```
ax2.plot(fg_grids,
        logistic(cal_shifted_odds(fg_
grids,slope,intercept)),
        linewidth=4,
        linestyle=":",
        c="green")


ax1.set_xlabel("Fear & Greedy Index",fontsize=20)
ax1.set_ylabel("Odds - 5",fontsize=20)
ax2.set_ylabel("Probability of Going Up",fontsize=20)
plt.legend(fontsize=20);
```

The result is a nice graph that shows the shifted odds and the transformed probability side by side. The dotted line corresponds to the right axis; it has an S shape and data points projected onto it are assigned probabilities:

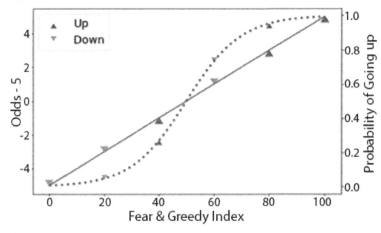

Figure 9.4 – Transformed probability and shifted odds

5. Now, you can pick a threshold of the probability to classify the data points. For example, a natural choice is 0.5. Check out the following graph where I use circles to mark out the up data points. I am going to call those points *positive*. The term comes from clinical testing where clinical experiments are done:

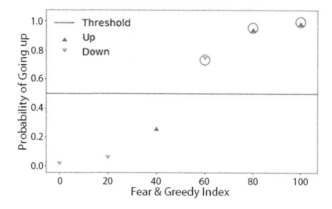

Figure 9.5 – Threshold and positive data points

As you can see, there is a negative data point that was misclassified as a positive data point, which means we misclassified a day that the stock index is going down as a day that the stock index goes up. If you buy a stock index on that day, you are going to lose money.

Positive and negative

The term positive is relative, as it depends on the problem. In general, when something interesting or significant happens, we call it positive. For example, if radar detects an incoming airplane, it is a positive event; if you test positive for a virus, it means you carry the virus.

Since our threshold is a linear line, we can't reach perfect classification. The following classifier with threshold 0.8 gets the misclassified negative data point right but won't fix the misclassified positive data point below it:

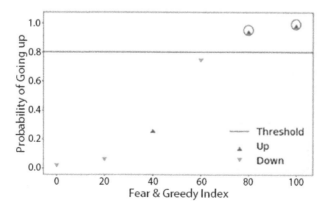

Figure 9.6 – Threshold = 0.8

Which one is *better*? In this section, we have converted a regression model into a classification model. However, we don't have the metrics to evaluate the performances of different choices of threshold. In the next section, let's examine the performance of the logistic regression classifier.

Evaluating the performance of the logistic regression classifier

In this section, we will approach the evaluation of our logistic regression classifiers in two ways.

The first way is to use the so-called confusion matrix, and the second way is to use the F1 score. To introduce the F1 score, we also need to introduce several other metrics as well, which will all be covered in this section.

Let's see what a confusion matrix looks like and define some terms. For that, let's take an example. The following table is a 2-by-2 confusion matrix for the threshold = 0.5 case:

	Ground truth positive	Ground truth negative
Predicted positive	TP=2	FP=1
Predicted negative	FN=1	TN=2

The 2 in the top-left cell means that there are two positive cases that we successfully classify as positive. Therefore, it is called **True Positive (TP)**. Correspondingly, the 1 in the bottom-left cell means that one positive case was misclassified as **False Negative (FN)**. We also have **True Negative (TN)** and **False Positive (FP)** by similar definition.

> **Note**
>
> A perfect classifier will have false positive and false negative being 0. The false positive error is also called a **type 1 error** and the false negative error is also called a **type 2 error**. As an example, if a doctor is going to claim a man is pregnant, it is a false positive error; if the doctor says a laboring woman is not pregnant, it is a false negative error.

In addition, the **recall** (or **sensitivity**, or **true positive**) rate is defined as follows:

$$\frac{TP}{TP + FN}$$

This means the ability of the classifier to correctly identify the positive ones from all the ground truth-positive examples. In our stock index example, if we set the threshold to 0, we reach a sensitivity of 1 because indeed we pick out all the positive ones.

The all-positive classifier is n ot acceptable, though. On the other hand, the **precision**, or **positive predictive value**, is defined as follows:

$$\frac{TP}{TP + FP}$$

This means among all the claimed positive results, how many of them are indeed positive? In our stock index example, setting the threshold to 1 will reach a precision of 1, because there won't be any false positive if there are no positive predictions at all!

A balance must be made. The F1 score is the balance; it is the **harmonic mean** of the precision and recall. The harmonic mean of a and b is defined as $\frac{2ab}{a + b}$:

$$F1 = \frac{2 * precision * recall}{precision + recall}$$

> **Notes on the harmonic mean**
>
> If two values are different, the harmonic mean is smaller than the geometric mean, which is smaller than the most common arithmetic mean.

We can calculate the metrics for the preceding confusion matrix. Recall and precision are both $\frac{2}{3} = \frac{2}{2 + 1}$. The F1 score is therefore also $\frac{2}{3}$.

If we pick a threshold of 0.8, the confusion matrix will look as follows:

	Ground true positive	Ground truth negative
Predicted positive	TP=2	FP=0
Predicted negative	FN=1	TN=3

Then, the recall will still be $\frac{2}{3}$, but the precision will be $\frac{2}{2}$. We reach a higher F1 score, 0.8. *We obtained a better result by simply changing the threshold.*

However, changing the threshold doesn't change the logistic function. To evaluate the model itself, we need to maximize the likelihood of our observation based on the regressed model. Let's take a look at the regressed probabilities with code:

```
logistic(cal_shifted_odds(fg_index,slope,intercept))
```

The result looks as follows:

```
array([0.00669285, 0.04742587, 0.26894142, 0.73105858,
0.95257413,
          0.99330715])
```

Here, I made the probabilities corresponding to positive data points bold. In this case, the likelihood function can be defined as follows:

$$L(slope, intercept) = \prod_{i=3,5,6} (P_i) \prod_{j=1,2,4} (1 - P_j)$$

Here, index i loops through the positive indexes, and index j loops through the negative indexes. Since we regress against the probabilities that the stock index will go up, we want the negative data points' probabilities to be small, which gives us the form $1 - P_j$.

In practice, we often calculate the log likelihood. Summation is easier to handle than multiplication numerically:

$$logL(slope, intercept) = \sum_{i=3,5,6} \left(log(P_i)\right) + \sum_{j=1,2,4} \left(log(1 - P_j)\right)$$

Let's calculate our log likelihood function for slope = 0.1 and intercept = -5 with the following code snippet:

```
np.prod(probs[stock_index_change>0])*np.prod(1-probs[stock_
index_change<0])
```

The result is about 0.065.

Let's try another set of parameters with the following code snippet:

```
probs = logistic(cal_shifted_odds(fg_index,
slope=0.11,intercept=-5.5))
np.prod(probs[stock_index_change>0])*np.prod(1-probs[stock_
index_change<0])
```

The result is about 0.058.

Our original choice set of parameters is actually better.

To find the parameters that maximize the likelihood function exactly, let's use the `sklearn` library. The following code snippet fits a regressor on our data points:

```
from sklearn.linear_model import LogisticRegression
regressor = LogisticRegression(penalty="none",
                               solver="newton-cg").fit(fg_index.
reshape(-1,1),
                                    stock_index_change>0)

print("slope: ",regressor.coef_[0][0])
print("intercept: ",regressor.intercept_[0])
```

The best possible slope and intercept are about 0.06 and -3.04, respectively. You can verify that this is true by plotting the likelihood function value against a grid of slopes and intercepts. I will leave the calculation to you as an exercise.

> **Note on the LogisticRegression( ) function**
>
> Note that I explicitly set the penalty to "`none`" in the initialization of the `LogisticRegression` instance. By default, `sklearn` will set an L2 penalty term and use another solver (a solver is a numerical algorithm to find the maximum) that doesn't support the no-penalty setting. I have to change these two arguments to make it match our approach in this section. The `newton-cg` solver uses the Newton conjugate gradient algorithm. If you are interested in finding out more about this, you can refer to a numerical mathematics textbook. The last thing I would like you to pay attention to is the reshaping of the input data to comply with the API.

Building a naïve Bayes classifier from scratch

In this section, we will study one of the most classic and important classification algorithms, the naïve Bayes classification. We covered Bayes' theorem in previous chapters several times, but now is a good time to revisit its form.

Suppose A and B are two random events; the following relationship holds as long as $P(B) \neq 0$:

$$P(A|B) = \frac{P(B|A)P(A)}{P(B)}$$

Some terminologies to review: $P(A|B)$ is called the **posterior probability** as it is the probability of event A *after* knowing the outcome of event B. $P(A)$, on another hand, is called the **prior probability** because it contains no information about event B.

Simply put, the idea of the Bayes classifier is to set the classification category variable as our *A* and the features (there can be many of them) as our *B*. We predict the classification results as posterior probabilities.

Then why the naïve Bayes classifier? The naïve Bayes classifier assumes that different features are mutually independent, and Bayes' theorem can be applied to them independently. This is a *very strong* assumption and likely incorrect. For example, to predict whether someone has a risk of stroke or obesity problems, or predicting their smoking habits and diet habits, are all valid. However, they are not independent. The naïve Bayes classifier assumes they are independent. Surprisingly, the simplest setting works well on many occasions, such as detecting spam emails.

> **Note**
>
> Features can be discrete or continuous. We will only cover a discrete version example. Continuous features can be naively assumed to have a Gaussian distribution.

I created a set of sample data, as shown here, which you can find in the book's official GitHub repository. Each row represents a set of information about a person. The `weight` feature has three levels, the `high_oil_diet` feature also has three, and the `smoking` feature has two levels. Our goal is to predict `stroke_risk`, which has three levels. The following table shows the profile of 15 patients:

	weight	high_oil_diet	smoking	stroke_risk
0	low	yes	no	low
1	low	no	yes	low
2	high	yes	yes	high
3	middle	no	no	low
4	high	yes	yes	high
5	high	no	yes	high
6	low	yes	no	middle
7	low	no	yes	low
8	low	no	no	low
9	middle	no	yes	high
10	middle	no	no	low
11	middle	yes	no	middle
12	middle	no	yes	middle
13	middle	yes	no	low
14	middle	no	no	low

Figure 9.7 – Stroke risk data

Let's start with the first feature, `weight`. Let's calculate $P(stroke\_risk|weight)$. According to Bayes' theorem, we have the following:

$$P(stroke_risk|weight) = \frac{P(weight|stroke_risk)P(stroke\_risk)}{P(weight)}$$

Let's calculate the prior probabilities first since they will be used again and again:

$$P(stroke\_risk = low) = \frac{8}{15}$$

$$P(stroke\_risk = middle) = \frac{3}{15}$$

$$P(stroke\_risk = high) = \frac{4}{15}$$

For the `weight` feature, we have the following:

$$P(weight = low) = \frac{5}{15}$$

$$P(weight = middle) = \frac{7}{15}$$

$$P(weight = high) = \frac{3}{15}$$

Now, let's find the 3-by-3 matrix of the conditional probability of $P(weight|stroke_risk)$. The column index is for the stroke risk and the row index is for the weight. The numbers in the cells are the conditional probabilities. To understand the table with an example, the first 0 in the last row means that $P(weight = low|stroke_risk = high) = 0$. If you count the table, you will find that among the four high-risk persons, none of them have a low weight:

	stroke_risk = high	stroke_risk = middle	stroke_risk = low
weight=high	3/4	0	0
weight= middle	1/4	2/3	4/8
weight= low	0	1/3	4/8

Let's do the same thing for the other two features:

	stroke_risk = high	stroke_risk = middle	stroke_risk = low
high_oil_diet = yes	2/4	2/3	2/8
high_oil_diet = no	2/4	1/3	2/6

The last one is for smoking, which is also binary:

	stroke_risk = high	stroke_risk = middle	stroke_risk = low
smoking = yes	4/4	1/3	2/8
smoking = no	0/4	2/3	6/8

OK, too many numbers; we will use Python to calculate them later in this chapter, but for now, let's look at an example.

What is the best stroke risk prediction if a person has middling weight, a high-oil diet, but no smoking habit?

We need to determine which of the following values is the highest. To simplify the expression, I will use abbreviations to represent the quantities. For example, *st* stands for `stroke_risk` and *oil* stands for a high-oil diet:

$$P(st = high|w = middle, oil = yes, sm = no) \text{ or}$$

$$P(st = middle|w = middle, oil = yes, sm = no) \text{ or}$$

$$P(st = low|w = middle, oil = yes, sm = no)$$

In the following example, I will use the *high stroke risk* case. With Bayes' theorem, we have the following:

$$P(st = high|w = middle, oil = yes, sm = no)$$
$$= \frac{P(st = high)P(w = middle, oil = yes, sm = no|st = high))}{P(w = middle, oil = yes, sm = no)}$$

> **Here is an interesting discovery**
>
> To get comparable quantitative values, we only care about the numerator because the denominator is the same for all classes. The numerator is nothing but the joint probability of both the features and the category variable.

Next, we use the assumption of independent features to decompose the numerator, as follows:

$$P(st = high|w = middle, oil = yes, sm = no)$$
$$\approx P(st = high)P(w = middle, oil = yes, sm = no|st = high)$$

We can further reduce the expression, as follows:

$$P(st = high)P(w = middle|st = high)P(oil = yes|st = high)P(sm = no|st = high)$$

Thus, the comparison of poster distributions boils down to the comparison of the preceding expression.

> **Note**
>
> It is always necessary to check the rules with intuition, to check whether they make sense. The preceding expression says that we should consider the prior probability and the conditional probabilities of specific feature values.

Let's get some real numbers. For the *stroke_risk = high* case, the expression gives us the following. The terms are in order. You can check the preceding tables to verify them:

$$\frac{4}{15}\frac{1}{4}\frac{2}{4}\frac{0}{4} = 0$$

The good habit of not smoking eliminates the possibility that this person has a high risk of getting a stroke.

How about *stroke_risk = middle*? The expression is as follows:

$$\frac{7}{15}\frac{2}{3}\frac{2}{3}\frac{2}{3} \approx 0.138$$

Note that this value is only meaningful when comparing it with other options since we omitted the denominator in the posterior probability's expression earlier.

How about *stroke_risk = low*? The expression is as follows:

$$\frac{8}{15}\frac{4}{8}\frac{2}{8}\frac{6}{8} = 0.05$$

The probabilities can therefore be normalized to a unit:

Stroke risk	Probability
High	0
Middle	73%
Low	27%

Therefore, according to our Bayes classifier, the person does not have a high risk of getting a stroke but has a middle or low stroke risk with a ratio of 3 to 1 after normalizing the probability.

Next, let's write code to automate this. The following code snippet builds the required prior probability for the category variable and the conditional probability for the features. It takes a pandas DataFrame and corresponding column names as input:

```python
def build_probabilities(df,feature_columns:list, category_
variable:str):
prior_probability = Counter(df[category_variable])
    conditional_probabilities = {}
    for key in prior_probability:
        conditional_probabilities[key] = {}
        for feature in feature_columns:
            feature_kinds = set(np.unique(df[feature]))
            feature_dict = Counter(df[df[category_
variable]==key][feature])
            for possible_feature in feature_kinds:
                if possible_feature not in feature_dict:
                    feature_dict[possible_feature] = 0
            total = sum(feature_dict.values())
            for feature_level in feature_dict:
                feature_dict[feature_level] /= total
            conditional_probabilities[key][feature] = feature_
dict
    return prior_probability, conditional_probabilities
```

Let's see what we get by calling this function on our stroke risk dataset with the following code snippet:

```
prior_prob, conditional_prob= build_probabilities(stroke_risk,
feature_columns=["weight","high_oil_diet","smoking"],category_
variable="stroke_risk")
```

I used the pprint module to print the conditional probabilities, as shown:

```
from pprint import pprint
pprint(conditional_prob)
```

The result is as follows:

```
{'high': {'high_oil_diet': Counter({'yes': 0.5, 'no': 0.5}),
          'smoking': Counter({'yes': 1.0, 'no': 0.0}),
          'weight': Counter({'high': 0.75, 'middle': 0.25,
'low': 0.0})},
 'low': {'high_oil_diet': Counter({'no': 0.75, 'yes': 0.25}),
         'smoking': Counter({'no': 0.75, 'yes': 0.25}),
         'weight': Counter({'low': 0.5, 'middle': 0.5, 'high':
0.0})},
 'middle': {'high_oil_diet': Counter({'yes':
0.6666666666666666,
                                      'no':
0.3333333333333333}),
            'smoking': Counter({'no': 0.6666666666666666,
                                'yes': 0.3333333333333333}),
            'weight': Counter({'middle': 0.6666666666666666,
                               'low': 0.3333333333333333,
                               'high': 0.0})}}
```

I highlighted a number; the way to interpret **0.75** is by reading the dictionary keys as the event we are conditioned on, and the event itself. You can verify that this does agree with our previous table counting. It corresponds to the following conditional probability expression:

$$P(weight = high | stroke\_risk = high)$$

Next, let's write another function to make the predictions displayed in the following code block:

```
def predict(prior_prob, conditional_prob, feature_values:dict):
    probs = {}
    total = sum(prior_prob.values())
    for key in prior_prob:
        probs[key] = prior_prob[key]/total
    for key in probs:
        posterior_dict = conditional_prob[key]
        for feature_name, feature_level in feature_values.
items():
            probs[key] *= posterior_dict[feature_name][feature_
level]
    total = sum(probs.values())
    if total == 0:
        print("Undetermined!")
    else:
        for key in probs:
            probs[key] /= total
        return probs
```

Note that it is totally possible that the probabilities are all 0 in the naïve Bayes classifier. This is usually due to an ill-posed dataset or an insufficient dataset. I will show you a couple of examples to demonstrate this:

- The first example is as follows:

```
predict(prior_prob,conditional_
prob,{"weight":"middle","high_oil_
diet":"no","smoking":"yes"})
```

The result is shown next, which indicates that the person is probably in the low-risk group:

```
{'low': 0.5094339622641509,
 'high': 0.33962264150943394,
 'middle': 0.15094339622641506}
```

- The second example is as follows:

```
predict(prior_prob, conditional_
prob,{"weight":"high","high_oil_
diet":"no","smoking":"no"})
```

The result is *undetermined*! If you check the conditional probabilities, you will find that the contradiction in the features and the insufficiency of the dataset lead to all zeros in the posterior probabilities. This is left to you as an exercise.

In the next section, let's look at another important concept in machine learning, especially classification tasks: cross-validation.

Underfitting, overfitting, and cross-validation

What is cross-validation and why is it needed? To talk about cross-validation, we must formally introduce two other important concepts first: **underfitting** and **overfitting**.

In order to obtain a good model for either a regression problem or a classification problem, we must fit the model with the data. The fitting process is usually referred to as *training*. In the training process, the model captures characteristics of the data, establishes numerical rules, and applies formulas or expressions.

> **Note**
>
> The training process is used to establish a mapping between the data and the output (classification, regression) we want. For example, when a baby learns how to distinguish an apple and a lemon, they may learn how to associate the colors of those fruits with the taste. Therefore, they will make the right decision to grab a sweet red apple rather than a sour yellow lemon.

Everything we have discussed so far is about the training technique. On the other hand, putting a model into a real job is called *testing*. Here is a little ambiguity that people often use carelessly. In principle, we should have no expectation of the model's output on the testing dataset, because that is the goal of the model: we need the model to predict or generate results on the testing set.

However, you may also hear the term *testing set* in a training process! Here, the word testing actually means an evaluation process of the trained model. Strictly speaking, a testing set is reserved for testing after the model is built. In this case, a model is trained on a training set, then applied on a so-called testing set, which we know the ground truth is to get a benchmark of the model's performance. So, be aware of the two meanings of testing.

In the following content, I will refer to testing in the training process. For example, if the baby we mentioned previously learned that red means sweetness, say one day the baby sees a red pepper for the first time and thinks it is sweet – what will happen? The baby's color-to-sweetness model will likely fail the testing on the testing set: a red pepper. What the baby learned is an **overfitted model**.

An overfitted model learns too much about the characteristics of the training data – for the baby, it is the apple – such that it cannot be generalized to unseen data easily.

How about an underfitted model? An underfitted model can be constructed this way. If the baby learns another feature that density is also a factor to indicate whether a fruit/ vegetable is sweet or not, the baby may likely avoid the red pepper. Compared to this model involving the fruit's density, the baby's simple color-only model is **underfitting**.

An underfitted model doesn't learn enough from the training data. It can be improved to perform better on the training data without potentially damaging its generalization capacity.

As you may have guessed, overfitting and underfitting are two cases that may not have clear boundaries. Here is a vivid example. Suppose we have the following data and we would like to have a polynomial regression model to fit it. A polynomial regression model uses a polynomial, rather than a linear line, to fit the data. The degree of the polynomial is a parameter we should choose for the model. Let's see which one we should choose.

The following code snippet plots the artificial data:

```
plt.figure(figsize=(10,6))
x_coor = [1,2,3,4,5,6,7]
y_coor = [3,8,5,7,10,9,15]
plt.scatter(x_coor,y_coor);
```

The result looks as follows:

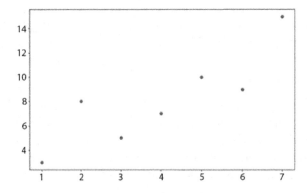

Figure 9.8 – Artificial data for polynomial fitting

Now, let me use 1st-, 3rd-, and 5th-order polynomials to fit the data points. The two functions I used are numpy.polyfit() and numpy.polyval(). The following code snippet plots the graph:

```python
styles=[":","--","-"]
plt.figure(figsize=(10,6))
x = np.linspace(1,7,20)
for idx, degree in enumerate(range(1,6,2)):
    coef = np.polyfit(x_coor,y_coor,degree)
    y = np.polyval(coef,x)
    plt.plot(x,y,
             linewidth=4,
             linestyle=styles[idx],
             label="degree {}".format(str(degree)))
plt.scatter(x_coor,y_coor,
            s=400,
            label="Original Data",
            marker="o");
plt.legend();
```

The result looks as in the following figure. Note that I made the original data points exceptionally large:

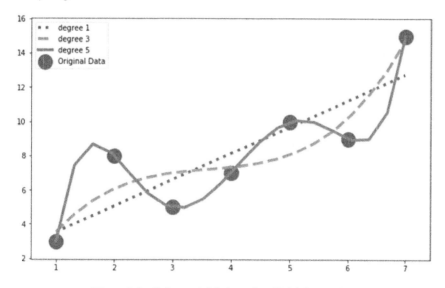

Figure 9.9 – Polynomial fitting of artificial data points

Well, it looks like the high-degree fitting almost overlaps with every data point and the linear regression line passes in between. However, with a degree of 5, the polynomial in principle can fit any five points in the plane, and we merely have seven points. This is clearly overfitting. Let's enlarge our vision a little bit. In the next figure, I slightly modified the range of the *x* variable from [1,7] to [0,8]. Let's see what happens. The modification is easy, so the code is omitted:

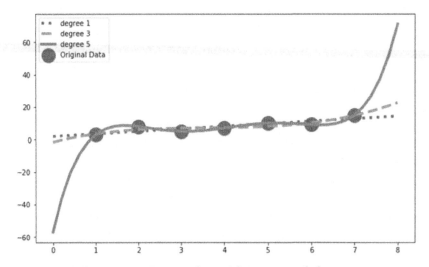

Figure 9.10 – Fitting polynomials in an extended range

Wow! See the penalty we pay to fit our training data? The higher-order polynomial just goes wild! Imagine if we have a testing data point between 0 and 1; what a counter-intuitive result we will get!

The question is, how do we prevent overfitting? We have already seen one tool, regularization. The other tool is called **cross-validation**.

Cross-validating requires another dataset called the *validation set* to validate the model *before* the model is applied to the testing set. Cross-validation can help to reduce the overfitting and reduce bias in the model learned in the training set early on. For example, the most common **k-fold cross-validation** splits the training set into *k* parts and leaves one part out of the training set to be the validation set. After the training is done, that validation set is used to evaluate the performance of the model. The same procedure is iterated *k* times. Bias can be detected early on if the model learned too much from the limited training set.

> **Note**
> Cross-validation can also be used to select parameters of the model.

Some sklearn classifiers have cross-validation built into the model classes. Since we have reached the end of the chapter, let's look at a logistic regression cross-validation example in sklearn. Here, I am going to use the stroke risk data for logistic regression cross-validation. I am going to convert some categorical variables into numerical variables. Recall that this is usually a bad practice, as we discussed in *Chapter 1, Fundamentals of Data Collection, Cleaning, and Preprocessing.*

However, it is doable here for a simple model such as logistic regression, because there is an ordered structure in the categories. For example, I can map low weight to 1, middle weight to 2, and high weight to 3. The logistic regression classifier will automatically learn the parameters to distinguish them. Another point is that the target stroke risk will now have three choices rather than two. This multi-class classification is also achievable by training more than two logistic regression classifiers and using them together to partition the outcome space. The code that does the category-to-numeric mapping is omitted due to space limitation; you can find it in the Jupyter notebook. The code that invokes logistic regression cross-validation reads as follows:

```
from sklearn.linear_model import LogisticRegressionCV
X = stroke_risk[["weight","high_oil_diet","smoking"]]
y = stroke_risk["stroke_risk"]
classifier = LogisticRegressionCV(cv=3,random_state=2020,multi_
class="auto").fit(X,y)
```

Note that the k-fold cross validation has a *k* value of 3. We shouldn't choose a *k* value larger than the total number of records. If we choose 15, which is exactly the number of records, it is called **leave-one-out cross-validation**.

You can obtain some parameters of the cross-validated classifier by calling `classifier.get_params`.

The result reads as follows:

```
<bound method BaseEstimator.get_params of
LogisticRegressionCV(Cs=10, class_weight=None, cv=3,
dual=False,
                     fit_intercept=True, intercept_scaling=1.0,
l1_ratios=None,
                     max_iter=100, multi_class='auto', n_
jobs=None,
                     penalty='l2', random_state=2020,
refit=True, scoring=None,
                     solver='lbfgs', tol=0.0001, verbose=0)>
```

Note that a regularization term is automatically introduced because of the `Cs` parameter. For more details, you can refer to the API of the function.

Now, let's call the `predict_prob()` function to predict the probabilities. Let's say the person is slightly overweight, so they have a weight value of *1.5*. Recall that *1* means middle and *2* means high for weight. This person also eats slightly more fatty foods but smokes a lot. So, they have *0.5* and *2* on another two features, respectively. The code reads as follows:

```
classifier.predict_proba(np.array([[1.5,0.5,2]]))
```

The results read as follows:

```
array([[0.20456731, 0.15382072, 0.64161197]])
```

So, this person likely falls into the high stroke risk group. Note that this model is very coarse due to the categorical variable-to-numerical variable conversion, but it gives you the capability to estimate on data, which is beyond the previous observations.

Summary

In this chapter, we thoroughly studied the logistic regression classifier and corresponding classification task concepts. Then, we built a naïve Bayes classifier from scratch. In the last part of this chapter, we discussed the concepts of underfitting and overfitting, and used sklearn to use cross-validation functions.

In the next chapter, we are going to study another big branch of machine learning models, tree-based models.

10
Statistics for Tree-Based Methods

In the previous chapter, we covered some important concepts in classification models. We also built a naïve Bayes classifier from scratch, which is very important because it requires you to understand every aspect of the details.

In this chapter, we are going to dive into another family of statistical models that are also widely used in statistical analysis as well as machine learning: tree-based models. Tree-based models can be used for both classification tasks and regression tasks.

By the end of this chapter, you will have achieved the following:

- Gained an overview of tree-based classification
- Understood the details of classification tree building
- Understood the mechanisms of regression trees
- Know how to use the `scikit-learn` library to build and regularize a tree-based method

Let's get started! All the code snippets used in this chapter can be found in the official GitHub repository here: `https://github.com/PacktPublishing/Essential-Statistics-for-Non-STEM-Data-Analysts`.

Overviewing tree-based methods for classification tasks

Tree-based methods have two major varieties: **classification trees** and **regression trees**. A classification tree predicts categorical outcomes from a finite set of possibilities, while a regression tree predicts numerical outcomes. Let's first look at the classification tree, especially the quality that makes it more popular and easy to use compared to other classification methods, such as the simple logistic regression classifier and the naïve Bayes classifier.

A classification tree creates a set of rules and partitions the data into various subspaces in the feature space (or feature domain) in an optimal way.

First question, what is a feature space?

Let's take our stroke risk data that we used in *Chapter 9, Statistics for Classification*, as sample data. Here's the dataset from the previous chapter for your reference. Each row is a profile for a patient that records their weight, diet habit, smoking habit, and corresponding stroke risk level:

	weight	high_oil_diet	smoking	stroke_risk
0	low	yes	no	low
1	low	no	yes	low
2	high	yes	yes	high
3	middle	no	no	low
4	high	yes	yes	high
5	high	no	yes	high
6	low	yes	no	high
7	low	no	yes	low
8	low	no	no	low
9	middle	no	yes	high
10	middle	no	no	low
11	middle	yes	no	high
12	middle	no	yes	high
13	middle	yes	no	low
14	middle	no	no	low

Figure 10.1 – Stroke risk data

We have three features for each record. If we only look at the `weight` feature, it can take three different levels: `low`, `middle`, and `high`. Imagine, in a one-dimensional line representing weight, that there are only three discrete points a value can take, namely the three levels. This is a one-dimensional feature space or feature domain.

On the other hand, *high-oil diet* and *smoking* habit are other two-feature dimensions with two possibilities. Therefore, a person can be on one of 12 (3*2*2) combinations of all features in this three-dimensional feature space.

A classification tree is built with rules to map these 12 points in the feature space to the outcome space, which has three possible outcomes. Each rule is a yes-no question and the answer will be non-ambiguous, so each data record has a certain path to go down the tree. The following is an example of such a classification tree:

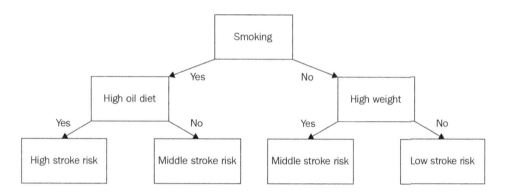

Figure 10.2 – An example of a classification tree for stroke risk data

Let's look at one example to better understand the tree. Suppose you are a guy who smokes but doesn't have a high-oil diet. Then, starting at the top of the tree, you will first go down to the left branch, and then go right to the **Middle stroke risk** box. The decision tree classifies you as a patient with middle stroke risk.

Now is a good time to introduce some terminology to mathematically describe a decision tree, rather than using casual terms such as *box*. A tree is usually drawn upside down, but this is a good thing as you follow down a chain of decisions to reach the final status. Here is some few important terminology that you need to be aware of:

- **Root node**: A root node is the only node/block that only has outgoing arrows. In the tree shown in the previous figure, it is the one at the top with the **Smoking** text. The root node contains all the records, and they haven't been divided into sub-categories, which corresponds to partitions of feature space.

- **Decision node**: A decision node is one node with both incoming and outgoing arrows. It splits the data feed into two groups. For example, the two nodes on the second level of the tree (**High oil diet?** and **High weight?**) are decision nodes. The one on the left splits the smoking group further into the smoking and high-oil diet group and the smoking and non-high-oil diet group. The one on the right splits the non-smoking group further into the non-smoking and high weight and non-smoking and non-high weight groups.

- **Leaf node**: A leaf node or a leaf is a node with only incoming arrows. A leaf node represents the final terminal of a classification process where no further splitting is needed or *allowed*. For example, the node at the bottom left is a leaf that indicates that people who smoke and have a high-oil diet are classified to have a high risk of stroke. It is not necessary for a leaf to only contain pure results. In this case, it is alright to have only low stroke risk and high stroke risk people in the leaf. What we optimized is the *pureness* of the classes in the node as the goal of classification is to reach unambiguous labeling. The label for the records in a leaf node is the *majority label*. If there is a tie, a common solution is to pick a random label of the tied candidates to make it the majority label.

- **Parent node and children nodes**: The node at the start of an arrow is the parent node of the nodes at the end of the arrows, which are called the child nodes. A node can simultaneously be a parent node and a child node, except the root node and the leaf. The process of determining which feature or criteria to use to generate children nodes is called *splitting*. It is common practice to do binary splitting, which means a parent node will have two child nodes.

- **Depth and pruning**: The depth of a decision tree is defined as the length of the chain from the root node to the furthest leaf. In the stroke risk case, the depth is 2. It is not necessary for a decision tree to be balanced. One branch of the tree can have more depth than another branch if accuracy requires. The operation of removing children nodes, including grandchild nodes and more, is called pruning, just like pruning a biological tree.

From now on, we will use the rigorous terms we just learned to describe a decision tree.

> **Note**
> One of the benefits of a decision tree is its universality. The features don't necessarily take discrete values; they can also take continuous numerical values. For example, if weight is replaced with continuous numerical values, the splitting on high weight or not will be replaced by a node with criteria such as *weight > 200 pounds?*.

Now, let's go over the advantages of decision trees:

- The biggest advantage of decision trees is that they are *easy to understand*. For a person without any statistics or machine learning background, decision trees are the easiest classification algorithms to understand.

- The decision tree is *not sensitive to data preprocessing and data incompletion*. For many machine learning algorithms, data preprocessing is vital. For example, the units of a feature in grams or kilograms will influence the coefficient values of logistic regression. However, decision trees are not sensitive to data preprocessing. The selection of the criteria will adjust automatically when the scale of the original data changes, but the splitting results will remain unchanged. If we apply logistic regression to the stroke risk data, a missing value of a feature will break the algorithm. However, decision trees are more robust to achieve relatively stable results. For example, if a person who doesn't smoke misses the weight data, they can be classified into the low-risk or middle-risk groups randomly (of course, there are better ways to decide, such as selecting the mode of records similar to it), but they won't be classified into high-risk groups. This result is sometimes good enough for practical use.

- **Explainability**: When a decision tree is trained, you are not only getting a model, but you also get a set of rules that you can explain to your boss or supervisor. This is also why I love the decision tree the most. The importance of features can also be extracted. For example, in general, the closer the feature is to the root, the more important the feature is in the model. In the stroke risk example, smoking is the root node that enjoys the highest feature importance. We will talk about how the positions of the features are decided in the next chapter.

Now, let's also talk about a few disadvantages of the decision tree:

- **It is easy to overfit**: Without control or penalization, decision trees can be very complex. How? Imagine that unless there are two records with exactly the same features but different outcome variables, the decision tree can actually build one leaf node for *every* record to reach 100% accuracy on the training set! However, the model will very likely not be generalized to another dataset. Pruning is a common approach to remove over-complex sub-branches. There are also constraints on the splitting step, which we will discuss soon.

- **The greedy approach doesn't necessarily give the best model**: A single decision tree is built by greedily selecting the best splitting feature sequentially. As a combination problem with an exponential number of possibilities, the greedy approach doesn't necessarily give the best model. In most cases, this isn't a problem. In some cases, a small change in the training dataset might generate a completely different decision tree and give a different set of rules. Make sure you double-check it before presenting it to your boss!

> **Note**
>
> To understand why building a decision tree involves selecting rules from a combination of choices, let's build a decision tree with a depth of 3, trained on a dataset of three continuous variable features. We have three decision nodes, including the root node, to generate four leaves. Each decision node can choose from three features for splitting, therefore resulting in a total of 27 possibilities. Yes, one child node can choose the same feature as its parent.
>
> Imagine we have four features; then, the total number of choices becomes 64. If the depth of the tree increases by 1, then we add four more decision nodes. Therefore, the total number of splitting feature choices is 16,384, which is huge for such a four-feature dataset. Most trees will obviously be useless, but the greedy approach doesn't guarantee the generation of the best decision tree.

We have covered the terminology, advantages, and disadvantages of decision trees. In the next section, we will dive deeper into decision trees, specifically how branches of a tree are grown and pruned.

Growing and pruning a classification tree

Let's start by examining the dataset one more time. We will first simplify our problem to a binary case so that the demonstration of decision tree growing is simpler. Let's examine *Figure 10.1* again.

For the purpose of this demonstration, I will just group the middle-risk and high-risk patients into the high-risk group. This way, the classification problem becomes a binary classification problem, which is easier to explain. After going through this section, you can try the exercises on the original three-category problem for practice.

The following code snippet generates the new dataset that groups middle-risk and high-risk patients together:

```
df["stroke_risk"] = df["stroke_risk"].apply(lambda x: "low" if
x == "low" else "high")
```

The new dataset will then look as follows:

	weight	high_oil_diet	smoking	stroke_risk
0	low	yes	no	low
1	low	no	yes	low
2	high	yes	yes	high
3	middle	no	no	low
4	high	yes	yes	high
5	high	no	yes	high
6	low	yes	no	high
7	low	no	yes	low
8	low	no	no	low
9	middle	no	yes	high
10	middle	no	no	low
11	middle	yes	no	high
12	middle	no	yes	high
13	middle	yes	no	low
14	middle	no	no	low

Figure 10.3 – Binary stroke risk data

Now, let's think about the root node. Which feature and what kind of criteria should we choose to generate two children nodes from the root node that contains all the records/data points? We will explore this topic in the next section.

Understanding how splitting works

The principle of splitting is that splitting, as a feature, must get us closer to a completely correct classification. We need a numerical metric to compare different choices of splitting features. The goal for classification is to classify records into pure states such that each leaf will contain records that are as *pure* as possible. Therefore, pureness or impureness becomes a natural choice of metric.

The most common metric is called **Gini impurity**. It measures how impure a set of data is. For a binary class set of data with class labels A and B, the definition of Gini impurity is the following:

$$Gini\ impurity\ =\ 1-\ P(A)^2-\ P(B)^2$$

If the set only contains A or B, the Gini impurity is 0. The maximum impurity is 0.5 when half of the records are A and the other half are B. For a three-class dataset, the minimum is still 0 but the maximum becomes $\frac{2}{3}$.

> **Note**
>
> Gini impurity is named after the Italian demographer and statistician Corrado Gini. Another well-known index named after him is the Gini index, which measures the inequality of wealth distribution in a society.

Let's see how this unfolds at the **root node**, without any splitting. The Gini impurity is calculated as $1 - \left(\frac{8}{15}\right)^2 - \left(\frac{7}{15}\right)^2$ because we have eight low-risk records and seven high-risk records. The value is about 0.498, close to the highest possible impurity.

After splitting by one criterion, we have two children nodes. The way to obtain the new, lower impurity is to calculate the weighted Gini impurity of the two children nodes.

First, let's take the high-oil diet group as an example. Let's examine the partition of the high-oil diet group. The following code snippet does the counting:

```
Counter(df[df["high_oil_diet"]=="yes"]["stroke_risk"])
```

There is a total of six records with two low-risk records and four high-risk records. Therefore, the impurity for the high-oil diet group is $1 - \left(\frac{1}{3}\right)^2 - \left(\frac{2}{3}\right)^2 = \frac{4}{9}$.

Meanwhile, we can calculate the non-high-oil diet group's statistics. Let's select and count them using the following code snippet:

```
Counter(df[df["high_oil_diet"]=="no"]["stroke_risk"])
```

There is a total of nine records with six low-risk records and three high-risk records. Note that the proportionalities are the same for the high-oil diet but with exchanging groups. Therefore, the Gini impurity is also $\frac{4}{9}$.

The weighted Gini impurity remains $\frac{4}{9}$ because $\frac{4}{9}\frac{6}{15} + \frac{4}{9}\frac{9}{15} = \frac{4}{9}$. It is about 0.444.

So, what do we get from such a classification? We have reduced the Gini impurity from 0.498 to 0.444, which is just a slight decrease, but better than nothing.

Next, let's examine the smoking behavior.

By the same token, let's first check the smoking group's statistics. The following code snippet does the counting:

```
Counter(df[df["smoking"]=="yes"]["stroke_risk"])
```

There is a total of seven smoking cases. Five of them are of high stroke risk and two of them are of low stroke risk. The Gini impurity is therefore about 0.408.

Let's check the non-smokers:

```
Counter(df[df["smoking"]=="no"]["stroke_risk"])
```

There are eight non-smokers: six of them are of low stroke risk and two of them are of high stroke risk. Therefore, the Gini impurity is 0.375.

Let's obtain the weighted impurity, which is about $0.408\frac{7}{15} + 0.375\frac{8}{15} = 0.390$.

This is a 0.108 decrease from the original impurity without splitting and it is better than the splitting on the high-oil diet group.

I will omit the calculation for the other feature, weight, but I will list the result for you in the following table. Note that the weight feature has three levels, so there can be multiple rules for splitting the feature. Here, I list all of them.

In the yes and no group statistics, I list the number of high-stroke risk records, the number of low-risk records, and the Gini impurity value separated by commas:

Splitting feature	Splitting rule	The *Yes* group	The *No* group	The *weighted* total Gini impurity
Smoking	Is smoking?	5, 2, 0.408	2, 6, 0.375	0.390
High oil diet	Is high oil diet?	4, 2, 0.444	3, 6, 0.444	0.444
Weight	Is low weight?	1, 4, 0.320	6, 4, 0.480	0.427
Weight	Is middle weight?	3, 4, 0.490	4, 4, 0.50	0.495
Weight	Is high weight?	3, 0, **0**	4, 8, 0.444	**0.356**

Figure 10.4 – The Gini impurity evaluation table for different splitting features at the root node

Note that I highlighted the Gini impurity for the high-weight group and the weighted Gini impurity for the last splitting choice. All high-weight patients have a high stroke risk, and this drives the weighted impurity down to 0.356, the lowest of all possible splitting rules. Therefore, we choose the last rule to build our decision tree. After the first splitting, the decision tree now looks like the following:

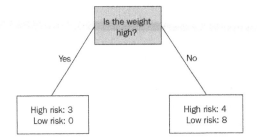

Figure 10.5 – The decision tree after the first splitting

Note that the left branch now contains a **pure** node, which becomes a leaf. Therefore, our next stop only focuses on the right branch. We naturally have an imbalanced tree now.

Now, we have four choices for the splitting of 12 records. First, I will select these 12 records out with the following one-line code snippet: df_right = df[df["weight"]!="high"].

The result looks as follows. The Gini impurity for the right splitting node is 0.444, as calculated previously. This will become our new baseline:

	weight	high_oil_diet	smoking	stroke_risk
0	low	yes	no	low
1	low	no	yes	low
3	middle	no	no	low
6	low	yes	no	high
7	low	no	yes	low
8	low	no	no	low
9	middle	no	yes	high
10	middle	no	no	low
11	middle	yes	no	high
12	middle	no	yes	high
13	middle	yes	no	low
14	middle	no	no	low

Figure 10.6 – The low-weight and middle-weight group

As we did earlier, let's build a table to compare different splitting choices for the splitting node on the right. The ordering of the numbers is the same as in the previous table:

Splitting feature	Splitting rule	The *Yes* group	The *No* group	The *weighted* total Gini impurity
Smoking	Is smoking?	2, 2, 0.5	2, 6, 0.375	0.417
High oil diet	Is high oil diet?	2, 2, 0.444	2, 6, 0.375	0.417
Weight	Is low weight?	1, 4, 0.320	3, 4, 0.490	0.420
Weight	Is middle weight?	4, 4, 0.490	1, 4, 0.320	0.420

Figure 10.7 – The Gini impurity evaluation table for different splitting features at the right splitting node

We essentially only have three choices because the two splitting rules on the feature weight are mirrors of each other.

Now, we have a tie. We can randomly select one criterion for building the trees further. This is one reason why decision trees don't theoretically generate the best results.

> **Note**
>
> An intuitive way to solve this issue is to build both possibilities and even more possible trees, which violates the greedy approach, and let them vote on the prediction results. This is a common method to build a more stable model or an ensemble of models. We will cover related techniques in the next chapter.

Let's say I choose high-oil diet as the criteria. The tree now looks like the following:

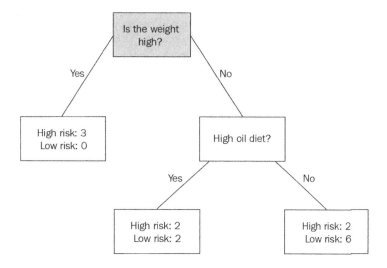

Figure 10.8 – The decision tree after the second splitting

Now, let's look at the two newly generated nodes. The first one at a depth of 2 contains two high stroke risk records and two low stroke risk records. They don't have a heavy weight, but do have a high-oil diet. Let's check out their profile with this line of code:

```
df_right[df_right["high_oil_diet"]=="yes"]
```

The result looks like the following:

	weight	high_oil_diet	smoking	stroke_risk
0	low	yes	no	low
6	low	yes	no	high
11	middle	yes	no	high
13	middle	yes	no	low

Figure 10.9 – Records classified into the first node at a depth of 2

Note that the low-weight category contains one low stroke risk record and a high stroke risk example. The same situation happens with the middle-weight category. This makes the decision tree incapable of further splitting on any feature. There won't be any Gini impurity decreasing for splitting. Therefore, we can stop here for this node.

> **Note**
>
> Well, what if we want to continue improving the classification results? As you just discovered, there is no way that the decision tree can classify these four records, and no other machine learning method can do it either. The problem is in the data, not in the model. There are two main approaches to solve this issue. The first option is to try to obtain more data. With more data, we may find that low weight is positively correlated with low stroke risk and further splitting on the weight feature might benefit decreasing the Gini impurity. Obtaining more data is always better because your training model gets to see more data, which therefore reduces possible bias. Another option is to introduce more features. This essentially expands the feature space by more dimensions. For example, blood pressure might be another useful feature that might help us further increase the accuracy of the decision tree.

Now, let's look at the second node at depth 2. The records classified into this node are the following, given by the `df_right[df_right["high_oil_diet"]!="yes"]` code:

	weight	high_oil_diet	smoking	stroke_risk
1	low	no	yes	low
3	middle	no	no	low
7	low	no	yes	low
8	low	no	no	low
9	middle	no	yes	high
10	middle	no	no	low
12	middle	no	yes	high
14	middle	no	no	low

Figure 10.10 – Records classified into the second node at a depth of 2

Note that only two high stroke risk records are in this node. If we stop here, the Gini impurity is $1 - 0.25^2 - 0.75^2 = 0.375$, which is quite a low value.

If we further split on the smoking feature, note that out of all the non-smokers, four of them have a low stroke risk. Half of the smokers have a high stroke risk and the other half have a low stroke risk. This will give us a weighted Gini impurity of 0.25 if we're splitting on smoking.

If we further split on the weight feature, all the low-weight patients are at low stroke risk. Two out of five middle-weight records are at high risk. This will give us a weighted Gini impurity of $\frac{5}{8}\left(1 - \left(\frac{2}{5}\right)^2 - \left(\frac{3}{5}\right)^2\right) = 0.3$, which is also not bad.

For the two cases, the final decision trees look as follows. The following decision tree has smoking as the last splitting feature:

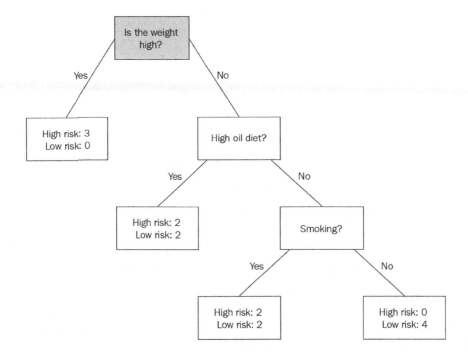

Figure 10.11 – Final decision tree, version 1

The other choice is splitting on weight, again at the second node, at depth 2. The following tree will be obtained:

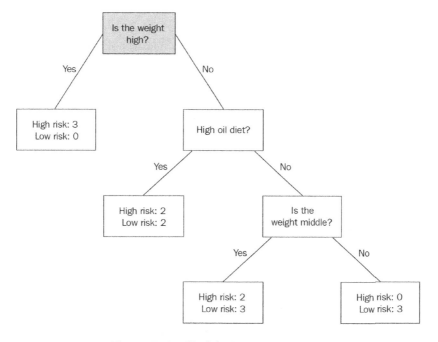

Figure 10.12 – Final decision tree, version 2

Now, we need to make some hard choices to decide the final shape of our decision trees.

Evaluating decision tree performance

In this section, let's evaluate the performance of the decision tree classifiers. If we stop at depth 2, we have the following confusion matrix. Note that for the unclassifiable first node at depth 2, we can randomly assign it a label. Here, I assign it as high stroke risk. The performance of our classifier can be summarized in the following table concisely:

	Ground truth high risk	Ground truth low risk
Predicted high risk	5	2
Predicted low risk	2	6

Figure 10.13 – Confusion matrix of a decision tree of depth 2

Generally, we identify high risk as positive, so the precision, recall, and F1 score are all $\frac{5}{7}$. If you have forgotten these concepts, you can review previous chapters.

If we don't stop at a depth of 2, the two finer decisions trees will have the following confusion matrices. Again, we assign the unclassifiable first node at depth 2 the label high stroke risk. However, the first node at depth 3 is also unclassifiable, because it contains equal high stroke risk and low stroke risk records. If they are classified as low-risk ones, then we essentially obtain the same result as the depth-of-2 one. Therefore, we assign the first leaf node at depth 3 a high stroke risk value. The new confusion matrix will look as follows:

	Ground truth high risk	Ground truth low risk
Predicted high risk	7	5
Predicted low risk	0	3

Figure 10.14 – Confusion matrix of a decision tree of depth 3, version 1

Note that we will have perfect recall, but the precision will be just slightly better than a random guess, $\frac{7}{12}$. The F1 score is $\frac{14}{19}$.

Next, let's check our final version. If we split with weight, the corresponding confusion matrix looks as shown in the following table:

	Ground truth high risk	Ground truth low risk
Predicted high risk	5	2
Predicted low risk	2	6

Figure 10.15 – Confusion matrix of a decision tree of depth 3, version 2

The precision recall and F1 score will be identical to the depth 2 decision tree. In real life, we usually prefer the simplest model possible if it is as good or almost as good as the complicated ones. Although the first depth 3 decision tree has a better F1 score, it also introduces one more unclassifiable node and one more rule. The second depth 3 decision tree does no better than the depth 2 one.

To constrain the complexity of the decision tree, there are usually three methods:

- **Constrain the depth of the tree**: This is probably the most direct way of constraining the complexity of the decision tree.

- **Constrain the lower bound of the number of records classified into a node**: For example, if after splitting one child node will only contain very few data points, then it is likely not a good splitting.

- **Constrain the lower bound of information gain**: In our case, the information gain means lower Gini impurity. For example, if we set a criterion that each splitting must lower the information gain by 0.1, then the splitting will likely stop soon, therefore confining the depth of the decision tree.

We will see algorithmic examples on a more complex dataset later in this chapter.

> **Note**
>
> When the number of records in a splitting node is small, the Gini impurity reduction is no longer as representative as before. It is the same idea as in statistical significance. The larger the sample size is, the more confident we are about the derived statistics.
>
> You may also hear the term *size of the decision tree*. Usually, the size is not the same as the depth. The size refers to the total number of nodes in a decision tree. For a symmetric decision tree, the relationship is exponential.

Exploring regression tree

The regression tree is very similar to a classification tree. A regression tree takes numerical features as input and predicts another numerical variable.

> **Note**
>
> It is perfectly fine to have mix-type features – for example, some of them are discrete and some of them are continuous. We won't cover these examples due to space limitations, but they are straightforward.

There are two very important visible differences:

- The output is not discrete labels but rather numerical values.

- The splitting rules are *not* similar to yes-or-no questions. They are usually inequalities for values of certain features.

In this section, we will just use a one-feature dataset to build a regression tree that the logistic regression classifier won't be able to classify. I created an artificial dataset with the following code snippet:

```
def price_2_revenue(price):
    if price < 85:
        return 70 * abs(price - 75)
    elif price < 95:
```

```
        return 10 * 80
    else:
        return 80 * (105 - price)

prices = np.linspace(80,100,8)
revenue = np.array([price_2_revenue(price) for price in
prices])
plt.rcParams.update({'font.size': 22})
plt.figure(figsize=(10,8))
plt.scatter(prices,revenue,s=300)
plt.xlabel("price")
plt.ylabel("total revenue")
plt.title("Price versus Revenue");
```

Let's say we want to investigate the relationship between the price of an item and its total revenue a day. If the price is set too low, the revenue will be lower because the price is low. If the price is too high, the revenue will also be low due to fewer amounts of the item being sold. The DataFrame looks as follows:

	Price	Revenue
0	80.000000	350.000000
1	82.857143	550.000000
2	85.714286	800.000000
3	88.571429	800.000000
4	91.428571	800.000000
5	94.285714	800.000000
6	97.142857	628.571429
7	100.000000	400.000000

Figure 10.16 – Price and total revenue DataFrame

The following visualization makes this scenario clearer:

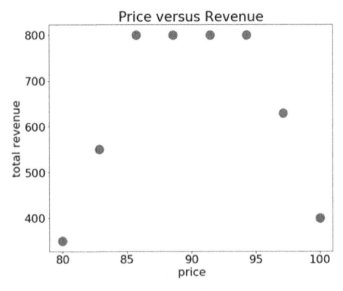

Figure 10.17 – The relationship between price and revenue

The relationship between price and revenue is clearly non-linear, and logistic regression won't be able to classify it. A linear regression will likely become a horizontal line. There are clearly three regions where different relationships between revenue and price apply.

Now, let's build a regression tree. Like the deduction of Gini impurity in the classification tree, we need a metric to measure the benefit of splitting. A natural choice is still the **sum of squared residuals**.

Let's start from the root node. We have eight data points, so there are essentially seven intervals where we can put the first splitting criteria into. For example, we can split at `price = 85`. Then, we use the average revenue on both sides to be our prediction, as follows. The code snippet for the visualization reads as follows:

```
plt.rcParams.update({'font.size': 22})
plt.figure(figsize=(12,8))
plt.scatter(prices,revenue,s=300)
plt.xlabel("price")
plt.ylabel("total revenue")
plt.title("Price versus Revenue")
threshold = 85
num_left = sum(prices < threshold)
ave_left = np.mean(revenue[prices < threshold])
```

```
num_right = sum(prices > threshold)
ave_right = np.mean(revenue[prices > threshold])


plt.axvline(threshold,color="red",linewidth=6)
plt.plot(prices[prices < threshold], [ave_left for _ in
range(num_left)],
         linewidth=6,linestyle=":",c="orange",
         label= "average revenue on the left half")
plt.plot(prices[prices > threshold], [ave_right for _ in
range(num_right)],
         linewidth=6,linestyle="--",c="green",
         label="average revenue on the right half");
plt.rcParams.update({'font.size': 16})
plt.legend(loc=[0.4,0]);
```

In the following figure, the dotted line represents the average price for the scenario when the price is lower than 85.0. The dashed line represents the average price for the scenario when the price is higher than 85.0:

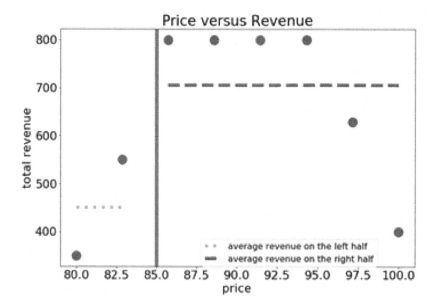

Figure 10.18 – Splitting at price 85.0

If we stop here, the regression tree will have a depth of 1 and looks like the following:

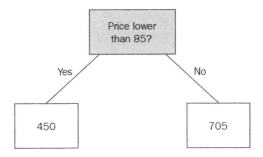

Figure 10.19 – A regression tree of depth 1

However, we haven't tested the other six splitting choices. Any splitting choice will have a corresponding sum of squared residuals and we would like to go over all the possibilities to determine the splitting that gives the minimal sum of squared residuals.

> **Note**
>
> Unlike Gini impurity, where we need to take a weighted average, the total sum of squared residuals is a simple summation. Gini impurity is not additive because it only takes a value between 0 and 1. Squared residuals are additive because each residual corresponds to one data point.

The following code snippet plots the sum of squared residuals against different choices of splitting. For completion, I plotted more than seven splitting values to visualize the stepped pattern:

```
def cal_ssr(arr):
    if len(arr)==0:
        return 0
    ave = np.mean(arr)
    return np.sum((arr-ave)**2)
splitting_values = np.linspace(80,100,20)
ssr_values = []
for splitting_value in splitting_values:
    ssr = cal_ssr(revenue[prices < splitting_value]) + cal_
ssr(revenue[prices > splitting_value])
    ssr_values.append(ssr)
```

```
plt.rcParams.update({'font.size': 22})
plt.figure(figsize=(12,8))
plt.xlabel("splitting prices")
plt.ylabel("sum of squared residuals")
plt.title("Splitting Price versus Sum of Squared Residuals")
plt.plot(splitting_values,ssr_values);
```

The result looks as in the following figure:

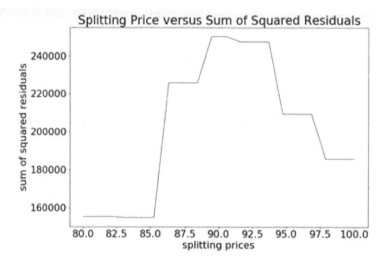

Figure 10.20 – Splitting value for the root node versus the sum of squared residuals

The visualization in the preceding figure indicates that 85.0, or any value between the second point and the third point, is the best splitting value for the root node.

There are only two records in the first node with a depth of 1, so we focus on the second node and repeat the process explained here. The code is omitted due to space limitations. The visualization of the sum of squared residuals is the following:

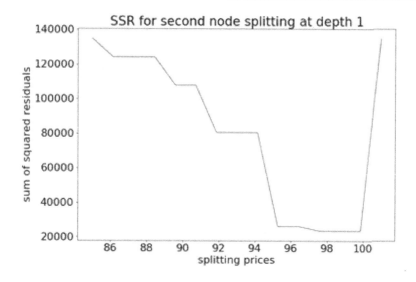

Figure 10.21 – Splitting choices at the second node at depth 1

Now, in order to achieve the minimum sum of squared error, we should put the last data point into one child node. However, you see that if we split at *98*, the penalty we pay is not increasing much. If we include another one, such as splitting at *96*, the penalty will soar. It may be a good idea to split at *96* rather than *98* because a leaf node containing too few records is not representative in general and often indicates overfitting. Here is the final look of our regression tree. You can calculate the regressed average prices in each region easily. The final regression tree looks as follows:

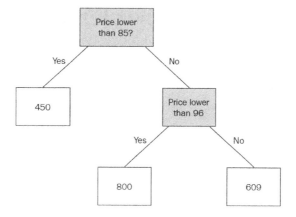

Figure 10.22 – Final regression tree

The following figure shows a visualization for the partition of the regions:

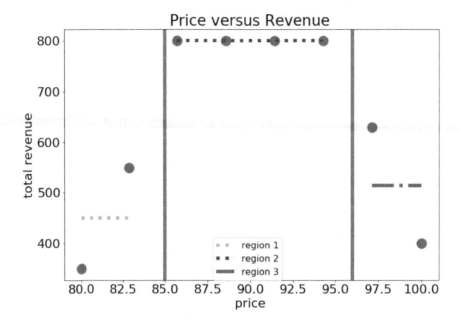

Figure 10.23 – Regressed values and region partitioning

In multi-feature cases, we will have more than one feature. The scanning of the best splitting value should include all the features, but the idea is the same.

Using tree models in scikit-learn

Before ending this chapter, let's try out the scikit-learn API. You can verify that the results agree with our models built from scratch. The following code snippet builds a regression tree with a maximum depth of 1 on the price-revenue data:

```
from sklearn.tree import DecisionTreeRegressor
from sklearn import tree
prices, revenue = prices.reshape(-1,1), revenue.reshape(-1,1)
regressor = DecisionTreeRegressor(random_state=0,max_depth=1)
regressor.fit(prices,revenue)
```

Now, we can visualize the tree with the following code snippet:

```
plt.figure(figsize=(12,8))
tree.plot_tree(regressor);
```

The tree structure looks as follows:

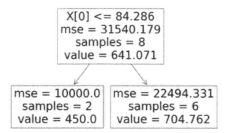

Figure 10.24 – Regression tree visualization of depth 1

Next, we limit the maximum depth to 2 and require the minimal number of records/samples in a leaf node to be 2. The code only requires a small change in the following line:

```
regressor = DecisionTreeRegressor(random_state=0,max_
depth=2,min_samples_leaf=2)
```

After running the code, we obtain the following tree structure:

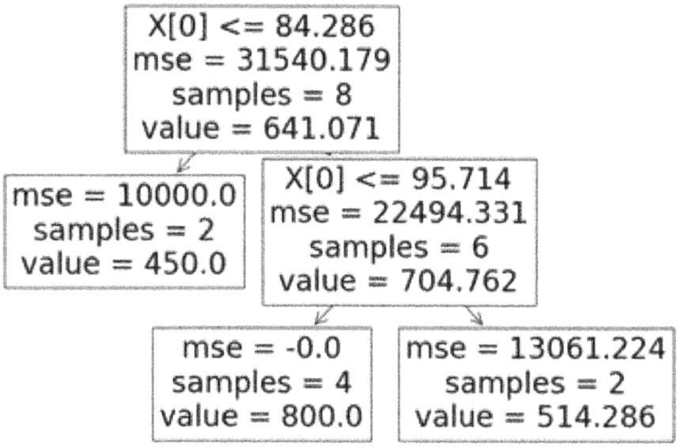

Figure 10.25 – Regression tree visualization of depth 2

As you can see, this produces exactly the same results as the one we built from scratch.

> **Note**
> The scikit-learn decision tree API can't explicitly handle categorical variables. There are various options, such as one-hot encoding, that you can use to bypass this limitation. You are welcome to explore the solutions on your own.

Summary

In this chapter, we started with the fundamental concepts of decision trees, and then built a simple classification tree and a regression tree from scratch. We went over the details and checked the consistency with the scikit-learn library API.

You may notice that tree methods do tend to overfit and might fail to reach the optimal model. In the next chapter, we will explore the so-called ensemble learning. They are meta-algorithms that can be used on top of many other machine learning algorithms as well.

11
Statistics for Ensemble Methods

In this chapter, we are going to investigate the ensemble method in terms of statistics and machine learning. The English word ensemble means a group of actors or musicians that work together as a whole. The ensemble method, or ensemble learning in machine learning, is not a specific machine learning algorithm, but a meta learning algorithm that builds on top of concrete machine learning algorithms to bundle them together to achieve better performance.

The ensemble method is not a single method, but a collection of many. In this chapter, we will cover the most important and representative ones.

We are going to cover the following in this chapter:

- Revisiting bias, variance, and memorization
- Understanding the bootstrapping and bagging techniques
- Understanding and using the boosting module
- Exploring random forests with scikit-learn

Let's get started!

Revisiting bias, variance, and memorization

Ensemble methods can improve the result of regression or classification tasks in that they can be applied to a group of classifiers or regressors to help build a final, augmented model.

Since we are talking about performance, we must have a metric for improving performance. Ensemble methods are designed to either reduce the variance or the bias of the model. Sometimes, we want to reduce both to reach a balanced point somewhere on the bias-variance trade-off curve.

We mentioned the concepts of bias and variance several times in earlier chapters. To help you understand how the idea of ensemble learning originated, I will revisit these concepts from the perspective of **data memorization**.

Let's say the following schematic visualization represents the relationship between the training dataset and the real-world total dataset. The solid line shown in the following diagram separates the *seen* world and the unseen part:

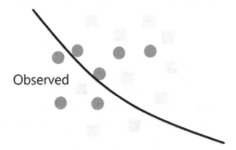

Figure 11.1 – A schematic representation of the observed data

Suppose we want to build a classifier that distinguishes between the circles and the squares. Unfortunately, our observed data is only a poor subset of the original data. In most cases, we *do not* know the entire set of real-world data, so we don't know how representative our accessible dataset is.

We want to train a model to classify the two classes; that is, square and circle. However, since our trained model will only be exposed to the limited observed data, different choices regarding which model we choose, as well as its complexity, will give us different results. Let's check out the following two decision boundaries.

First, we can draw a decision boundary as a horizontal line, as shown in the following diagram. This way, one square data point is misclassified as a round one:

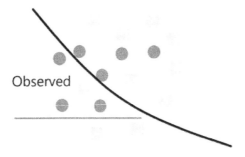

Figure 11.2 – A simple decision boundary

Alternatively, we can draw a decision boundary the other way, as shown in the following diagram. This zigzagging boundary will correctly classify both the square data points and the round data points:

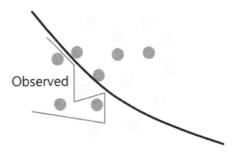

Figure 11.3 – A more complex decision boundary

Can you tell which classification method is better? With our hindsight of knowing what the entire dataset looks like, we can tell that neither is great. However, the difference is how much we want our model to learn from the known data. The structure of the training dataset will be *memorized* by the model. The question is, how much?

> **Note on memorization**
>
> Data memorization means that when a model is being trained, it is exposed to the training set, so it remembers the characteristics or structure of the training data. This is a good thing when the model has high bias because we want it to learn, but it becomes notoriously bad when its memory gets *stuck* in the training data and fails to generalize. Simply put, when a model memorizes and learns too little of the training data, it has high bias. When it learns too much, it has high variance.

Because of this, we have the following famous curve of the relationship between model complexity and error. This is probably the most important graph for any data scientist interview:

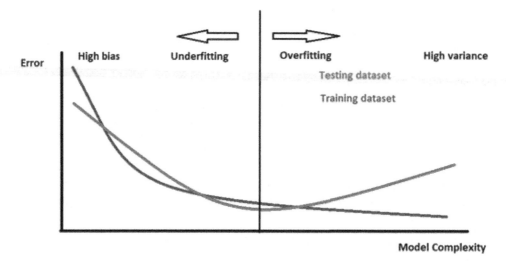

Figure 11.4 – The relationship between model complexity and error

When model complexity increases, the error – in terms of mean squared error or any other form – will always decrease monotonically. Recall that when we discussed R^2, we said that adding any predictor feature will increase the R^2 rate.

On the other hand, the performance of the learned model will start to decrease on the test dataset or other unseen datasets. This is because the model learns too many ungeneralizable characteristics, such as the random noise of the training data. In the preceding example, the zigzagging boundary doesn't apply to the rest of the dataset.

To summarize, underfitting means that the model is biased toward its original assumption, which means there's information that's missing from the training set. On the other hand, overfitting means that too many training set-specific properties were learned, so the model's complexity is too high.

> **Underfitting and overfitting**
>
> High bias corresponds to underfitting, while high variance corresponds to overfitting. Humans also fall into similar traps. For example, a CEO is very busy, so he/she does not have a lot of free time to spend with his/her kids. What is the most likely job of the kids' mother? Most people will likely say homemaker. However, I didn't specify the gender of the CEO. Well, the CEO is the mother!

As the power of machine learning algorithms grows, the necessity to curb overfitting and find a balance between bias and variance is prominent. Next, we'll learn about the bootstrapping and bagging techniques, both of which can help us solve these issues.

Understanding the bootstrapping and bagging techniques

Bootstrapping is a pictorial word. It allows us to imagine someone pulling themselves up by their bootstraps. In other words, if no one is going to help us, then we need to help ourselves. In statistics, however, this is a sampling method. If there is not enough data, we help ourselves by creating more data.

Imagine that you have a small dataset and you want to build a classifier/estimator with this limited amount of data. In this case, you can perform cross-validation. Cross-validation techniques such as 10-fold cross-validation will decrease the number of records in each fold even further. We can take all the data as the training data, but you likely will end up with a model with very high variance. What should we do, then?

The bootstrapping method says that if the dataset being used is a sample of the unknown data in the dataset, why not try **resampling** again? *The bootstrap method creates new training sets by uniformly sampling from the dataset and then replacing it.* This process can be repeated as many times as it's necessary to create many new training datasets. Each new training set can be used to train a classifier/regressor.

Besides the magic of creating training datasets from thin air, bootstrapping has two significant advantages:

- Bootstrapping increases the randomness in the training set. It is likely that such randomness will help us avoid capturing the intrinsic random noise in the original training set.

- Bootstrapping can help build the confidence interval of calculated statistics (plural form of statistic). Suppose we run bootstrapping N times and obtain N new samples. By doing this, we can calculate the standard variation of a selected statistic, which is not possible without bootstrapping.

Before we move on, let's examine how bootstrapping works on a real dataset. We are going to use the Boston Housing Dataset, which you can find in its official GitHub repository: `https://github.com/PacktPublishing/Essential-Statistics-for-Non-STEM-Data-Analysts`. You can also find the meanings of each column in the respective Jupyter notebook. It contains information regarding the *per capita crime rate by town, average number of rooms per dwelling*, and so on.

Later in this chapter, we will use these features to predict the target feature; that is, *the median value of owner-occupied homes* (medv).

> **Turning a regression problem into a classification problem**
>
> I am going to build a classifier for demonstration purposes, so I will transform the continuous variable, medv, into a binary variable that indicates whether a house's price is in the upper 50% or lower 50% of the market.

The first few lines of records in the original dataset look as follows. Due to space limitations, most of the code, except for the crucial pieces, will be omitted here:

	crim	zn	indus	chas	nox	rm	age	dis	rad	tax	ptratio	b	lstat	medv
0	0.00632	18.0	2.31	0	0.538	6.575	65.2	4.0900	1	296	15.3	396.90	4.98	24.0
1	0.02731	0.0	7.07	0	0.469	6.421	78.9	4.9671	2	242	17.8	396.90	9.14	21.6
2	0.02729	0.0	7.07	0	0.469	7.185	61.1	4.9671	2	242	17.8	392.83	4.03	34.7
3	0.03237	0.0	2.18	0	0.458	6.998	45.8	6.0622	3	222	18.7	394.63	2.94	33.4
4	0.06905	0.0	2.18	0	0.458	7.147	54.2	6.0622	3	222	18.7	396.90	5.33	36.2

Figure 11.5 – Main section of the Boston Housing Dataset

First, let's plot the distribution of the *index of accessibility to radial highways* variable. Here, you can see that this distribution is quite messy; no simple distribution can model it parametrically. Let's say that this is our entire dataset for selecting the training dataset in this demo:

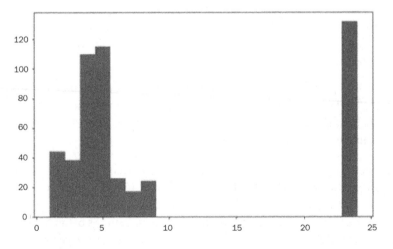

Figure 11.6 – Index of accessibility to radial highways distribution (the dataset contains 506 records)

Now, let's select 50 pieces of data to be our training/observed data. This distribution looks as follows. Notice that the *y*-axis has a different scale. The functions we'll be using to perform sampling can be found in the scikit-learn library. Please refer to the relevant Jupyter notebook for details:

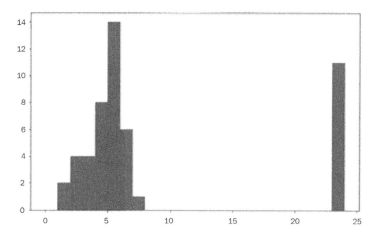

Figure 11.7 – Index of accessibility to radial highways distribution (our original sample, which contains 50 records)

Next, let's run bootstrapping 1,000 times. For each round, we'll sample 25 records. Then, we will plot these new samples on the same histogram plot. Here, you can see that the overlapping behavior drops some characteristics of the 50-record sample, such as the very high peak on the left-hand side:

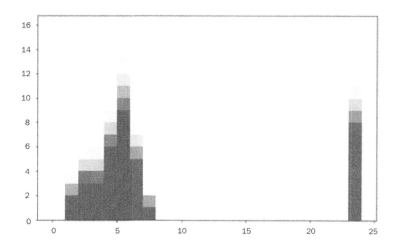

Figure 11.8 – Overlapping 1,000 times with our bootstrapped sample containing 25 records

Next, we will learn how this will help decrease the variance of our classifiers by aggregating the classifiers that were trained on the bootstrapped sets. The word bagging is essentially an abbreviation of bootstrap aggregation. This is what we will study in the remainder of this section.

The premise of bagging is to train some weak classifiers or regressors on the newly bootstrapped training sets and then aggregating them together through a majority vote/averaging mechanism to obtain the final prediction.

The following code performs preprocessing and dataset splitting. I am going to use a decision tree as our default weak classifier, so feature normalization won't be necessary:

```python
from sklearn.model_selection import train_test_split
import numpy as np
boston_bag = boston.copy()
boston_bag["medv"] = boston_bag["medv"].apply(lambda x: int(x>=
np.median(boston_bag["medv"])))
boston_bag_train, boston_bag_test = train_test_split(boston_
bag,train_size=0.7,shuffle=True,random_state=1)
boston_bag_train_X, boston_bag_train_y = boston_bag_train.
drop(["medv"],axis=1).to_numpy(),  boston_bag_train["medv"].
to_numpy()
boston_bag_test_X, boston_bag_test_y = boston_bag_test.
drop(["medv"],axis=1).to_numpy(),  boston_bag_test["medv"].
to_numpy()
```

Note that I explicitly made a copy of the boston DataFrame.

Now, I'm going to try and reproduce something to show the overfitting on the test set with a single decision tree. I will control the maximal depth of the single decision tree in order to control the complexity of the model. Then, I'll plot the F1 score with respect to the tree depth, both on the training set and the test set.

Without any constraints regarding model complexity, let's take a look at how the classification tree performs on the training dataset. The following code snippet plots the unconstrained classification tree:

```python
from sklearn.tree import DecisionTreeClassifier
from sklearn.metrics import f1_score
from sklearn import tree
clf = DecisionTreeClassifier(random_state=0)
clf.fit(boston_bag_train_X, boston_bag_train_y)
```

```
plt.figure(figsize=(12,8))
tree.plot_tree(clf);
```

By doing this, we obtain a huge decision tree with a depth of 10. It is hard to see the details clearly, but the visualization of this is shown in the following diagram:

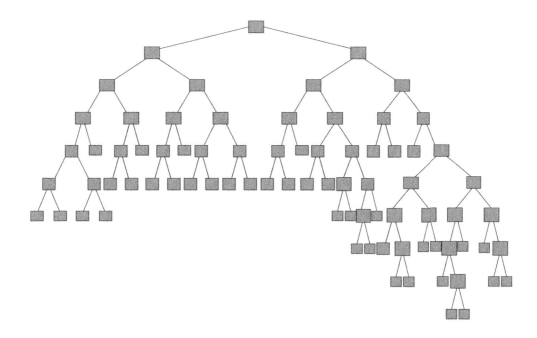

Figure 11.9 – Unconstrained single decision tree

The F1 score can be calculated by running the following:

```
f1_score(boston_bag_train_y,clf.predict(boston_bag_train_X))
```

This is exactly 1. This means we've obtained the best performance possible.

Next, I'll build a sequence of classifiers and limit the maximal depth it can span. I'll calculate the F1 score of the model on the train set and test set in the same way. The code for this is as follows:

```
train_f1 = []
test_f1 = []
depths = range(1,11)
for depth in depths:
    clf = DecisionTreeClassifier(random_state=0,max_
```

```
depth=depth)
    clf.fit(boston_bag_train_X, boston_bag_train_y)
    train_f1.append(f1_score(boston_bag_train_y,clf.
predict(boston_bag_train_X)))
    test_f1.append(f1_score(boston_bag_test_y,clf.
predict(boston_bag_test_X)))
```

The following code snippet plots the two curves:

```
plt.figure(figsize=(10,6))
plt.rcParams.update({'font.size': 22})
plt.plot(depths,train_f1,label="Train Set F1 Score")
plt.plot(depths,test_f1, label="Test Set F1 Score")
plt.legend()
plt.xlabel("Model Complexity")
plt.ylabel("F1 Score")
plt.title("F1 Score on Train and Test Set");
```

The following graph is what we get. Note that the F1 score is an inverse indicator/metric of the error. The higher the F1 score is, the better the model is in general:

Figure 11.10 – F1 score versus model complexity

Although the F1 score on the training set continues increasing to reach the maximum, the F1 score on the test set stops increasing once the depth reaches 4 and gradually decreases beyond that. It is clear that after a depth of 4, we are basically overfitting the decision tree.

Next, let's see how bagging would help. We are going to utilize the BaggingClassifier API in scikit-learn. First, since we roughly know that the critical depth is 4, we'll build a base estimator of such depth before creating a bagging classifier marked out of 10 for it. Each time, we'll draw samples from the training dataset to build a base estimator. The code for this reads as follows:

```
from sklearn.ensemble import BaggingClassifier


base_estimator = DecisionTreeClassifier(random_state = 0, max_
depth = 4)
bagging_clf = BaggingClassifier(base_estimator=base_estimator,
                                n_estimators=10,
                                n_jobs=20,
                                max_samples=0.7,
                                random_state=0,)


bagging_clf.fit(boston_bag_train_X, boston_bag_train_y)
```

Next, let's plot the relationship between the F1 score and the number of base estimators:

```
train_f1 = []
test_f1 = []
n_estimators = [2**i+1 for i in range(1,8)]
for n_estimator in n_estimators:
    bagging_clf = BaggingClassifier(base_estimator=base_
estimator,
                                    n_estimators=n_estimator,
                                    n_jobs=20,
                                    random_state=0,)
    bagging_clf.fit(boston_bag_train_X, boston_bag_train_y);
    train_f1.append(f1_score(boston_bag_train_y, bagging_clf.
predict(boston_bag_train_X)))
    test_f1.append(f1_score(boston_bag_test_y, bagging_clf.
predict(boston_bag_test_X)))
plt.figure(figsize=(10,6))
plt.plot(n_estimators,train_f1,label="Train Set F1 Score")
plt.plot(n_estimators,test_f1, label="Test Set F1 Score")
plt.xscale("log")
plt.legend()
```

```
plt.xlabel("Number of Estimators")
plt.ylabel("F1 Score")
plt.title("F1 Score on Train and Test Set");
```

The resulting of running the preceding code is displayed in the following graph. Note that the *x*-axis is on the log scale:

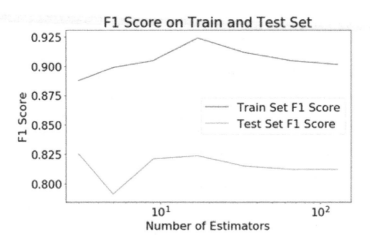

Figure 11.11 – F1 score versus number of estimators

As you can see, even on the training set, the F1 score stops increasing and begins to saturate and decline a little bit (pay attention to the *y*-axis), which indicates that there is still an intrinsic difference between the training set and the test set. There may be several reasons for this performance, and I will point out two here:

- The first reason is that it is possible that we are intrinsically unlucky; that is, there was some significant difference between the training set and the test set in the splitting step.

- The second reason is that our depth restriction doesn't successfully constrain the complexity of the decision tree.

What we can do here is try another random seed and impose more constraints on the splitting condition. For example, changing the following two lines will produce different results:

- First, we'll change how the dataset is split:

```
boston_bag_train, boston_bag_test = train_test_
split(boston_bag,train_size=0.7,shuffle=True,random_
state=1)
```

- Second, we'll impose a new constraint on the base estimator so that a node must be large enough to be split:

```
base_estimator = DecisionTreeClassifier(random_state = 0,
max_depth = 4,min_samples_split=30)
```

Due to further imposed regularization, it is somewhat clearer that the performance of both the training set and the test set is consistent:

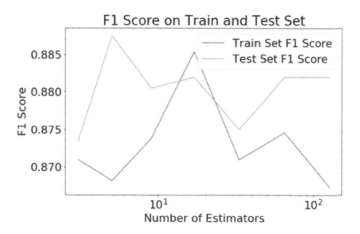

Figure 11.12 – F1 score under more regularization

Note that the scale on the *y*-axis is much smaller than the previous one.

> **Dealing with inconsistent results**
>
> It is totally normal if the result is not very consistent when you're training/ evaluating machine learning models. In such cases, try different sets of data to eliminate the effect of randomness or run cross-validation.
>
> If your result is inconsistent with the expected behavior, take steps to examine the whole pipeline. Start with dataset completeness and tidiness, then preprocessing and model assumptions. It is also possible that the way the results are being visualized or presented is flawed.

Understanding and using the boosting module

Unlike bagging, which focuses on reducing variance, the goal of boosting is to reduce bias without increasing variance.

Bagging creates a bunch of base estimators with *equal* importance, or weights, in terms of determining the final prediction. The data that's fed into the base estimators is also *uniformly* resampled from the training set.

Determining the possibility of parallel processing

From the description of bagging we provided, you may imagine that it is relatively easy to run bagging algorithms. Each process can independently perform sampling and model training. Aggregation is only performed at the last step, when all the base estimators have been trained.

In the preceding code snippet, I set n_jobs = 20 to build the bagging classifier. When it is being trained, 20 cores on the host machine will be used at most.

Boosting solves a different problem. The primary goal is to create an estimator with low bias. In the world of boosting, both the samples and the weak classifiers are not equal. During the training process, some will be more important than others. Here is how it works:

1. First, we assign a weight to each record in the training data. Without special prior knowledge, all the weights are equal.

2. We then train our first base/weak estimator on the entire dataset. After training, we increase the weights of those records, which are predicted with wrong labels.

3. Once the weights have been updated, we create the next base estimator. The difference here is that those records that were misclassified by previous estimators, or whose values seriously deviated from the true value provided by regression, now receive higher attention. Misclassifying them again will result in higher penalties, which will, in turn, increase their weight.

4. Finally, we iterate *step 3* until the preset iteration limit is reached or accuracy stops improving.

Note that boosting is also a meta algorithm. This means that at different iterations, the base estimator can be completely different from the previous one. You can use logistic regression in the first iteration, use a neural network at the second iteration, and then use a decision tree at the final iteration.

There are two classical boosting methods we can use: **adaptive boosting (AdaBoost)** and **gradient descent boosting**.

First, we'll look at AdaBoost, where there are two kinds of weights:

- The weights of the training set records, which change at every iteration
- The weights of the estimators, which are determined inversely by their training errors

The weight of a record indicates the probability that this record will be selected in the training set for the next base estimator. For the estimator, the lower its training error is, the more voting power it has in the final weighted classifier.

The following is the pseudo-algorithm for AdaBoost:

1. Initialize the equal-weight training data with weight $\{w_i\}$ and a maximal iteration of k.

2. At round k, sample the data according to weight $\{w_i\}$ and build a weak classifier, c_k.

3. Obtain e_k, the error of c_k, and calculate its corresponding weight; that is,

$$\alpha_k = \frac{1}{2} ln\left(\frac{1 - e_k}{e_k}\right)$$

4. Update the weight of each record for round $k + 1$, $w_i(k + 1) \approx w_i(k)e^{-\alpha_k}$ if classified right; otherwise, $w_i(k + 1) \approx w_i(k)e^{+\alpha_k}$.

5. Repeat *steps 2* to *4 k* times and obtain the final classifier, which should be proportional to the form $\Sigma \; \alpha_k c_k$.

> **Intuition behind the AdaBoost algorithm**
>
> At *step 3*, if there are no errors, c_k will have an infinitely large weight. This intuitively makes sense because if one weak classifier does the job, why bother creating more?
>
> At *step 4*, if a record is misclassified, its weight will be increased exponentially; otherwise, its weight will be decreased exponentially. Do a thought experiment here: if a classifier correctly classifies most records but only a few, then those records that have been misclassified will be $e^{2\alpha_k}$ times more likely to be selected in the next round. This also makes sense.

AdaBoost is only suitable for classification tasks. For regression tasks, we can use the **Gradient Descent Boost (GDB)** algorithm. However, please note that GDB can also be used to perform classification tasks or even ranking tasks.

Let's take a look at the intuition behind GDB. In regression tasks, often, we want to minimize the mean squared error, which takes the form $\frac{1}{n}\Sigma\ (y_i-y_i')^2$, where y_i' means the true value and y_i is a regressed value, $y_i = f_k(x_i)$. The weak estimator, f_k, at round k has a sum of residual $r_k = \Sigma\ (y_i'-y_i)$.

Sequentially, at iteration $k + 1$, we want to build another base estimator to remove such residuals. If you know calculus and look closely, you'll see that the form of the residual is proportional to the derivative of the mean squared error, also known as the loss function.

This is the key: improving the base estimator is not achieved by weighing records like it is in AdaBoost, but by deliberately constructing it to predict the residuals, which happens to be the gradient of the MSE. If a different loss function is used, the residual argument won't be valid, but we still want to predict the gradients. The math here is beyond the scope of this book, but you get the point.

> **Does GDB work with the logistic regression base learner?**
>
> The answer is a conditional *no*. In general, GDB doesn't work on simple logistic regression or other simple linear models. The reason is that the addition of linear models is still a linear mode. This is basically the essence of being linear. If a linear model misclassifies some records, another linear model will likely misclassify them. If it doesn't, the effect will be smeared at the last averaging step too.
>
> This is probably the reason behind the illusion that ensemble algorithms are only applicable to tree-based methods. Most examples are only given with tree base estimators/learners. People just don't use them on linear models.

As an example, let's see how GDB works on the regression task of predicting the median price of Boston housing.

The following code snippet builds the training dataset, the test dataset, and the regressor:

```
from sklearn.ensemble import GradientBoostingRegressor
from sklearn.metrics import mean_squared_error


boston_boost = boston.copy()
boston_boost_train, boston_boost_test = train_test_
split(boston_boost,
                                                     train_
size=0.7,

shuffle=True,
```

```
                                                     random_
state=1)
```

```
boston_boost_train_X, boston_boost_train_y = boston_boost_
train.drop(["medv"],axis=1).to_numpy(), boston_boost_
train["medv"].to_numpy()
```

```
boston_boost_test_X, boston_boost_test_y = boston_boost_test.
drop(["medv"],axis=1).to_numpy(), boston_boost_test["medv"].
to_numpy()
```

```
gdb_reg = GradientBoostingRegressor(random_state=0)
```

```
reg.fit(boston_boost_train_X, boston_boost_train_y);
```

```
print(mean_squared_error(reg.predict(boston_boost_train_X),
boston_boost_train_y))
```

Here, the MSE on the training set is about **1.5**. On the test set, it is about **7.1**, which is likely due to overfitting. Now, let's limit the number of iterations so that we can inspect the turning point. The following code snippet will help us visualize this:

```
train_mse = []
test_mse = []
n_estimators = range(10,300,20)
for n_estimator in n_estimators:
    gdb_reg = GradientBoostingRegressor(random_state=0,n_
estimators=n_estimator)
    gdb_reg.fit(boston_boost_train_X, boston_boost_train_y);
    train_mse.append(mean_squared_error(gdb_reg.predict(boston_
boost_train_X), boston_boost_train_y))
    test_mse.append(mean_squared_error(gdb_reg.predict(boston_
boost_test_X), boston_boost_test_y))
plt.figure(figsize=(10,6))
plt.plot(n_estimators,train_mse,label="Train Set MSE")
plt.plot(n_estimators,test_mse, label="Test Set MSE")
plt.legend()
plt.xlabel("Number of Estimators")
plt.ylabel("MSE")
plt.title("MSE Score on Train and Test Set");
```

What we've obtained here is the classic behavior of bias-variance trade-off, as shown in the following graph. Note that the error doesn't grow significantly after the turning point. This is the idea behind decreasing bias without exploding the variance of boosting:

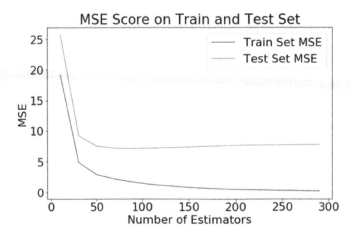

Figure 11.13 – Number of estimators in terms of boosting and MSE

At this point, you have seen how boosting works. In the next section, we will examine a model so that you fully understand the what bagging is.

Exploring random forests with scikit-learn

Now that we're near the end of this chapter, I would like to briefly discuss random forests. Random forests are not strictly ensemble algorithms because they are an extension of tree methods. However, unlike bagging decision trees, they are different in an important way.

In *Chapter 10, Statistical Techniques for Tree-Based Methods*, we discussed how splitting the nodes in a decision tree is a greedy approach. The greedy approach doesn't always yield the best possible tree and it's easy to overfit without proper penalization. *The random forest algorithm does not only bootstrap the samples, but also the features.* Let's take our stroke risk dataset as an example. The heavy weight is the optimal feature to split on, but this rules out 80% of all possible trees, along with the other features of the root node. The random forest algorithm, at every splitting decision point, samples a subset of the features and picks the best among them. This way, it is possible for the suboptimal features to be selected.

Non-greedy algorithms

The idea of not using a greedy algorithm to achieve the potential optimal is a key concept in AI. For example, in the game Go, performing a short-term optimal move may lead to a long-term strategic disadvantage. A human Go master is capable of farseeing such consequences. The most advanced AI can also make decisions regarding what a human does, but at the cost of exponentially expensive computation power. The balance between short-term gain and long-term gain is also a key concept in reinforcement learning.

Let's take a look a code example of random forest regression to understand how the corresponding API in scikit-learn is called:

```
train_mse = []
test_mse = []
n_estimators = range(10,300,20)
for n_estimator in n_estimators:
    regr = RandomForestRegressor(max_depth=6,
                                 random_state=0,
                                 n_estimators=n_estimator,
                                 max_features="sqrt")
    regr.fit(boston_boost_train_X, boston_boost_train_y);
    train_mse.append(mean_squared_error(regr.predict(boston_
boost_train_X), boston_boost_train_y))
    test_mse.append(mean_squared_error(regr.predict(boston_
boost_test_X), boston_boost_test_y))
plt.figure(figsize=(10,6))
plt.plot(n_estimators,train_mse,label="Train Set MSE")
plt.plot(n_estimators,test_mse, label="Test Set MSE")
plt.legend()
plt.xlabel("Number of Estimators")
plt.ylabel("MSE")
plt.title("MSE Score on Train and Test Set");
```

The visualization we receive is also a typical bias-variance trade-off. Note that the limitation of the max depth for each individual decision tree being set to 6 can significantly decrease the power of the model anyway:

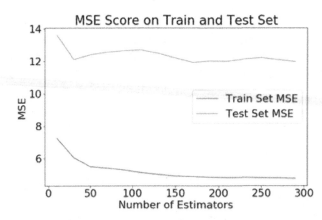

Figure 11.14 – Estimators versus MSE in random forest regression

One of the key features of random forests is their robustness against overfitting. The relative flat curve of the test set's MSE is proof of this claim.

Summary

In this chapter, we discussed several important ensemble learning algorithms, including bootstrapping for creating more training sets, bagging for aggregating weak estimators, boosting for improving accuracy without increasing variance too much, and the random forest algorithm.

Ensemble algorithms are very powerful as they are models that build on top of basic models. Understanding them will benefit you in the long run in terms of your data science career.

In the next chapter, we will examine some common mistakes and go over some best practices in data science.

Section 4:
Appendix

Section 4 covers some real-world best practices that I have collected in my experience. It also identifies common pitfalls that you should avoid. Exercises, projects, and instructions for further learning are also provided.

This section consists of the following chapters:

12
A Collection of Best Practices

This chapter serves as a special chapter to investigate three important topics that are prevalent in data science nowadays: **data source quality**, **data visualization quality**, and **causality interpretation**. This has generally been a missing chapter in peer publications, but I consider it essential to stress the following topics. I want to affirm that you, as a future data scientist, will practice data science while following the best practice tips as introduced in this chapter.

After finishing this chapter, you will be able to do the following:

- Understand the importance of data quality
- Avoid using misleading data visualization
- Spot common errors in causality arguments

First, let's start with the beginning of any data science project: the data itself.

Understanding the importance of data quality

Remember the old adage that says *garbage in, garbage out*? This is especially true in data science. The quality of data will influence the entire downstream project. It is difficult for people who work on the downstream tasks to identify the sources of possible issues.

In the following section, I will present three examples in which poor data quality causes difficulties.

Understanding why data can be problematic

The three examples fall into three different categories that represent three different problems:

- Inherent bias in data
- Miscommunication in large-scale projects
- Insufficient documentation and irreversible preprocessing

Let's start with the first example, which is quite a recent one and is pretty much a hot topic—face generation.

Bias in data sources

The first example we are going to look at is bias in data. *Face-Depixelizer* is a tool that is capable of significantly increasing the resolution of a human face in an image. You are recommended to give it a try on the Colab file the developers released. It is impressive that **Generative Adversarial Network (GAN)** is able to create faces of human in images that are indistinguishable from real photos.

Generative adversarial learning

Generative adversarial learning is a class of machine learning frameworks that enable the algorithms to compete with each other. One algorithm creates new data, such as sounds or images, by imitating original data, while another algorithm tries to distinguish the original data and the created data. This adversarial process can result in powerful machine learning models that can create images, sounds, or even videos where humans are unable to tell whether they are real.

However, people soon started encountering this issue within the model. Among all of them, I found the following example discovered by Twitter user @Chicken3egg to be the most disturbing one. The image on the left is the original picture, with low resolution, and the one on the right is the picture that Face-Depixelizer generated:

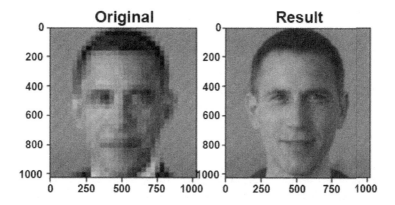

Figure 12.1 – Face-Depixelizer example on the Obama picture

If you are familiar with American politics, you know the picture on the left is former President Barack Obama. However, the generated picture turns out to be a completely different guy. For a discussion on this behavior, please refer to the original tweet: `https://twitter.com/Chicken3gg/status/1274314622447820801`.

This issue is nothing new in today's machine learning research and has attracted the attention of the community. A machine learning model is nothing but a digestor of data, which outputs what it learns from the data. Nowadays, there is little diversity in human facial datasets, especially in the case of people from minority backgrounds, such as African Americans. Not only will the characteristics of the human face be learned by the model, but also its inherent bias.

This is a good example where flawed data may cause issues. If such models are deployed in systems such as CCTV (closed-circuit television), the ethical consequences could be problematic. To minimize such effects, we need to scrutinize our data before feeding it into machine learning models.

The machine learning community has been working to address the data bias issue. As the author of this book, I fully support the ethical progress in data science and machine learning. For example, as of October 2020, the author of Face-Depixelizer has addressed the data bias issue. You can find the latest updates in the official repository at `https://github.com/tg-bomze/Face-Depixelizer`.

Miscommunication in large-scale projects

When a project increases in size, miscommunication can lead to inconsistent data and cause difficulties. Here, size may refer to code base size, team size, or the complexity of the organizational structure. The most famous example is the loss of the 125 million-dollar Mars climate orbiter from NASA in September 1999.

Back then, NASA's Jet Propulsion Laboratory and Lockheed Martin collaborated and built a Mars orbiter. However, the engineering team at Lockheed Martin used English units of measurement and the team at Jet Propulsion Laboratory used the conventional metric system. For readers who are not familiar with the English unit, here is an example. Miles are used to measure long distances, where 1 mile is about 1,600 meters, which is 1.6 kilometers.

The orbiter took more than 280 days to reach Mars but failed to function. The reason was later identified to be a mistake in unit usage.

Lorelle Young, president of the U.S. Metric Association, commented that two measurement systems should not be used as the metric system is the standard measurement language of all sophisticated science.

> **Units in the United States**
>
> Technically speaking, the unit system in the United States is also different from the English unit system. There are some subtle differences. Some states choose the so-called United States customary, while others have adopted metric units as official units.

This may not be a perfect example for our data science project since none of our projects will ever be as grand or important as NASA's Mars mission. The point is that as projects become more complex and teams grow larger, it is also easier to introduce data inconsistency into projects.

> **The weakest stage of a project**
>
> A point when a team upgrades their systems, dependencies, or algorithms is the easiest stage to make mistakes and it is imperative that you pay the utmost attention at this stage.

Insufficient documentation and irreversible preprocessing

The third most common reason for poor quality data is the absence of documentation and irreversible preprocessing. We briefly talked about this in *Chapter 1, Fundamentals of Data Collection, Cleaning, and Preprocessing*. Data documentation is sometimes referred to as metadata. It is the data about the dataset itself; for example, information about how the data was obtained, who is responsible for queries with respect to the data, and the meanings of abbreviations in the dataset.

In data science teams, especially for cross-team communication, such information is often omitted based on my observations, but they are actually very important. You cannot assume that the data speaks for itself. For example, I have used the Texas county dataset throughout this book, but the meaning of the rural code can't be revealed unless you read the specs carefully.

Even if the original dataset is accompanied by metadata, irreversible (pre)processing still has the potential to damage the data's quality. One example I introduced earlier in *Chapter 2, Essential Statistics for Data Assessment*, is the categorization of numerical values. Such preprocessing results in the loss of information and there isn't a way for people who take the data from you to recover it. Similar processing includes imputation and min-max scaling.

The key to solving such issues is to *embrace the culture of documentation and reproducibility*. In a data science team, it is not enough to share a result or a presentation; it is important to share a reproducible result with well-written and easy-to-understand documentation. In such instances, a Jupyter notebook is better than a script because you can put text nicely with the code together. For the R ecosystem, there is R Markdown, which is similar to a Jupyter notebook. You can demonstrate the pipeline of preprocessing and algorithm functioning in an interactive fashion.

The idea of painless reproducibility comes from different levels, and not only in a data science project. For a general Python project, a `requirements.txt` file specifying versions of dependencies can ensure the consistency of a Python environment. For our book, in order to avoid possible hassles for readers who are not familiar with pip or virtualenv, the Python package management and virtual environment management tools, I have chosen Google Colab so that you can run the companying codes directly in the browser.

A general idea of reproducibility

A common developer joke you might hear is 'This works on my machine." Reproducibility has been a true headache at different levels. For data science projects, in order to make code and presentations reproducible, Jupyter Notebooks, R Markdown, and many other tools were developed. In terms of the consistency of libraries and packages, we have package management tools such as pip for Python and npm for JavaScript. In order to enable large systems to work across different hardware and environments, Docker was created to isolate configurations of a running instance from its host machine. All these technologies solve the same problem of painlessly reproducing a result or performance consistently. This is a philosophical concept in engineering that you should keep in mind.

In the next section, we'll look at another aspect of common pitfalls in data science–misleading graphs.

Avoiding the use of misleading graphs

Graphics convey much more information than words. Not everyone understands P-values or statistical arguments, but almost everyone can tell if one piece of a pie plot is larger than another piece of pie plot, or if two-line plots share a similar trend. However, there are many ways in which graphs can also damage the quality of a visualization or mislead readers.

In this section, we will examine two examples. Let's start with the first example – misleading graphs.

Example 1 – COVID-19 trend

The following graph is a screenshot taken in early April 2020. A news channel showed this graph of new COVID-19 cases per day in the United States. Do you spot anything strange?

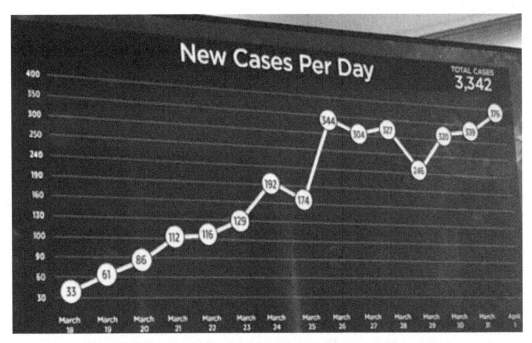

Figure 12.2 – A screenshot of COVID-19 coverage of a news channel

The issue is on the *y* axis. If you look closely, the *y* axis tickers are not separated equally but in a strange pattern. For example, the space between 30 and 60 is the same as the space between 240 and 250. The distances vary from 10 up to 50.

Now, I will regenerate this plot without mashing the *y* axis tickers with the following code snippet:

```python
import pandas as pd
import matplotlib.pyplot as plt
dates =  pd.date_range('2020-03-18', periods=15, freq='D')
daily_cases = [33,61,86,112,116,129,192,174,344,304,327,246,32
0,339,376]
plt.rcParams.update({'font.size': 22})
plt.figure(figsize=(10,6))
plt.plot( dates,daily_cases, label='Daily Cases', marker='o')
plt.legend()
plt.gca().tick_params(axis='x', which='major', labelsize=14)
plt.xlabel('Dates')
plt.ylabel('New Daily Cases')
plt.title('New Daily Cases Versus Dates')
plt.xticks(rotation=45)
for x,y in zip(dates, daily_cases):
    plt.text(x, y, str(y))
```

You will see the following visualization:

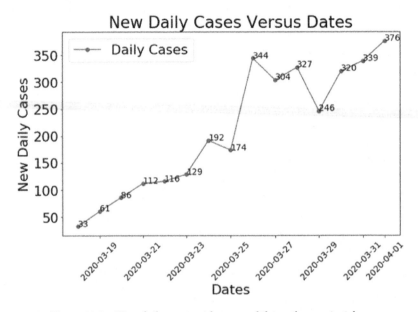

Figure 12.3 – New daily cases without modifying the *y*-axis tickers

What's the difference between this one and the one that the news channel showed to its audience? The jump from 174 to 344 is much more significant, while the increase from 246 to 376 is also more dramatic. The news channel manipulated the space used to represent 10 or 30 to represent 50 when the number grew large. This way, the visual impression is much weaker.

Next, let's look at another example that has the ability to confuse readers.

Example 2 – Bar plot cropping

We are going to use the US county data for this example. Here, I am loading the data with the following code snippet we used in *Chapter 4, Sampling and Inferential Statistics*. The difference is that this time, I am looking at the influence code of all counties in the United States, and not limited to just Texas. The following code snippet performs the visualization:

```
from collections import Counter
df = pd.read_excel('PopulationEstimates.xls',skiprows=2)
counter = Counter(df.tail(-1)['Urban_Influence_Code_2003'])
codes = [key for key in counter.keys() if str(key) != 'nan']
heights = [counter[code] for code in codes]
```

```
plt.figure(figsize=(10,6))
plt.bar(list(map(lambda x: str(x),codes)), heights)
plt.xticks(rotation=45);
plt.title('Urban Influence Code for All Counties in the US')
plt.xlabel('Urban Influence Code')
plt.ylabel('Count');
```

The result looks like the following:

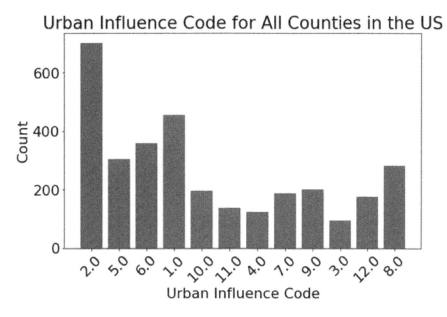

Figure 12.4 – Urban influence code counting for all counties in the US

Note that I deliberately changed the urban influence code to a string and indicated that it is a categorical variable, and not a numerical one. According to the definition, the urban influence code is a 12-level classification of metropolitan counties developed by the United States Department of Agriculture.

Now, this is what happens if I add one more line to the previous code snippet:

```
plt.gca().set_ylim([80,800])
```

We then obtain the data as shown in the following diagram:

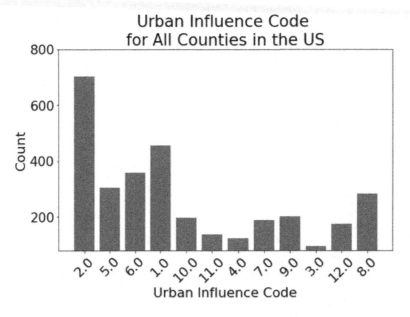

Figure 12.5 – Urban influence code counting with limited *y* axis values

The new graph uses the same data and the exact same kind of bar plot. This visualization is not wrong, but it is confusing as much as it is misleading. There are more than 100 counties with an urban influence code of 3.0, the third bar from right-hand side, but the second visualization shows that there are probably no such counties.

The difference between being confusing and misleading is that misleading graphs are usually coined carefully and deliberately to convey the wrong message; confusing graphs may not. The visualizer might not realize the confusion that such data transformation or capping will cause.

There are other causes that may result in bad visualizations, for example, the improper use of fonts and color. The more intense a color is, the greater the importance we place on that element. Opacity is an important factor, too. The perception of linear opacity doesn't always result in a linear impression of quantities. *It is not safe to purely rely on visual elements to make a quantitative judgement.*

In the next section, we will talk about another good practice: You should always question causality arguments:

Spot the common errors in this causality argument. A popular conspiracy theory in early 2020 is that the coronavirus is caused by 5G towers being built around the world. People who support such a theory have a powerful graph to support their argument. I can't trace the origin of such a widespread theory, but here are the two popular visualizations:

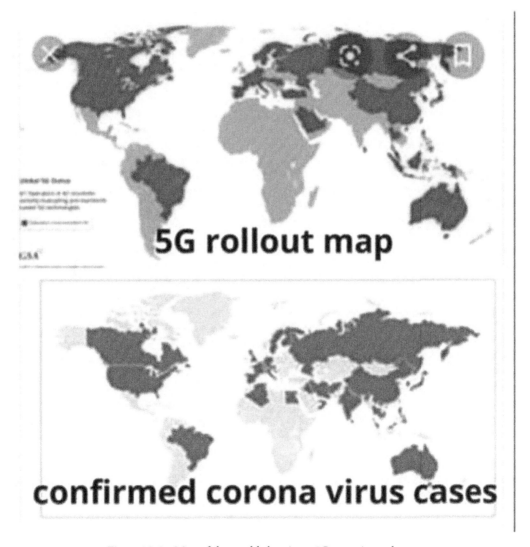

Figure 12.6 – Map of the world showing a 5G conspiracy theory

The following map is similar, but this time limited to the United States:

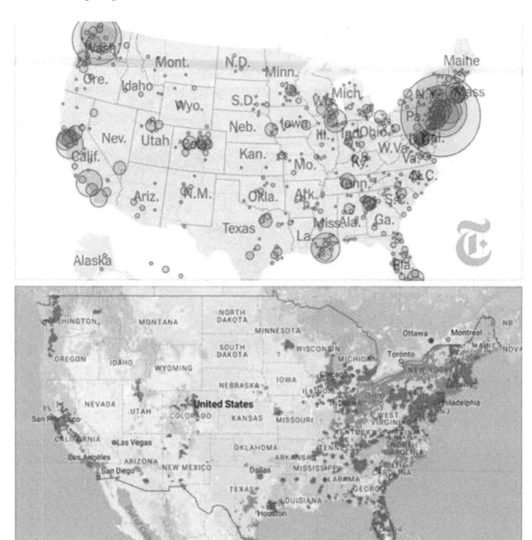

Figure 12.7 – Map of the United States showing a 5G conspiracy theory

The top portion shows the number of COVID-19 cases in the United States, while the lower portion shows the installation of 5G towers in the United States.

These two graphs are used to support the idea that 5G causes the spread of COVID-19. Do you believe it?

Let's study this problem step by step from the following perspectives.

- Is the data behind the graphics accurate?

- Do the graphics correctly represent the data?

- Does the visualization support the argument that 5G is resulting in the spread of COVID-19?

For the first question, following some research, you will find that Korea, China, and the United States are indeed the leading players in 5G installation. For example, as of February 2020, Korea has 5G coverage in 85 cities, while China has 5G coverage in 57 cities. However, Russia's first 5G zone was only deployed in central Moscow in August 2019. For the first question, the answer can roughly be true.

However, the second question is definitively false. All of Russia and Brazil are colored to indicate the seriousness of the spread of COVID-19 and 5G rollout. The visual elements do not represent the data proportionally. Note that the maps first appeared online long before cases in the United States and Brazil exploded. People can't tell the quantitative relationship between the rollout/coverage of 5G and the number of COVID-19 cases. The graphic is both misleading and confusing.

Onto the last question. The answer to this is also definitively false. However, the misrepresentation issue got confused with the interpretation of the data for the world map, so let's focus on the map of the United States. There are many ways to generate maps such as the COVID-19 cases map or the 5G tower installation map, for example, by means of population or urbanization maps. Since COVID-19 is transmitted mainly in the air and by touching droplets containing the virus, population density and lifestyles play a key role in its diffusion. This explains why areas with a high population are also areas where there are more confirmed cases.

From a business standpoint, AT&T and Verizon will focus heavily on offering 5G services to high population density regions such as New York. This explains the density map concerning 5G tower installation.

Factors such as population density are called **confounding factors**. A confounding factor is a factor that is a true cause behind another two or more factors. The causal relationships are between the confounding factor and the other factors, not between the non-confounding factors. It is a common trick to use visualization to suggest or represent a causal relationship between two variables without stating the underlying reasons.

That said, how do we detect and rebut the entire causal argument? Let's understand this in the next section.

Fighting against false arguments

To refute false arguments, you need to do the following:

- Maintain your curiosity to dig deeper into domain knowledge
- Gather different perspectives from credible experts

To refute false arguments, domain knowledge is the key because domain knowledge can reveal the details that loose causal arguments often hide from their audience.

Take the case of COVID-19, for example. To ascertain the possible confounding factor of population density, you need to know how the virus spreads, which falls into the domain of epidemiology. The first question you need to ask is whether there is a more science-based explanation. During the process of finding such an explanation, you need to learn domain knowledge and can often easily poke a hole in the false arguments.

> **Proving causal relations scientifically**
>
> Proving a causal relation between variables is hard, but to fake one is quite easy. In a rigorous academic research environment, to prove a cause and effect relationship, you need to control variables that leave the target variable as being the only explanation of the observed behavior. Often, such experiments must have the ability to be reproduced in other labs with different groups of researchers. However, this is sometimes hard, or even impossible, to reproduce in the case of social science research.

A second great way of refuting such false arguments is to gather opinions from credible experts. A credible expert is someone who has verifiable knowledge and experience in specific domains that is trustworthy. As the saying goes, *given enough eyes on the codes, there won't be any bugs*. Seeking opinions from true experts will often easily reveal the fallacy in false causal arguments.

In your data science team, pair coding and coding reviews will help you to detect errors, including, but not limited to, causal relation arguments. An even better way to do this is to show your work to the world – put your code on GitHub or build a website to show it to anyone on the internet. This is how academic publishing works, and includes two important elements—peer review and open access to other researchers.

Summary

In this chapter, we discussed three best practices in data science. They are also three warnings I give to you: always be cautious about data quality; always be vigilant about visualization; and pay more attention to detect (and thereby help avoid) false cause and effect relationship claims.

In the next and final chapter of this book, we will use what you have learned so far to solve the exercises and problems.

13
Exercises and Projects

This chapter is dedicated to exercises and projects that will enhance your understanding of statistics, as well as your practical programming skills.

This chapter contains three sections. The first section contains exercises that are direct derivatives of the code examples you saw throughout this book. The second section contains some projects I would recommend you try out; some of these will be partially independent of what we covered concretely in previous chapters. The last section is for those of you who want to dive more into the theory and math aspects of this book. Each section is organized according to the contents of the corresponding chapter.

Once you've finished this final chapter, you will be able to do the following:

- Reinforce your basic knowledge about the concepts and knowledge points that were covered in this book
- Gain working experience of a project's life cycle
- Understand the math and theoretical foundations at a higher level

Let's get started!

> **Note on the usage of this chapter**
>
> You are not expected to read or use this chapter sequentially. You may use this chapter to help you review the topics that were covered in a certain chapter once you've finished it. You can also use it as reference for your data scientist interview.

Exercises

Most of the exercises in each chapter don't depend on each other. However, if the exercises do depend on each other, this relationship will be stated clearly.

Chapter 1 – Fundamentals of Data Collection, Cleaning, and Preprocessing

Exercises related to Chapter 1, *Fundamentals of Data Collection, Cleaning, and Preprocessing*, are listed in this section.

Exercise 1 – Loading data

Load the auto-mpg data as a pandas DataFrame by using the `pandas.read_csv()` function. This data can be found at `https://archive.ics.uci.edu/ml/machine-learning-databases/auto-mpg/`.

> **Hint**
>
> You may find that the default argument fails to load the data properly. Search the document of the `read_csv()` function, identify the problem, and find the solution.

Exercise 2 – Preprocessing

Once you've loaded the `auto-mpg` data, preprocess the data like so:

1. Identify the type of each column/feature as numerical or categorical.

2. Perform min-max scaling for the numerical variables.

3. Impute the data with the median value.

> **Hint**
>
> This dataset, which I chose on purpose, can be ambiguous in terms of determining the variable type. Think about different choices and their possible consequences for downstream tasks.

Exercise 3 – Pandas and API calling

Sign up for a free account at `https://openweathermap.org/api`, obtain an API key, and read the API documentation carefully. Make some API calls to obtain the hourly temperature for the city you live in for the next 24 hours. Build a pandas DataFrame and plot a time versus temperature graph.

> **Hint**
>
> You may need Python's `datetime` module to convert a string into a valid datetime object.

Chapter 2 – Essential Statistics for Data Assessment

Exercises related to *Chapter 2, Essential Statistics for Data Assessment*, are listed in this section.

Exercise 1 – Other definitions of skewness

There are several different definitions of skewness. Use the data that we used to examine skewness in *Chapter 2, Essential Statistics for Data Assessment*, to calculate the following versions of skewness according to Wikipedia (`https://en.wikipedia.org/wiki/Skewness`):

- Pearson's second skewness coefficient
- Quantile-based measures
- Groeneveld and Meeden's coefficient

Exercise 2 – Bivariate statistics

Load the auto-mpg dataset that we introduced in *Exercise 1 – Loading data*, for *Chapter 1, Fundamentals of Data Collection, Cleaning and Preprocessing*. Identify the bivariate correlation with all the numerical variables. Which variables are positively correlated, and which ones are negatively correlated? Do these correlations make real-life sense to you?

Exercise 3 – The crosstab() function

Can you implement your own `crosstab()` function? It can take two lists of equal length as input and generate a `DataFrame` as output. You can also set an optional parameter, such as the name of the input lists.

> **Hint**
>
> Use the `zip()` function for a one-pass loop.

Chapter 3 – Visualization with Statistical Graphs

Exercises related to *Chapter 3, Visualization with Statistical Graphs*, are listed in this section.

Exercise 1 – Identifying the components

This is an open question. Try to identify the three components shown on Seaborn's gallery page: `https://seaborn.pydata.org/examples/index.html`. The three components of any statistical graph are data, geometry, and aesthetics. You may encounter new kinds of graph types here, which makes this a great opportunity to learn!

Exercise 2 – Query-oriented transformation

Use the auto-mpg data we introduced in *Exercise 1 – Loading data*, for *Chapter 1, Fundamentals of Data Collection, Cleaning and Preprocessing*, transform it into the long format, and generate a boxplot called the *Seaborn tips boxplot*. Namely, you want the *x*-axis to be the cylinders variable and the *y*-axis to be the mpg data.

Exercise 3 – Overlaying two graphs

For the birth rate and death rate of the Anderson county, overlay the line plot and the bar plot in the same graph.

Some possible enhancements you can make here are as follows:

- Choose a proper font and indicate the value of the data with numbers.
- Choose different symbols for the death rate and the birth rate.

Exercise 4 – Layout

Create a 2x2 layout and create a scatter plot of the birth rate and death rate of your four favorite states in the US. Properly set the opacity and marker size so that it is visually appealing.

Exercise 5 – The pairplot() function

The `pairplot()` function of the seaborn library is a very powerful function. Use it to visualize all the numerical variables of the auto-mpg dataset we introduced in *Exercise 1 – Loading data*, of *Chapter 1, Fundamentals of Data Collection, Cleaning and Preprocessing*. Study its documentation so that you know how to add a regression line to the off-diagonal plots. Does the regression line make sense to you? Compare the result with the correlation result you obtained in *Exercise 2 – Bivariate statistics*, of *Chapter 2, Essential Statistics for Data Assessment*.

> **Hint**
>
> Read the documentation regarding `pairplot()` for more information:
> `https://seaborn.pydata.org/generated/seaborn.`
> `pairplot.html`.

Chapter 4 – Sampling and Inferential Statistics

Exercises related to *Chapter 4, Sampling and Inferential Statistics*, are listed in this section.

Exercise 1 – Simple sampling with replacement

Create a set of data that follows a standard normal distribution of size 1,000. Run simple random sampling with and without replacement. Increase the sampling size. What happens if the sampling size of your replacement sampling exceeds 1,000?

Exercise 2 – Stratified sampling

Run stratified sampling on the population of county, stratified with respect to states rather than rural-urban Continuum Code_2013. Sample two data points from each state and compare the results by running the sampling multiple times.

Exercise 3 – Central limit theorem

Verify the central limit theorem by summing non-normal random variables by following the distributions listed here (just pick the easiest form for each). If you are not familiar with these distributions, please refer to *Chapter 5, Common Probability Distributions*:

- Binomial distribution

- Uniform distribution

- Poisson distribution

- Exponential distribution

Can you visually examine the number of random variables that need to be summed together to approach a normal distribution for each of the aforementioned distributions? What is the intuition behind your observation?

Chapter 5 – Common Probability Distributions

Exercises related to *Chapter 5, Common Probability Distributions*, are listed in this section.

Exercise 1 – Identify the sample space and the event corresponding to the probability being asked in the following statements:

- By tossing four fair coins, find the probability of at least getting two heads.

- The probability that a bus arrives between 8:00 A.M. and 8:30 A.M.

- A battleship fires three missiles. The battleship's target will be destroyed if at least two missiles hit its target. Find the probability that the battleship's target will be destroyed.

- Assume that the likelihood of a woman giving birth to a boy or a girl are the same. If we know a family that has three kids has a girl in the family, find the probability that the family has at least one girl. How about the probability of having at least a boy?

Exercise 2 – Proof of probability equations

Prove the following equation:

- $P(A \cup B) = P(A) + P(B) - P(A \cap B)$

> **Hint**
>
> Enumerate all possibilities of both the left-hand side and the right-hand side of the equation. Prove that if an event is in the left-hand side – that is, the union of A and B – then it is in the expression of the right-hand side. In the same regard, if it is in the right-hand side, then prove it is also in the left-hand side.

Exercise 3 – Proof of De Morgan's law

De Morgan's law states two important transformation rules, as stated here: `https://en.wikipedia.org/wiki/De_Morgan%27s_laws`. Use the same technique you used in the previous exercise to prove them.

Exercise 4 – Three dice sum

Write a program that calculates the distribution in a sum of three fair dice. Write a program that will simulate the case where the dice are not fair so that for each dice, it is two times more likely to have an even outcome than an odd outcome.

> **Hint**
>
> Write some general simulation code so that you can specify the probability associated with each face of the dice and the total number of dice. Then, you are free to recover the central limit theorem easily.

Exercise 5 – Approximate the binomial distribution with the Poisson distribution

The binomial distribution with a large n can sometimes be very difficult to calculate because of the involvement of factorials. However, you can approximate this with Poisson distribution. The condition for this is as follows:

- $n \to \infty$

- $p \to 0$

- $np \to \lambda$, where λ is a constant

If all three conditions are met, then the binomial distribution can be approximated by the Poisson distribution with the corresponding parameter, λ.

Prove this visually. Most of the time, n must be larger than 100 and p must be smaller than 0.01.

Exercise 6 – Conditional distribution for a discrete case

In the following table, the first column indicates the grades of all the students in an English class, while the first row indicates the math grades for the same class. The values shown are the count of students and the corresponding students:

	Math: A	Math: B	Math: C	Math: D
English: A	3	6	3	0
English: B	5	9	4	3
English: C	1	5	8	2
English: D	1	4	7	2

Figure 13.1 – Scores

Answer the following questions. Some of these question descriptions are quite complicated, so read them carefully:

- What is the probability of a randomly selected student having a B in math?

- What is the probability of a randomly selected student having a math grade that's no worse than a C and an English grade that's no worse than a B?

- If we know that a randomly selected student has a D in math, what's the probability that this student has no worse than a B in English?

- What's the minimal math grade a randomly selected student should have where you have the confidence to say that this student has at least a 70% chance of having no worse than a B in English?

Chapter 6 – Parameter Estimation

Exercises related to *Chapter 6, Parameter Estimation*, are listed in this section.

Exercise 1 – Distinguishing between estimation and prediction

Which of the following scenarios belong to the estimation process and which belong to the prediction process?

- Find out the weather next week.

- Find out the battery capacity of your phone based on your usage profile.

- Find out the arrival time of the next train based on the previous trains' arrival time.

Exercise 2 – Properties of estimators

If you were to use the method of moments to estimate a uniform distribution's boundaries, is the estimator that's obtained unbiased? Is the estimator that's obtained consistent?

Exercise 3 – Method of moments

Randomly generate two variables between 0 and 1 without checking their values. Set them as the μ and σ of a Gaussian random distribution. Generate 1,000 samples and use the method of moments to estimate these two variables. Do they agree?

Exercise 4 – Maximum likelihood – I

We toss a coin 100 times and for 60 cases we get heads. It's possible for the coin to be either fair, or biased to getting heads with a probability of 70%. Which is more likely?

Exercise 5 – Maximum likelihood – II

In this chapter, we discussed an example in which we used normal distribution or Laplace distribution to model the noise in a dataset. What if the noise follows a uniform distribution between -1 and 1? What result will be yielded? Does it make sense?

Exercise 6 – Law of total probability

Let's say the weather tomorrow has a 40% chance of being windy and a 60% chance of being sunny. On a windy day, you have a 50% chance of going hiking, while on a sunny day, the probability goes up to 80%. What's the probability of you going hiking tomorrow without knowing tomorrow's weather? What about after knowing that it's 90% likely to be sunny tomorrow?

Exercise 7 – Monty Hall question calculation

Calculate the quantity, $P(C|E_B)$, that we left in the Monty Hall question. Check its value with the provided answer.

Chapter 7 – Statistical Hypothesis Testing

Exercises related to *Chapter 7, Statistical Hypothesis Testing*, are listed in this section.

Exercise 1 – One-tailed and two-tailed tests

Is the following statement correct?

The significant level for a one-tailed test will be twice as large as it is for the two-tailed test.

Exercise 2 – P-value concept – I

Is the following statement correct?

For a discrete random variable where every outcome shares an equal probability, any outcome has a P-value of 1.

Exercise 3 – P-value concept – II

Are the following statements correct?

- The value of the P-value is obtained by assuming the null hypothesis is correct.

- The P-value, by definition, has a false-positive ratio.

> **Hint**
> False-positive naively means something isn't positive but you misclassify or mistreat it as being positive.

Exercise 4 – Calculating the P-value

Calculate the P-value of observing five heads when tossing an independent fair coin six times.

Exercise 5 – Table looking

Find the corresponding value in a one-tailed t-distribution table where the degree of freedom is 5 and the significance level is 0.002.

Exercise 6 – Decomposition of variance

Prove the following formula mathematically:

$$S_T^2 = S_B^2 + S_W^2$$

Exercise 7 – Fisher's exact test

For the link-clicking example we discussed in this chapter, read through the Fisher's exact test page: `https://en.wikipedia.org/wiki/Fisher%27s_exact_test`. Run a Fisher's exact test on the *device* and *browser* variables.

> **Hint**
> Build a crosstab first. It may be easier to refer to the accompanying notebook for reusable code.

Exercise 8 – Normality test with central limit theorem

In *Exercise 3 – Central limit theorem*, of *Chapter 4, Sampling and Inferential Statistics*, we tested the central limit theorem visually. In this exercise, use the normality test provided in *Chapter 7, Statistical Hypothesis Testing*, to test the normality of the random variable that was generated from summing non-normal random variables.

Exercise 9 – Goodness of fit*

In *Chapter 7, Statistical Hypothesis Testing*, we ran a goodness of fit test on the casino card game data. Now, let's assume the number of hearts no longer follows a binomial distribution, but a Poisson distribution. Now, run a goodness of fit test by doing the following:

1. Find the most likely parameter for the Poisson distribution by maximizing the likelihood function.

2. Run the goodness of fit test.

> **Suggestion**
> This question is a little tricky. You may need to review the procedure of building and maximizing a likelihood function to complete this exercise.

Exercise 10 – Stationary test*

Find the data for the total number of COVID-19 deaths in the United States from the date when the first death happened to July 29th, where the number of patients that died had reached 150,000. Run a stationary test on the data and the first difference of the data.

Chapter 8 – Statistics for Regression

Exercises related to *Chapter 8, Statistics for Regression*, are listed in this section.

Exercise 1 – R-squared

Are the following statements correct?

- A bigger R^2 is always a good indicator of good fit for a single-variable linear model.
- For a multivariable linear model, an adjusted R^2 is a better choice when evaluating the quality of the model.

Exercise 2 – Polynomial regression

Is the following statement correct?

To run a regression variable, y, over single variable, x, an 8th order polynomial can fit an arbitrary dataset of size 8. If yes, why?

Exercise 3 – Doubled R^2

Is the following statement correct?

If a regression model has an R^2 of 0.9, suppose we obtained another set of data that happens to match the original dataset *exactly*, similar to a duplicate. What will happen to the regression coefficients? What will happen to the R^2?

Exercise 4 – Linear regression on the auto-mpg dataset

Run simple linear regression on the auto-mpg dataset. Obtain the coefficients between the make year and mpg variables. Try to do this by using different methods, as we did in the example provided in this chapter.

Exercise 5 – Collinearity

Run multivariable linear regression to fit the *mpg* in the auto-mpg dataset to the rest of the numerical variables. Are the other variables highly collinear? Calculate VIF to eliminate two variables and run the model again. Is the adjusted R^2 decreasing or increasing?

Exercise 6 – Lasso regression and ridge regression

Repeat *Exercise 5 – Collinearity*, but this time with lasso regularization or ridge regularization. Change the regularization coefficient to control the strength of the regularization and plot a set of line plots regarding the regularization parameter versus the coefficient magnitude.

Chapter 9 – Statistics for Classification

Exercises related to *Chapter 9, Statistics for Classification*, are listed in this section.

Exercise 1 – Odds and log of odds

Determine the correctness of the following statements:

- The odds of an event can take any value between 0 and infinity.

- The log of odds has the meaning as a probability.

> **Hint**
> Plot the relationship between the probability and the log of odds.

Exercise 2 – Confusion matrix

Determine the proper quadrant for the following scenarios in the coefficient matrix:

- Diagnose a man as pregnant.

- If there are incoming planes and the detector failed to find them.

- A COVID-19 patient was correctly diagnosed as positive.

Exercise 3 – F1 score

Calculate the F1 score for the following confusion matrix:

	Ground true positive	**Ground truth negative**
Predicted positive	TP=45	FP=35
Predicted negative	FN=55	TN=65

Figure 13.2 – Confusion matrix

Exercise 4 – Grid search for optimal logistic regression coefficients

When we maximized the loglikelihood function of the stock prediction example, I suggested that you use grid search to find the optimal set of slopes and intercepts. Write a function that will find the optimal values and compare them with the ones I provided there.

Exercise 5 – The linregress() function

Use the `linregress()` function to run linear regression on the Netflix stock data. Then, verify the R^2 value's agreement with our manually calculated values.

Exercise 6 – Insufficient data issue with the Bayes classifier

For a naïve Bayes classifier, if the data is categorical and there's not enough of it, we may encounter an issue where the prediction encounters a tie between two or even more possibilities. For the stroke risk prediction example, verify that the following data gives us an undetermined prediction:

```
{"weight":"high","high_oil_diet":"no","smoking":"no"}
```

Exercise 7 – Laplace smoothing

One solution for solving the insufficient data problem is to use Laplace smoothing, also known as additive smoothing. Please read the wiki page at `https://en.wikipedia.org/wiki/Additive_smoothing` and the lecture note from Toronto university at `http://www.cs.toronto.edu/~bonner/courses/2007s/csc411/lectures/03bayes.zemel.pdf` before re-solving the issue that was raised in *Exercise 4 – Grid search for optimal logistic regression coefficients*.

Exercise 8 – Cross-validation

For the auto-mpg data we introduced in *Exercise 1 – Loading data*, of *Chapter 1, Fundamentals of Data Collection, Cleaning, and Preprocessing*, use 5-fold cross-validation to train multivariable linear regression models and evaluate their performance using the mean squared error metric.

Exercise 9 – ROC curve

One important concept I skipped due to space limitations is the ROC curve. However, it is easy to replicate. For the stock prediction logistic regression model, pick a series of equally spaced thresholds between 0 and 1, and then create a scatter plot of the true positive rates and the true positive rates. Examine the result. What you will have obtained is an ROC curve. You can find more information about the ROC curve at `https://en.wikipedia.org/wiki/Receiver_operating_characteristic`.

Exercise 10 – Predicting cylinders

Use the `mpg`, `horsepower`, and `displacement` variables of the auto-mpg dataset to classify the `cylinder` variable using a Gaussian Naïve classifier. Check out the documentation at `https://scikit-learn.org/stable/modules/naive_bayes.html#gaussian-naive-bayes` to find out more.

> **Hint**
>
> Gaussian Naïve Bayes is the continuous version of the categorical Naïve Bayes method. However, it is not the only option. Feel free to explore other Naïve Bayes classifiers and compare their performance. You are also permitted to remove odd-number cylinder samples since they are very rare and not informative in general.

Chapter 10 – Statistics for Tree-Based Methods

Exercises related to *Chapter 10*, *Statistics for Tree-Based Methods*, are listed in this section.

Exercise 1 – Tree concepts

Determine the correctness of the following statements:

- A tree can only have a single root node.

- A decision node can only have, at most, two child nodes.

- A node can only have one parent node.

Exercise 2 – Gini impurity visualized

For a three-category dataset with categories A, B, and C, produce a 2D visualization of the Gini impurity as a function of $P(A)$ and $P(B)$, where $0 < P(A) + P(B) < 1$.

> **Hint**
>
> Although we have three categories, the requirement of summing to one leaves us with two degrees of freedom.

Exercise 3 – Comparing Gini impurity with entropy

Another criterion for tree node splitting is known as entropy. Read the Wikipedia page at `https://en.wikipedia.org/wiki/Entropy_(information_theory)` and write functions that will help you redo *Exercise 2 – Gini impurity revisited*, but with entropy being used instead. What do you find? In terms of splitting nodes, which method is more aggressive/conservative? What if you increase the number of possible categories? Can you perform a Monte Carlo simulation?

Exercise 4 – Entropy-based tree building

Use entropy instead of Gini impurity to rebuild the stroke risk decision tree.

Exercise 5 – Non-binary tree

Without grouping low-risk and middle-risk groups, build a three-category decision tree from scratch for the stroke risk dataset. You can use either Gini impurity or entropy for this.

Exercise 6 – Regression tree concepts

Determine the correctness of the following statements:

- The number of possible outputs a regression tree has is the same as the number of partitions it has for the feature space.

- Using absolute error rather than MSE will yield the same partition result.

- To split over a continuous variable, the algorithm has to try all possible values, so for each splitting, the time complexity of the naïve approach will be $O(NM)$, where N is the number of continuous features and M is the number of samples in the node.

Exercise 7 – Efficiency of regression tree building

Write some pseudocode to demonstrate how the tree partition process can be paralleled. If you can't, please explain which step or steps prohibit this.

Exercise 8 – sklearn example

Use sklearn to build a regression tree that predicts the value of *mpg* in the *auto-mpg* dataset with the rest of the features. Then, build a classification tree that predicts the number of *cylinders* alongside the rest of the features.

Exercise 9 – Overfitting and pruning*

This is a hard question that may involve higher coding requirements.

The sklearn API provides a parameter that helps us control the depth of the tree, which prevents overfitting. Another way we can do this is to build the tree so that it's as deep as needed first, then prune the tree backward from the leaves. Can you implement a helper/utility function to achieve this? You may need to dive into the details of the `DecisionTreeClassifier()` class to directly manipulate the tree object.

Chapter 11 – Statistics for Ensemble Methods

Exercises related to *Chapter 11, Statistics for Ensemble Methods*, are listed in this section.

Exercise 1 – Bias-variance trade-off concepts

Determine the correctness of the following statements:

- Train set and test set splitting will prevent both underfitting and overfitting.
- Non-randomized sampling will likely cause overfitting.
- Variance in terms of the concept of bias-variance trade-off means the variance of the model, not the variance of the data.

Exercise 2 – Bootstrapping concept

Determine the correctness of the following statements. If there is any ambiguity, please illustrate your answer(s) with examples:

- The bigger the variance of the sample data, the more performant bootstrapping will be.
- Bootstrapping doesn't generate new information from the original dataset.

Exercise 3 – Bagging concept

Determine the correctness of the following statements:

- Each aggregated weak learner is the same weight.
- `BaggingClassifier()` can be set so that it's trained in parallel.
- The differences between weak learners are caused by the differences in the sampled data that they are exposed to.

Exercise 4 – From using a bagging tree classifier to random forests*

You may have heard about random forests before. They are tree-based machine learning models that are known for their robustness to overfitting. The key difference between bagging decision trees and random forests is that a random forest not only samples the records, but also samples the features. For example, let's say we're performing a regression task where we're using the *auto-mpg* dataset. Here, the *cylinder* feature may not be available during one iteration of the node splitting process.

Implement your own simple random forest class. Compare its performance with the sklearn bagging classifier.

Exercise 5 – Boosting concepts

Determine the correctness of the following statements:

- In principle, boosting is not trainable in parallel.
- Boosting, in principle, can decrease the bias of the training set indefinitely.
- Boosting linear weak learners is not efficient because the linear combinations of a linear model is also a linear model.

Exercise 6 – AdaBoost

Use AdaBoost to predict the number of cylinders in the *auto-mpg* dataset against the rest of the variables.

Exercise 7 – Gradient boosting tree visualization

Using the tree visualization code that was introduced in *Chapter 12, Statistics for Tree-Based Methods*, visualize the decision rules of the weak learners/trees for a gradient descent model. Select trees from the first 10 iterations, first 40 iterations, and then every 100 iterations. Do you notice any patterns?

Everything up to this point has all been exercises I've prepared for you. The next section is dedicated to the projects you can carry out. Each project is associated with a chapter and a topic, but it's recommended that you integrate these projects to build a comprehensive project that you can show to future employers.

Project suggestions

These projects will be classified into three different categories, as listed here:

- **Elementary projects**: Elementary projects are ones where you only need knowledge from one or two chapters and are easy to complete. Elementary projects only require that you have basic Python programming skills.

- **Comprehensive projects**: Comprehensive projects are ones that require you to review knowledge from several chapters. Having a thorough understanding of the example code provided in this book is required to complete a comprehensive project.

- **Capstone projects**: Capstone projects are projects that involve almost all the contents of this book. In addition to the examples provided in this book, you are expected to learn a significant amount of new knowledge and programming skills to complete the task at hand.

Let's get started!

Non-tabular data

This is an elementary project. The knowledge points in this project can be found in *Chapter 1, Fundamentals of Data Collection, Cleaning, and Preprocessing*, and *Chapter 2, Essential Statistics for Data Assessment*.

The university dataset in the UCI machine learning repository is stored in a non-tabular format: `https://archive.ics.uci.edu/ml/datasets/University`. Please examine its format and perform the following tasks:

1. Examine the data format visually and then write down some patterns to see whether such patterns can be used to extract the data at specific lines.

2. Write a function that will systematically read the data file and store the data contained within in a pandas DataFrame.

3. The data description mentioned the existence of both missing data and duplicate data. Identify the missing data and deduplicate the duplicated data.

4. Classify the features into numerical features and categorical features.

5. Apply min-max normalization to all the numerical variables.

6. Apply median imputation to the missing data.

> **Non-tabular format**
>
> Legacy data may be stored in non-tabular format for historical reasons. The format the university data is stored in is a LISP-readable format, which is a powerful old programming language that was invented more than 60 years ago.

Real-time weather data

This is a comprehensive project. The knowledge points are mainly from *Chapter 1, Fundamentals of Data Collection, Cleaning, and Preprocessing*, and *Chapter 3, Visualization with Statistical Graphs*.

The free weather API provides current weather data for more than 200,000 cities in the world. You can apply for a free trial here: `https://openweathermap.org/api`. In this example, you will build a visualization of the temperature for major US cities. Refer to the following instructions:

1. Read the API documentation for the current endpoint: `https://openweathermap.org/current`. Write some short scripts to test the validity of your API key by querying the current weather in New York. If you don't have one, apply for a free trial.

2. Write another function that will parse the returned data into tabular format.

3. Query the current weather in Los Angeles, Chicago, Miami, and Denver as well. You may want to store their zip codes in a dictionary for reference. Properly set the fonts, legends, and size of markers. The color of the line will be determined by the main field of the returned JSON object. You are encouraged to choose a color map that associates warmer colors with higher temperatures, for example.

4. Write another function that re-queries the weather information in each city and re-plots the visualization every 20 minutes.

Colormap

In data science-related visualization, a colormap is a mapping from ordered quantities or indices to an array of colors. Different colormaps significantly change the feeling of viewers. For more information, please refer to `https://matplotlib.org/3.1.1/tutorials/colors/ colormaps.html`.

I also pointed out the `main` field in the returned JSON for you:

```
{
  "coord": {
    "lon": -122.08,
    "lat": 37.39
  },
  "weather": [
    {
      "id": 800,
      "main": "Clear",
      "description": "clear sky",
      "icon": "01d"
    }
  ],
  "base": "stations",
  "main": {
    "temp": 282.55,
    "feels_like": 281.86,
    "temp_min": 280.37,
    "temp_max": 284.26,
    "pressure": 1023,
    "humidity": 100
  },
  "visibility": 16093,
```

Figure 13.3 – The main field of the returned json object

We will use the functions and code you developed in this project for a capstone project, later in this chapter. The rest of this project is quite flexible and up to you.

Goodness of fit for discrete distributions

This is an elementary project. The topics involved are from *Chapter 3, Visualization with Statistical Graphs*, to *Chapter 7, Statistical Hypothesis Testing*. The description is fancy, but you should be able to divide it into small parts. This is also a project where many details are ambiguous, and you should define your own questions specifically.

In this project, you will write a "bot" that can guess the parameters of discrete distributions. You also need to visualize this process.

Suppose there is a program that randomly selects integer λ from the list [5,10,20] first, then generates Poisson-distributed samples based on the pre-generated λ. The program will also recreate λ after generating n samples, where n is another random integer variable that's uniformly distributed between 500 and 600.

By doing this, you will have obtained 100,000 data points generated by this program. Write a function that will calculate the possibilities of λ behind every data point. Then, visualize this.

You can approach this problem by using the following instructions:

1. First, you need to clarify the definition. Let's say you can calculate the goodness of fit test's P-value and then use this P-value to indicate how likely a specific λ is for the parameter of a distribution. You can also calculate the likelihoods and compare them. The point is that you need to define quantities that can describe the ambiguous term possibilities in the question. This is up to you, but I used the goodness of fit test as an example.

2. Then, you should write a program that will generate 100,000 pieces of data.

3. Next, define a window size. The window will be moved to capture the data and run the goodness of fit test on the windowed data. Choose a window size and justify your choice. What's the problem with a window size being too small and what's the problem with a window size being too large?

4. Calculate the P-values for the goodness of fit results. Plot them along with the original data. Choose your aesthetics wisely.

> **The idea behind this exercise**
>
> There are many observations that can be modeled as a process that's controlled by a hidden parameter. It's key to model such a process and determine the parameter(s). In this project, you already know that the mechanism behind the random variable generation is a Poisson process, but in most cases, you won't know this. This project is a simplified scenario.

Building a weather prediction web app

This is a capstone project.

To complete this project, you should get your hands on the Dash framework: `https://dash-gallery.plotly.host/Portal/`. Dash is a framework that you can use to quickly turn a Python script into a deployable data science application. You should at least go over the first four sessions of the tutorial and focus on the Dash map demo to learn how to render maps: `https://dash-gallery.plotly.host/dash-mapd-demo/`.

To finish this project, follow these steps:

1. Finish the prerequisite mentioned in the project description.

2. Write a function that will map a list of city zip codes to markers on a US map and render them. Learn how to change the contents on the map when hovering over it with your mouse.

3. Use the weather API to obtain a weather report for the last 7 days for the major cities we listed in earlier projects. Build a linear regressor that will predict the temperature for the following data. Write a function that will automate this step so that every time you invoke the function, new data will be queried.

4. Design a layout where the page is split into two parts.

5. The left panel should be a map where each city is highlighted with today's temperature value.

6. The right panel should be a line chart where regression is performed so that tomorrow's temperature is predicted and distinguished from known previous temperature.

7. This step is optional*. You are encouraged to use other machine learning algorithms rather than simple linear regression to allow the users to switch between different algorithms. For example, you can use both simple linear regression and regression trees.

8. To train a regression tree, you might need more historical data. Explore the API options and give it a try.

9. You need a UI component to allow the users to change between algorithms. The toggle button may be what you need: `https://dash.plotly.com/dash-daq/toggleswitch`.

This project is particularly useful because as a data scientist, an interactive app is probably the best way to demonstrate your skills in terms of both statistics and programming. The last project is similar in this regard.

Building a typing suggestion app

This is a capstone project. In this project, you are going to build a web app that predicts what the user's typing by training them on large word corpus. There are three components in this app, but they are not strongly correlated. You can start from any of them:

- **Processing word data**: The typing suggestion is based on Bayes' theorem, where the most likely or top-k predictions are made by examining a large set of sentences. You can obtain an English text corpus from the English Corpora website: `https://www.english-corpora.org/history.asp`. You can start from a small corpus, such as the manually annotated sub-corpus project: `http://www.anc.org/data/masc/downloads/data-download/`. You need to tokenize the data by sequencing words. You are encouraged to start with tutorials from SpaCy or NLTK. You should find material online, such as `https://realpython.com/natural-language-processing-spacy-python/`, to help with this.

- **Building the model**: You need to build a two-gram model, which means counting the number of appearances of neighboring word pairs. For example, "I eat" is likely to be more frequent than "I fly", so the word "eat" will be more likely to show up than "fly". You need to create a model or module that can perform such a task quickly. Also, you may want to save your data in a local disk persistently so that you don't need to run the model building process every time your app starts.

- **Building the app**: The last step is to create a UI. The documentation for the input component can be found here: `https://dash.plotly.com/dash-core-components/input`. You need to decide on how you want your user to see your suggestions. You can achieve this by creating a new UI component.

One additional feature you may wish to add to your app is a spam filter. By doing this, you can inform your user of how likely the input text looks like a spam message in real time.

Further reading

With that, you have reached the last part of this book. In this section, I am going to recommend some of the best books on data science, statistics, and machine learning I've found, all of which can act as companions to this book. I have grouped them into categories and shared my personal thoughts on them.

Textbooks

Books that fall into this category are read like textbooks and are often used as textbooks or at least reference books in universities. Their quality has been proven and their value is timeless.

The first one is *Statistical Inference by George Casella, 2nd Edition,* which book covers the first several chapters of this book. It contains a multitude of useful exercises and practices, all of which are explained in detail. It is hard to get lost when reading this book.

The second book is *The Elements of Statistical Learning* by *Trevor Hastie, Robert Tibshirani, and Jerome Friedman, 2nd Edition.* This book is the bible of traditional statistical learning. It's not easy for beginners who are not comfortable with the conciseness of math proof. There is another book, *An Introduction to Statistical Learning: With Application in R by Gareth James and Daniela Witten,* that is simpler and easier to digest. Both books cover all the topics in this book starting from *Chapter 6, Parametric Estimation.*

Visualization

The first book I recommend about visualization is *The Visual Display of Quantitative Information* by *Edward R. Tufte.* This book will not teach you how to code or plot a real visualization, instead teaching you the philosophy surrounding visualization.

The second book I recommend is also by Edward R. Tufte. It is called *Visual and Statistical Thinking: Displays of Evidence for Making Decisions.* It contains many examples where visualizations are done correctly and incorrectly. It is also very entertaining to read.

I won't recommend any specific books that dedicate full content to coding examples for visualization here. The easiest way to learn about visualization is by referring to this book's GitHub repository and replicating the examples provided. Of course, it would be great if you were to get a hard copy so that you can look up information quickly and review it frequently.

Exercising your mind

This category contains books that don't read like textbooks but also require significant effort to read, think about, and digest.

The first book is *Common Errors in Statistics (and How to Avoid Them)* by *Phillip I. Good and James W. Hardin.* This book contains concepts surrounding the usage of visualizations that are widely misunderstood.

The second book is *Stat Labs: Mathematical Statistics Through Applications (Springer Texts in Statistics)* by *Deborah Nolan and Terry P. Speed*. This book is unique because it starts every topic with real-world data and meaningful questions that should be asked. You will find that this book's reading difficulty increases quickly. I highly recommend this book. You may need to use a pen and paper to perform any calculations and tabulation that's required of you.

Summary

Congratulations on reaching the end of this book! In this chapter, we introduced exercises and projects of varying difficulty. You were also provided with a list of additional books that will help you as you progress through the exercises and projects mentioned in this chapter. I hope these additional materials will boost your statistical learning progress and make you an even better data scientist.

If you have any questions about the content of this book, please feel free to light up any issues on the official GitHub repository for this book: `https://github.com/PacktPublishing/Essential-Statistics-for-Non-STEM-Data-Analysts`. We are always happy to answer your questions there.

Other Books You May Enjoy

If you enjoyed this book, you may be interested in these other books by Packt:

Practical Data Analysis Using Jupyter Notebook

Marc Wintjen

ISBN: 978-1-83882-603-1

- Understand the importance of data literacy and how to communicate effectively using data

- Find out how to use Python packages such as NumPy, pandas, Matplotlib, and the Natural Language Toolkit (NLTK) for data analysis

- Wrangle data and create DataFrames using pandas

- Produce charts and data visualizations using time-series datasets

- Discover relationships and how to join data together using SQL

- Use NLP techniques to work with unstructured data to create sentiment analysis models

Hands-On Mathematics for Deep Learning

Jay Dawani

ISBN: 978-1-83864-729-2

- Understand the key mathematical concepts for building neural network models

- Discover core multivariable calculus concepts

- Improve the performance of deep learning models using optimization techniques

- Cover optimization algorithms, from basic stochastic gradient descent (SGD) to the advanced Adam optimizer

- Understand computational graphs and their importance in DL

- Explore the backpropagation algorithm to reduce output error

- Cover DL algorithms such as convolutional neural networks (CNNs), sequence models, and generative adversarial networks (GANs)

Leave a review - let other readers know what you think

Please share your thoughts on this book with others by leaving a review on the site that you bought it from. If you purchased the book from Amazon, please leave us an honest review on this book's Amazon page. This is vital so that other potential readers can see and use your unbiased opinion to make purchasing decisions, we can understand what our customers think about our products, and our authors can see your feedback on the title that they have worked with Packt to create. It will only take a few minutes of your time, but is valuable to other potential customers, our authors, and Packt. Thank you!

Index

Made in the USA
Middletown, DE
08 June 2021